Jill :
merry Christmas
_2007_

Wisdom for the
Busy SportsLeader

250 Daily Devotions on Leadership
that can be read in 60 seconds or less

Pat Richie

[signature]

Foreword by
Mike Holmgren

Dedicated to My Family
*Whose sacrifice has far surpassed what anyone outside the
five of us will ever know.*

To My Wife -
Nico
*Your Love, Faithfulness, and Strength
Has owned my heart for nearly 30 years*

To My Daughter –
*Cristina Sofia whose name means: Christian Wisdom
Your Pursuit of God and His Wisdom
Inspires me to faithfully Seek the Lord in Every Endeavor*

To My Son –
*Matteo Patrick whose name means: Noble Gift of God
Your Indomitable Spirit
Is an Example for me to Never Give Up*

To My Daughter –
*Angelica Nicolette whose name means: Victorious Angel
Your Competitive Character
Challenges me to Always do my Best*

Contents

Foreword

Dear Reader:

I know that I am not alone when I say that my life is busy. For me, the schedule becomes even more intense during football season when it seems like every minute is filled with film review, game preparation, coaches meetings, press conferences, football practice, not to mention the game on Sunday. In addition, my work schedule is just part of my busy life-sometimes trying to keep up with my wife, four daughters, and four granddaughters, makes football seem routine by comparison.

Though it has been a constant challenge to keep my priorities straight and stay connected to God while trying to develop as a leader in my profession, I believe that God puts people in our lives to help us keep on track. For me, one of those people has been Pat Richie. I have known Pat for more than 20 years, since my first days in the National Football League when I was an assistant coach at the San Francisco 49ers and he was the team chaplain. Throughout our relationship, I have been privileged to call him friend and spiritual mentor. In contrast to the sometimes turbulent nature of the job, he has been a consistent presence in my life, helping me keep a proper perspective about winning and losing, challenging me to be a better person who is as committed to my relationship with Jesus Christ as I am to my job as an NFL head coach.

Seven years ago, Pat began sending a group of 30 coaches and sports administrators a short devotion each week entitled "Wisdom for the Busy SportsLeader" that combined a thought-provoking quote, a lesson in leadership, and a Biblical passage. These devotions became so popular that within a year more than 500 leaders from all walks of life requested to receive these powerful messages. A couple of years ago many of us who had been receiving these devotions suggested to Pat that he compile his weekly emails into a book.

In his book, Pat has included 250 devotions-one for each work day of the year-full of interesting quotes, practical wisdom, and most importantly verses from God's Word. Regardless of the pressure at work and the demands of my schedule, I try to take a few minutes each day to read the devotion and use the space on the page below to jot a note to myself, whether it is a commitment to improve an area of my life or an important lesson I want to remember. They are not very long, but these messages help me to remember what is really important on a daily basis.

Each Thursday at practice during the season, I ask my offense to run our two-minute drill, a series of plays designed to get our team down the field to score in under two minutes. It isn't a lot of time to get things done, but it is an important aspect of our game plan. I have seen many times when a score resulting from a two minute drill has been the difference in the game. I encourage you to take two minutes each day in your busy schedule for these pieces of wisdom and see the difference they can make in your life.

Mike Holmgren

Marvin Lewis, Head Coach Cincinnati Bengals
"Wisdom for the Busy SportsLeader is timely, relevant and to the point. A great way to jump start each and every day."

Greg Jamison, President & CEO San Jose Sharks
"I look forward to reading Wisdom for the Busy SportsLeader every day. It is an encouraging and practical devotional which provides great food for thought."

Jon Richardson, President Carolina Panthers Stadium
"Wisdom for the Busy Sports Leader provides great encouragement and perspective to make the "right" decisions in our businesses and in our personal lives. I share Pat's messages with many of my friends and teammates at work, and I can see the impact it is making as our relationships and faith continue to grow."

Scott Radecic, Senior Principal HOK Sport
"Wisdom for the Busy Sports Leader devotions penetrate the heart of every leadership issue that I am challenged with daily, providing spiritual insight, direction and inspiration all at once."

John A. Weber, Chaplain Dallas Cowboys
"Pat is a gifted communicator. His words are pithy, powerful, passionate. Best of all, he's a trusted friend. Write on, Pat, write on."

Jim Mora Jr., Former Head Coach Atlanta Falcons
"I love starting my day with a reading from Wisdom for the Busy SportsLeader; it helps gets my mind right for the challenges that lie ahead."

Jeff Kemp, Former NFL Quarterback
"This is a daily compass to gain balance and direction for life and leadership."

Jeff Farrar, Chaplain Phoenix Coyotes Hockey Club
"Pat is the real deal. He has lived in the sports world and knows its opportunities, challenges and battles. Anyone living in the heat of that world would be encouraged and challenged by his words."

Jack Mula, New England Patriots General Counsel, Player Personnel
"Wisdom for the Busy SportsLeader is a wonderful up, down and up again read, thoughtful, entertaining, practical and oh yeah, once you put it down....you're sure to pick it up again and again and again."

Mike Nolan, San Francisco 49'ers Head Coach
"I have found Wisdom for the Busy Sports Leader to be a very helpful and enlightening book."

Kevin Warren Vice President of Operations & Legal Counsel Minnesota Vikings Football, LLC.
"Wisdom for the Busy Sports Leader is a fascinating book that is guaranteed to touch the core of your soul."

Norm Evans, Starter 1972 Undefeated Miami Dolphins, President Pro Athletes Outreach *"Busy SportsLeader – to the point and wisdom in bite size morsels."*

Tom Cousineau, Ohio State University All-America, First Overall Pick 1978 NFL Draft, Cleveland Browns Linebacker
"Reading Wisdom for the Busy Sports Leader is like using oxygen after the confusion and exhaustion of having unsuccessfully attempted to defend a 15 play scoring drive versus a hurry-up offense in 100 degree heat. It calms, refreshes, and brings everything into focus. I love this book! "

Preface

"Wisdom is not what you know about the world but how well you know God." - *Henry Blackaby.*

It can be very time efficient for the *Busy SportsLeader* to make decisions based on his comfort level and pool of knowledge. Tasks can be checked off, projects delegated, opportunities rejected or accepted based on what he already knows. But the organization can only go as far as its leader's experience will take it.

To break through the ceiling of competence to a new level of dynamic leadership it takes growth, care and new insights. Knowing where to search for those insights is the key.

The word *"wisdom"* appears 234 times in the Bible. It is the principal source of God's wisdom to us. In its pages God is revealed.

A queen visiting from Africa observed King Solomon's knowledge of God when she declared, *"How happy these people must be! What a privilege for your officials to stand here day after day listening to your wisdom"! I Kings 10:8.*

You may not get that kind of praise from royalty, but your people will be happy in your growing wisdom.

Winter

"Honesty is the first chapter in the book of wisdom".
- Thomas Jefferson.

Desire wisdom? Know where to start? Be honest in your relationship with God. Honest about your struggles, fears, weaknesses. Honestly seek Him, know Him and follow Him. God wants *Busy SportsLeaders* to have His wisdom, but He doesn't reveal it to those who are not forthright.

As the psalmist writes, *"You desire honesty from the heart, so You can teach me to be wise in my inmost being."* *Psalm 51:6.*

"No notice is taken of a little evil, but when it increases it strikes the eye." - Aristotle.

Temptation by full frontal attack rarely works. The real danger is in the small things that are easy to let slide. The *Busy SportsLeader* has a lot to do. Putting up some barriers to protect yourself from big time spiritual disaster is a good thing, but it is not enough.

Ancient vintners put up fences to protect their grapes from the animals that would feed on them; it worked well…most of the time.

The following piece of wisdom comes from a rarely read book of the Old Testament. Its truth is powerful for all of life, but note – the book's primary focus is about enjoying and maintaining a love relationship with our spouse.

"It is the little foxes that spoil the vines".
Song of Songs 2:15.

Ethics have become a hot topic in sports and business over the past two years. Committees have been formed, executives have been fired and entire companies have gone bankrupt all because of "ethics". Millions, no billions, of dollars have been lost along with our ethics.

At its essence the problem lies in determining, and acting upon, that which is "right" or "wrong". But what is right for you might be wrong for me. What is wrong in one industry might not be regulated in another. What is questionable today, well, perhaps no one will care about in 10 or 20 years.

The *Busy Sports Leader* whose ethics are derived from the God of the Bible does not have to hide, doubt or debate his ethics. The person of God and biblical ethics are universal, timeless and not situational.

"...the Father of heavenly lights, with whom there is no variation, or shifting shadow." James 1:17.

"We love playing together and we love adversity." - Steve Nash.

Knowing where you're going and why you're going there will help you overcome a lot of problems. This simple truth often gets lost in the complexities of leading. The *Busy SportsLeader* needs to remind himself and those who travel with him regularly of their destination.

"Can two people walk together without agreeing on a direction?" Amos 3:3.

"The key to successful leadership today is influence, not authority." - Ken Blanchard.

It should be obvious when a *Busy SportsLeader* with Christian convictions is leading an organization. Their presence should be felt in three distinct ways, and will be analogous to salt.

1. Preserves: Slows or halts the moral decay of those around them.
2. Cleanses: Helps change or remove corruption.
3. Thirst: Creates a desire for others to seek God.

"You are the salt of the earth; but if the salt has become tasteless, how can it be made salty again? It is no longer good for anything, except to be thrown out and trampled by men." Matthew 5:13.

"Nobody roots for Goliath." - Wilt Chamberlian.

I have never met a *Busy SportsLeader* who wanted their team to be smaller, slower, and weaker. Only when forced to, do leaders play the *"David"* card to inspire the troops. There is nothing wrong with physical advantages, or being the best. The thing that set David apart from Goliath was *where* he placed his confidence.

Goliath was amazed that anyone would defy HIM. David was amazed anyone would defy GOD.

"David spoke and said, 'Who is this uncircumcised Philistine that he should defy the armies of the living God?'" I Samuel 17:26.

"Give light, and the darkness will disappear of itself." - *Desiderius Erasmus, 15th Century philosopher.*

If you work in a dark place don't blame the darkness, it comes swiftly when there is no light.

For the *Busy SportsLeader,* unveiling their beliefs to a darkened world can be frightening, but it never fails; light diminishes the darkness. It is our responsibility to be light and not fear the darkness.

"Don't hide your light under a basket"! Matthew 5:15.

"He that cannot forgive others breaks the bridge over which he must pass himself; for every man has need to be forgiven." - Thomas Fuller.

Broken promises, disloyalty, and betrayal. Every *Busy SportsLeader* has been through some painful experiences. You may choose to never work with those who have harmed you, but you must avoid the allure of holding a grudge. The soil in which the bitter weed "grudge" grows is called "lack of forgiveness".

"...and forgive us our sins, just as we have forgiven those who have sinned against us." Matthew 6:12.

"Therefore, since we have so great a cloud of witnesses surrounding us, let us also lay aside every encumbrance and the sin which so easily entangles us and let us run with endurance the race that is set before us." Hebrews 12:1.

Media day at the Super Bowl is a perfect picture of a "cloud" of witnesses. With the Super Bowl and two major All-Star games upon us, the *Busy SportsLeader* should encourage and prepare the men of faith who are the focus of attention. Athletes and coaches should be reminded that: pride costs credibility, sin surrenders integrity, and sharing Christ out of context forfeits believability. When dealing with the press, (or anyone else), sharing the personal results of a relationship with Christ as it applies to real life issues is very powerful.

"Let us never put confidence in man, or in any sanctity of position, office, or dress. If apostleship did not make Judas a saint, neither will position, office, nor dress make thee a saint." - Johann Fenis.

The GPS unit in my car gives me voice directions for every turn. Finally it announces "You have arrived!"

Go to college, marry a great spouse, have kids, attend church, climb the ladder, become a *Busy SportsLeader* with a good reputation, maybe even get voted an elder at church. A little voice on your shoulder says, "You have arrived!" Memorize the six words below, and walk humbly before your God.

"...put no confidence in the flesh". Philippians 3:3.

Searching, scouring, and hunting for the gifts that will delight our loved ones; we can do it on the net or on the street. It's difficult to know what to get, it is even more difficult to find it. We can try to remind ourselves of the *"true meaning of Christmas"* but the clamor is so loud, the pressure so great, that it is easy for the ***Busy SportsLeader*** to forget the gift already purchased.

"Praise be to the God and Father of our Lord Jesus Christ, who has blessed us in the heavenly realms with <u>every</u> spiritual blessing in Christ." Ephesians 1:3.

"A man's behavior is the index of the man, and his discourse is the index of his understanding," - Ali.

The radio commercial declares, "People judge you by the words you speak!" It then implores us to build our vocabulary so we can be more effective.

Many *Busy SportsLeaders* don't need more words; they need to lose some they already have.

Ask God to give you the words that will motivate, direct, and correct others *and* proclaim your understanding of God.

"The words of the godly are like sterling silver". Proverbs 10:20.

Tom Landry's record was impressive: an all-pro defensive back in '54, a coach with 270 wins, 5 Super Bowl appearances and two World Championships.

Several friends of mine attended his funeral. None mentioned the remarkable statistics listed above. All talked of how *"Coach Landry"* had deeply touched their life in a personal way.

Last week when I usually send *"Wisdom for the Busy SportsLeader"* I was with my wife at her mother's bedside. As we prayed for her and let her know of our love, she passed to be with the Lord. This week we will lay her to rest at a military national cemetery. I expect little will be said of her many accomplishments. I expect much will be said of her touch on the lives of others.

Living life with a perspective from the "right-side of the dash" will help anyone live like God asks them to live. From there we can see what is important. The dash I speak of is the one that will be on our headstone someday. Left of the dash is our birth date, the right marks our death.

"There is an appointed time for everything. And there is a time for every event under heaven. A time to give birth and a time to die; a time to plant and a time to uproot what is planted." Ecclesiastes 3:1, 2.

"No man is able to make progress when he is wavering between opposite things." - Epictetus.

Many churches offer "seeker services" on Sunday mornings. These are aimed at people who are investigating the faith before making a decision about placing Christ in their life.

Regrettably many ***Busy SportsLeaders*** will remain in "seeker-mode" for countless years to create an appearance of godliness without having to live by the convictions of faith.

"For he that waverth is like a wave of the sea driven with the wind and tossed." James 1:6.

"We consider Christmas as the encounter, the great encounter, the historical encounter, the decisive encounter, between God and mankind. He who has faith knows this truly; let him rejoice." - Pope Paul VI.

Music blaring, arena jammed, crowd on its feet. The **Busy SportsLeader** knows the joy of anticipation like no other. It is the moment when our quiet toil is about to encounter public reality. These are the moments for which many of us live.

Don't miss it this year: the foretaste of the Great Encounter. Create the environment, anticipate the moment, and celebrate the provision for atonement.

"When they saw the star, they rejoiced with exceedingly great joy." Matthew 2:10.

Can the *Busy SportsLeader* gain wisdom from the old, worn out Christmas story? Let's look at the "wise-men". What made them so wise?

"Now after Jesus was born in Bethlehem of Judea in the days of Herod the king, behold, magi from the east arrived in Jerusalem, saying, 'Where is He who has been born King of the Jews? For we saw His star in the east, and have come to worship Him.'" Matthew 2:1, 2.

These men were leaders, who looked for direction from above and acted on it. The *Busy SportsLeader* must take time to look for God's direction and then act on it.

If the magi simply gave intellectual ascent to the coming of the King and didn't act on that information, they may have been knowledgeable but they would not have been **wise**.

"Where do you want the ransom dropped?" the anxious father asked.

"Somewhere out of the way, where no one will notice, a cave in a small town, used by livestock will do," the kidnapper snapped back. "And I want your son to be the bagman. Do you understand me?"

"Yes....what price do you want? I'll pay anything to get them back," the father sighed.

"Anything?" the known killer inquired.

"To get them away from you? Yes...anything," repeated the father.

"Then instead of your son being the bagman, let him be the price you pay!"

It seemed as though the prisoners waited two thousand years for the answer. This price was certainly far too high, for the loving father had only one son. Finally the answer came.

"I agree to the price, he'll be delivered in Bethlehem."

"O come, o come Emmanuel, and ransom captive Israel."
From a traditional Christmas hymn. Lyrics translated from
9th century Latin. Music by Thomas Helmore.

If you're reading this early Christmas morning at work you're probably feeling the disappointment of not being with family.

This day over 2000 years ago The Son of The King willing left his heavenly home to do His work. It was a work we would never wish on our own sons. It was a place we would never send our own sons. Yet the Son of God came, freely, for you and me. We know of the sacrifice of Jesus, but rarely do we think of the sacrifice of the Father. He gave His most precious gift to us.

Today as you offer your gift of work for your family, remember the gift given for you.

"Glory to God in the highest, and on earth peace to men on whom his favor rests." Luke 2:14.

"Wisdom, thoroughly learned, will never be forgotten." -
Pythagoras.

The goal of Bible reading and study is not interpretation but application. Thoroughly learning God's Word requires the *Busy SportsLeader* putting into practice what is read. Only then will you truly live.

"Keep sound wisdom and discretion, and they will be life for your soul." Proverbs 3:21, 22.

The only thing that travels as fast as the **speed of light** is the **speed of darkness**. It's a basic truth of physics. The moment light invades darkness the darkness is gone. Remove the light and at the same speed darkness returns.

It is almost shocking how fast the *Busy SportsLeader* can move past the focus on Christ and the sense of the lasting love of family. In those few hours of "light" you had with those you love, perhaps you sensed the joy they had in your presence, not just your presents. **Perhaps too you imagined things would be different from now on, you and your family would be more Christ-centered**. Only 48 hours have passed, has the darkness swept over those hopes? Are you so far into the darkness you can't remember what you saw in the light? Don't forget. Let Christ be the center of every day for your family.

"For if anyone is a hearer of the word and not a doer, he is like a man who looks at his natural face in a mirror; for once he has looked at himself and gone away, he has immediately forgotten what kind of person he was."
James 1: 23.

"When you come to the end of all the light you know, and it's time to step into the darkness of the unknown, faith is knowing that one of two things shall happen: Either you will be given something solid to stand on or you will be taught to fly." - Edward Teller.

Important decisions on the athletes and coaches you bring into your organization are made after much of research. But at the end of the day you, "come to the end of all the light you know" as Edward Teller says. Here it takes an act of faith. The *Busy SportsLeader* has to have a vision for what the candidate will bring; those are the leaders who see the potential in others.

"Now faith is the substance of things hoped for, the evidence of things not seen." Hebrews 11:1.

"Success is not final, failure is not fatal: it is the courage to continue that counts." - Anonymous.

Courage is rarely found anymore.

Risk-management is a growth industry.

Looking bad is worse than being bad.

How is it then, that the **Busy SportsLeader** can take his or her organization to the next level?

Look beyond the horizon...plot a route that is in line with God's law...set sail and... *"be strong and very courageous, being careful to do according to all the law which Moses my servant commanded you; turn not from it to the right hand or to the left, that you may have good success wherever you go." Joshua 1:7.*

"I can't change the direction of the wind, but I can adjust my sails to always reach my destination." - Jimmy Dean.

Busy SportsLeaders find that change generates many questions which must be answered quickly. "How will this affect my family, my career, my new team, the future?" Unfortunately we can be so hurried and feel we have so few options that little time is taken to hear what God wants.

I urge anyone in the throes of decision making to take at least one hour of quiet before God to read, pray, and listen.

"Let integrity and uprightness preserve me, For I wait for You." Psalm 25:21.

A lengthy hike through the forest requires strength, perseverance, and if the terrain is difficult, a compass. A few steps in the wrong direction at the beginning of your trip can very quickly put you far off your target. A regular check of the compass and appropriate adjustments will get you where you intend to go.

Paul knew where he intended to go. In *Galatians 1:15, 16* He writes, *(God) "called me through His grace...that I would preach Him among the Gentiles..."* His calling was his compass.

Many of us have written our life's purpose statement; for the Christian *Busy SportsLeader* this should be the unique mission God has called you to do. In other words the reason **He** put **you** here.

This is far more than goal setting, like winning a certain title or making "x" amount of dollars. Many people *could* do that. Your personal mission is far more than being a good father and faithful husband. We are *all* **commanded** to do that.

Perhaps God has called you to build men for Christ in your sphere of influence, or provide educational opportunities for missionary children. It could be many things, but He's called YOU to do it.

Before you wander far into the forest this year, recheck your compass. Are you still on track? If not, make the adjustments necessary now before you're too far down the wrong trail.

"Making good decisions is a crucial skill at every level." -
Peter Drucker.

The *Busy SportsLeader* is responsible for the values of his
team. He must clearly set and read the moral compass of the
organization. He must also frequently communicate the values
to everyone in the group.

A leader cannot effectively lead without a values based
atlas. Followers look for direction from their leader. If people
sense the direction of the team is vague and not based on
timeless truths, they can make serious errors in judgment.

Lead - and tell others where you're going, in case they can't
always see you.

"Folly is joy to him who is destitute of discernment, But a
man of understanding walks uprightly." Proverbs 15:21.

"Hard work without talent is a shame; talent without hard work is a tragedy." – Robert Haff.

Investing the gifts God gives you is not just a good idea, it's an eternal principle.

The *Busy SportsLeader* is always evaluating talent, but how often do you evaluate the investment of talent? Look to surround yourself with talented people who work diligently to improve, not only in their areas of weakness, but in their strengths.

"'And I was afraid, and went away and hid your talent in the ground. See, you have what is yours.' But his master answered and said to him, 'You wicked, lazy slave'". *Matthew 25:25-26.*

"Acclaim is a distraction." - James Broughton.

Success has its down side. No longer can you go about your work in anonymity. It's easy to give in to fame; take a little less time to prepare, be a little more self assured, and enjoy things you previously felt were off-limits.

The **Busy SportsLeader** should fear the pitfalls on the path to success as much as he fears failure. Never forget the goal. Enjoy the process but don't stop.

"So I run straight to the goal with purpose in every step. I am not like a boxer who misses his punches." I Corinthians 9:6.

This time of year often brings some amount of uncertainty to the **Busy SportsLeader**. Change is in the air: if not for you, for many of your friends. A lot of big decisions are made now. You may have to make them, or others may ask your advice in big decisions.

Proverbs 24:3- 4 says, "By wisdom a house is built, and by understanding it is established, and by knowledge the rooms are filled with all precious and pleasant riches."

Prior to this passage we find a clue about God's "wisdom". Associate with people of **high character**, and avoid "evil men", as Proverbs 24:1 calls them. This little advice may help you or those you know today.

When looking at candidates for job openings the ***Busy SportsLeader*** has to make a decision as to what he is hiring...*to*? Is he hiring to....*profit*? Is he hiring to....*skill-set*? Is he hiring to....*team chemistry*? Of course he would like to have it all, but he will have preferences for the things he needs. Whatever his priorities are will disclose much about the leader and his organization.

The greatest leader of the Old Testament, Moses, became overworked and needed help. God revealed His wisdom for adding people to leadership through Moses' father-in-law. God's wisdom involves proper training and inspection of an individual's **character** before they are selected.

"Show them the way to live and the duties they are to perform. (Then) select capable men from all the people, men who fear God, trustworthy men who hate dishonest gain, and appoint them as officials over thousands, hundreds, fifties and tens." Exodus 18:20-21.

When hiring never overlook hiring to....*moral fiber*.

"It is a great consolation for me to remember that the Lord, to whom I had drawn near in humble and child-like faith, has suffered and died for me, and that He will look on me in love and compassion." - Wolfgang Amadeus Mozart.

Busy SportsLeaders usually hate mistakes. It's in their nature to get the team to strive for perfection. This drive is often reflected in their personal lives as they set goals, seek excellence, and achieve success. Dealing with setbacks and mistakes in their private life can be as tough as losses in their professional life.

It's important to remember how God sees you: the same way you hurt when your children hurt, He hurts for you. He cares for you, as you do for yours. Remember how you feel toward your sons and daughters when they struggle and you will have a sense of how God feels toward you.

"The Lord is like a father to his children, tender and compassionate to those who fear him." Psalm 103:13.

"If you lose your wealth, you have lost nothing, If you lose your health, you have lost something, But if you lose your character, you have lost everything." - Woodrow Wilson.

It is amazing how smart some people are when they begin to attain wealth. They see things clearer, their opinions are sure, and they dismiss those with an opposing point of view.

Hubris is the enemy of the *Busy SportsLeader*. Money cannot make you smarter. A humble search for truth and wisdom will secure what you need.

"The rich man is wise in his own eyes, But the poor who has understanding sees through him." Proverbs 28: 11.

"The one who cannot restrain their anger will wish undone, what their temper and irritation prompted them to do." - Horace.

The **Busy SportsLeader** lives in a world of passion. At times leaders need to stir the passions of the team, at other times they need to bridle violence. Great leadership in this area takes a powerful combination of conviction and modeling. Leaders must verbally express their beliefs and also demonstrate appropriate behavior in their own demeanor. If frustration is appropriate, show it without destruction. If celebration is called for, express it without arrogance. Mature leaders can teach valuable lessons to a generation who has had few healthy examples in this area.

"He who is slow to anger is better than the mighty, and he who rules his spirit than he who takes a city." Proverbs 16:32.

Profitability and efficiency are hallmarks of good business. **Bankruptcy and downtime** *(read jail-time)* were hallmarks of the apostle Paul's work. Yet it was in that poverty and in those periods of incarceration Paul had some of his greatest successes.

The *Busy SportsLeader* has a responsibility to watch the bottom line. But in that task is an even greater duty to find ways and places for God to work through him into the lives of others. Those activities may not generate revenue in the short run, but will have long-term impact.

"Each man's work will become evident; for the day will show it, because it is to be revealed with fire; and the fire itself will test the quality of each man's work. If any man's work, which he has built upon, remains, he shall receive a reward." I Corinthians 3: 13, 14.

"An appeaser is one who feeds a crocodile, hoping it will eat him last." - Winston Churchill.

Hoping that turning a blind eye will solve the problem, *this one time*, is a common tactic of many **Busy SportsLeaders**.

"The timing isn't right" or *"this person needs to be handled in a special way"* or *"I just don't have time to deal with that kind of stuff."* Each of these reasons to delay confronting a difficult situation may be true, or they may simply be appeasement that has its root in fear.

"An open rebuke is better than hidden love". **Proverbs 27:5.**

"Public behavior is merely private character writ large." - Stephen Covey.

Often **Busy SportsLeaders** feel like they are walking a tight rope when dealing with the bad behavior of their top performers. Everyone knows you need their production, but you can't stand their conduct. The easiest solution seems to be to attribute the behavior to a momentary lapse in judgment and assure the world the person is really made of solid character. Unfortunately this is rarely the case.

As leaders we must address the core issues. It may sound corny and out of date but developing character in others is still part of our job; even when the person in need is an adult. Not everyone will receive instruction, but many will. They will be forever grateful for your care and leadership in their life.

"He who ignores discipline comes to poverty and shame, but whoever heeds correction is honored." Proverbs 13:18.

"Effort only fully releases its reward after a person refuses to quit." - Napoleon Hill.

Discouragement is the precursor to surrender. The *Busy SportsLeader* must sense the early signs of pessimism and look for the building blocks of hope. This takes faith and strength; faith to believe you can get to the light, and strength to provide the effort to get there. It won't be easy, but with strong leadership, it is possible.

"Be on the alert, stand firm in the faith, act like men, be strong." I Corinthians 16:13.

Recently the commissioner of a major sport said one of his jobs is to, "add value to existing franchises". His comments were in response to the sale of a franchise where the announced price reflected a loss for the current owner.

There are several reasons why the value of a team can go down: deteriorating fan base, higher costs of salaries, and uncertainty over the future of the general economy are all real issues for the *Busy SportsLeader*.

It is a blessing to have a place where we can "add value" everyday without the worry of weakening interest, evaporating capital and doubt over the horizon.

"Sell your possessions and give to the poor. Provide purses for yourselves that will not wear out, a treasure in heaven that will not be exhausted, where no thief comes near and no moth destroys. For where your treasure is, there your heart will be also." Luke 12:33, 34.

"Every life is a march from innocence through temptation, to virtue or vice."- Lyman Abbott.

You <u>will</u> face temptation today.

So will those you lead.

What will happen?

You get to chose!

Can you expect those you lead to resist if you don't? The *Busy SportsLeader* has many who will find strength in their leadership. Don't let them down. The strategy to overcome temptation is NO SECRET.

"Watch and pray, lest you enter into temptation, The spirit indeed is willing, but the flesh is weak." Matthew 26:41.

"Life is one of those precious fleeting gifts, and everything can change in a heartbeat." -Anonymous.

Head down, nose to the grindstone, putting out fires and pushing onward. *Busy SportsLeaders* know how to work, but every once in a while they might need to get away to see the big picture. This is an important discipline in business and in life.

"Focus" can eventually cause us to forget the larger context. Like the golfer who takes a glance at the target before beginning the swing, make sure your work today is still in line with where you want to be.

"The hot sun rises and the grass withers; the little flower droops and falls, and its beauty fades away. In the same way, the rich will fade away with all of their achievements." James 1: 11.

If we could negotiate for ourselves a guaranteed, no cut, and no trade contract with the **perfect** team doing the **perfect** job, in the **perfect** city, and at the **perfect** salary, *for life*, **regardless of our performance**, most of us would jump at it. It's natural to seek security and safety for our families and ourselves, but hard to for the ***Busy SportsLeader*** to find.

There are so many things that can happen in the future to turn even a good situation bad. Ownership can changes hands or the marketplace could go sour, or maybe your talent begins to fade.

We all would like to secure the future for those who are precious to us. Incredibly, there is an ironclad guarantee for the future, and the most wonderful thing you can experience today. God lists ten powerful forces that will try to separate us from His **perfect** love. But He won't let that happen.

"For I am convinced that neither death, nor life, nor angels, nor principalities, nor things present, nor things to come, nor powers, nor height, nor depth, nor any other created thing, shall be able to separate us from the love of God, which is in Christ Jesus our Lord." Romans 8: 38, 39.

"Delusions of grandeur make me feel a lot better about myself." - Lily Tomlin.

The more successful leaders become, the harder it is to get good information from those around them. Many times, a *Busy SportsLeader* has complained to me that one of their biggest frustrations is the feeling that they are flying in the dark because others only tell them filtered truth, not what is really going on.

If you experience this phenomenon, it most likely comes from either fear or ignorance: fear - that you will react badly toward the person bringing the information, or ignorance - not theirs, yours. You've probably been told about things that needed changing…and ignored it.

"Don't just listen to God's word. You must do what it says. Otherwise, you are only fooling yourselves. For if you listen to the word and don't obey, it is like glancing at your face in a mirror. You see yourself, walk away, and forget what you look like." James 1: 22-24.

SportsLeadership is usually an exciting occupation. But all good things come with a price. I know very few SportsLeaders that have great marriages. If you disagree with me, ask your wife. If you're a woman, you already know this reality.

God has given us the road map to a better relationship. *"Let marriage be held in honor among all"*. *Hebrews 13:4.* The Greek word for honor here is TIMAÓ, which means, "valuing at a price". TIMAÓ is derived from another Greek word, TIMÉ, which literally means, "a price paid". You may be thinking, "I am a *Busy SportsLeader* and if I had more of that TIME stuff, I'd have a better marriage!"

To have a great marriage it literally takes TIME. To have TIME, you have to pay a price; that may mean something gets left undone or done later. Choosing what gets done later, or not at all, can be a daunting task, especially during the season. But if busyness is eroding your marriage, tough choices must be made.

As a Leader consider how you can bring TIME or honor, to the marriages of the people who work for you. Perhaps your organization will be known as a place of great marriages.

I know of no Christian *SportsLeader* who wants to be thought of as a person with a **"BIG EGO"**. But sometimes as the wins come and praise follows, we can unlock the cage we keep our ego crammed into, and let it out for a little stroll. It can be kind of fun. Lots of people are willing to stroke it and fawn over it; besides it's not all *that* big and could use a little encouragement!

On the other hand if the wins aren't coming sometimes we feel it **necessary** to remind those around us of our past accomplishments. I know I often wear one of my *many* Super Bowl rings on those days. I only wear one at a time, but I usually mention *I do have others*.

The Israelites let the old ego out for a party once in a while too...then they got this message from God.

"Is the axe to boast itself over the one who chops with it? Is the saw to exalt itself over the one who wields it? That would be like a club wielding those who lift it, or like a rod lifting him who is not wood." Isaiah 10:15.

How true Isaiah's words are. The imagination, the ingenuity, sound mind and body, all are gifts from God. We are just the instrument. Staying sharp and clean is partly our responsibility for sure. But the real work is done by the Master craftsman, not the tool.

"All wise men share one trait in common, the ability to listen." - Frank Tyger.

The trouble with "know-it-alls" is that they never do…and they never will. God offers us wisdom, but most people rarely access it. The *Busy SportsLeader* is often giving directions, solving problems and providing clarity. They are used to doing the talking. But it's not the talking that makes us wise, it's the listening. When was the last time you *listened* to God?

"Come here and listen to me! I'll pour out the spirit of wisdom and make you wise." Proverbs 1:23.

"It's not about 'who wants it the most', we are both professionals...we both want it! It's about - Who Executes.'"- Bill Walsh, Head Coach San Francisco 49'ers, just days before Super Bowl XXIII against the Cincinnati Bengals.

When the *Busy SportsLeader* loses a mentor, they are bound to consider all the lessons learned in the relationship: the changes in their life the mentor encouraged, the difference this one person made.

I served the 49'ers as team chaplain for 18 years. Eight of those years Bill Walsh was the head coach. We were not particularly close, but I know he appreciated me, my work, and the contributions I made. I appreciated his professionalism, kindness to me, and the lesson of execution. It served me well as a chaplain, and now as a consultant, to know my good intentions and desires are not enough. It is the execution of my job that produces results.

"But prove yourselves doers of the word, and not merely hearers (with simply good intentions) who delude themselves." James 1:22.

The television graphic showed that each of the past four Super Bowls produced first time championships for four different franchises.

With stunning similarity the fans, players, coaches and owners of the Rams, Ravens, Patriots and Buccaneers rejoiced at the achievement of a long time goal. It was a fond reminder of what I experienced in January of 1982 as the 49'ers won their first ever Lombardi trophy.

Three years later another 49'ers Super Bowl victory caused one player to ask, "Is that all there is?" Five years after that a grizzled veteran of several Super Bowl wins confessed to me on the charter flight home after a 55-10 blowout win over the Broncos, "I thought it would feel better than this." The *Busy SportsLeader* with wisdom seeks joy beyond victory, knowing that the celebration is fleeting. Championships should always be your goal, but not your god.

"For who can eat and who can have enjoyment without Him?" Ecclesiastes 2:25.

"The real problem with hunting elephants is carrying the decoys." - Anonymous.

A New Yorker Magazine cartoon shows an elephant on a psychiatrists couch. The elephant says, "I don't know...I'm right there in the middle of the room and everyone acts like they can't see me!"

Wise *Busy SportsLeaders* don't need decoys to find and get rid of the "elephants" no one wants to talk about. They need honesty and courage.

"Oh Lord who may dwell in Your tent? He who...speaks truth in his heart and does not slander with his tongue." Psalm 15:2-3.

In modern elite sports, it is common to see the marriage of high performance and illegal behavior. In addition, if a conviction can't be made, the behavior may not be considered "bad", just "expected".

The **Busy SportsLeader** has to make tough decisions in the face of ever increasing competition to retain talent. In their leadership position they set the standards for their team.

Professional batters are required to hit the most difficult pitches in the world, Olympic sprinters must run faster than those in past games, NFL wide receivers are obliged to create space between themselves and some of the best athletes on the planet.

Why set the bar LOWER for YOUR organization? It is not consistent with high performance, nor does it inspire high achievers.

"Abstain from all appearance of evil." I Thessalonians 5:22.

"I find it true in my life that what I enjoy does not satisfy and what satisfies I do not enjoy." - Walter A. Henrichsen.

Winning a world championship is always followed by a joyous celebration. After months and years of effort finally the fruit of the labor is realized. Now is the time to hug, laugh, and soak in champagne.

The celebrating Super Bowl wins were awesome. But on the trip home in a quiet moment on the plane, a player or coach would eventually pull me aside and say, "You know, I thought I would feel different. It's great…but not as great as I thought it would be."

True contentment doesn't usually come from what is enjoyable at the moment. The deeply satisfying can only come from the hand of God. He seems to give a depth of joy from faithfulness in doing the difficult things: raising children, physical exercise, study, and work to name a few. Prayer, bearing one another's burdens, and patience, would be a few more.

For the *Busy SportsLeader* then, being handed the trophy may not be that which ultimately satisfies, but the knowledge that you were faithful and disciplined on the journey.

"Those who love money will never have enough. How absurd to think that wealth brings true happiness." Ecclesiastes 5:10.

In the film, *"Ground Hog Day"*, Bill Murray portrays a television reporter who discovers that he will always wake up and live Ground Hog day over and over again, no matter what he does. With this sense of security he begins to throw himself into traffic, jump off buildings, and dare heroic deeds. No matter what he does, he wakes up in the same bed, and faces the day again.

Of course fear keeps us from tempting fate, which is wise. We know the truth of the results of high-speed impact on our bodies. But fear can also keep a *Busy SportsLeader* from daring to do right things. The fear of rejection, ridicule, or loss of profits keeps many from following Christ.

Even in the face of real physical persecution the writer of *Hebrews 13:6* says, *"The Lord is my helper; I will not be afraid. What can man do to me?"* A truth well worth considering next time you are fearful of tomorrow. Go ahead. Take a stand. It won't kill you!

"All wisdom is not new wisdom." - Winston Churchill.

People regularly comment to me that many of the best leadership and business books have the same threads running through them. These books are often advertised as "*groundbreaking*".

In reality, it is timeless principles that should guide the **Busy SportsLeader**. Great wisdom is not new, just repackaged. That is fine, if it helps you and others learn it.

"What has been will be again, what has been done will be done again; there is nothing new under the sun."
Ecclesiastes 1:9.

"The aim and final end of all music should be none other than the glory of God and the refreshment of the soul." - Johannes Sebastian Bach.

Five times I was fortunate enough to be part of a Super Bowl championship. Five other times I was only one game away. For many years I have contemplated *"the aim and final end of all sport"*. Business leaders, architects, entertainers, or any person of faith who receives public acclaim should consider the aim and final end of their work.

I know that God, ultimately, is the rightful recipient of all the glory that comes with a championship. But how do we, as a practical matter, glorify God and not ourselves? Examine two key areas of your life to glorify God: the effort and quality of your work - is it the best you can do; and your internal pride meter - is it singing your praises or God's?

"For ye are bought with a price: therefore glorify God in your body, and in your spirit, which are God's."
I Corinthians 6:20.

Scandal is an ugly word. Who is ultimately responsible for the integrity of a sport? Is it the commissioner? Is it the head of the Federation, or chief of referees? One thing is obvious, the broader responsibility is accepted, the greater the integrity. Perhaps the professional sport with the highest level of integrity is golf. The reason for this perception is that the competitors take on much of the responsibility. They preserve the values of the game, even when it costs them success. They were taught these values.

Integrity is taught. Competitors want to win, that is their nature. But values are carefully developed.

Titus 2:6-8 says, "Similarly, encourage the young men to be self-controlled. In everything set them an example by doing what is good. In your teaching show integrity, seriousness and soundness of speech that cannot be condemned, so that those who oppose you may be ashamed because they have nothing bad to say about us."

The *Busy SportsLeader* has many responsibilities. One of them is teaching and demonstrating integrity.

"Then Jesus said, 'Were there not ten cleansed? But the other nine—where are they?'" Luke 17:17.

Jesus was omniscient; he didn't ask a question to get an answer. He asked so that we would discover the answer!

Well, I suppose the other nine were too *busy* to thank Jesus for their healing. By-the-way, when was the last time you thanked Him?

"Go the extra mile. It's never crowded."- Anonymous.

"Truth is so obscure in these times, and falsehood so established, that, unless we love the truth, we cannot know it." - Blaise Pascal.

So much information, so little time. The *Busy SportsLeader* often has to make important decisions quickly. Reliance on generally accepted *"truth"* can be hazardous to your career. Make truth a priority in your own life, and make that priority known to others. You'll get better information faster.

"Therefore love truth and peace." Zechariah 8:19.

"**Negotiations**" and "**Trust**" are words that seem both mutually exclusive, and at the same time, in sync. During negotiations you protect your own interests while at the same time trying to reach a compromise. But to reach a compromise, you need mutual trust, at least to some degree.

There are some whose personal principles dictate that the solution is the one that benefits *only* them. They walk in self-justification believing their actions are right, because their personal agenda has been fulfilled. The *Busy SportsLeader* encounters many people like this. The only thing worse is **becoming...one of them**.

Proverbs 21:2 reads, "Every man's way is right in his own eyes, but the Lord weighs the heart."

Ask God daily to reveal to you what He finds in your heart. **Is it jaded?** He desires us to have a pure heart; trust Him that He can make yours a **heart of gold**.

"Catch on fire with enthusiasm and people will come for miles to watch you burn." - Charles Wesley

My local bookstore has shelves of titles on leadership, motivation, incentivization, inspiration, and stimulation. The key for a *Busy SportsLeader* to get others to work with more fervor isn't in them, it's in you.

"...your enthusiasm has stirred most of them to action".
II Corinthians 8:17.

"The real war is inward of which the outer action is but the echo and reverberation." - Harry Emerson Fosdick.

At first many **Busy SportsLeaders** appear confident, calm, articulate and in control. But if their internal personal battles are not being won their facade will soon shatter. Strengthen the inside first, the outside will follow.

"So we fix our eyes not on what is seen, but on what is unseen. For what is seen is temporary, but what is unseen is eternal." II Corinthians 4:18.

"We serve God by serving others. The world defines greatness in terms of power, possessions, prestige, and position. If you can demand service from others, you've arrived. In our self-serving culture with its me-first mentality, acting like a servant is not a popular concept." - Rick Warren.

One day I asked an NFL head coach if he thought his relationships with his friends had changed much since he had taken the position. He really didn't think they had; he felt those closest to him treated him the same as always. Then I inquired if any of his friends had asked him to help move furniture, paint a room, lay cement or any of the typical things guys ask guys to do. After a pause he said, "No, I guess no one asks that of me anymore."

The *Busy SportsLeader* can easily avoid service to others and justify it by citing the overwhelming demands of the job. From time to time though, the call to service outside of the PR department is expected from God. A practical step this summer is to seek out one day or half day when you can serve a friend. It will bless him, and strengthen your understanding of Biblical leadership.

"If anyone serves Me, let him follow Me; and where I am, there My servant will be also. If anyone serves Me, him My Father will honor." John 12:26.

Middle managers often evaluate the performance of those they manage. **Leaders** carry an extra burden, they not only evaluate performance, but they **must evaluate the motives** of people whom they trust in to run large portions of the organization. In addition many *Busy SportsLeaders* regularly enter into high-stakes, high-profile, high-pressure negotiations. Reading intentions of good-faith or deceit are usually the fulcrum for moving forward.

Evaluating others' motives can be very difficult. God speaks to this issue in *Titus 1:15: "To the pure, all things are pure; but to those who are defiled and unbelieving, nothing is pure, but both their mind and their conscience are defiled."*

The first step in seeing others rightly is purifying your own heart! We all see others through glasses tinted by our own faults. If we hedge the truth we'll expect others to do so also. If we have our own selfish interests as our top priority, we'll look at others as competition for our "stuff".

With a pure heart you will look more rightly at others and become a better judge of motives and character. The fear of being naïve or gullible can be relieved by the knowledge that you will now see others through God's eyes.

Spring

"Motivation is what gets you started. Habit is what keeps you going." - Jim Ryun.

Behaviors are predictors of results.
Habits are our regular behaviors.
Our basic nature as humans draws us to our habits.
Understanding the basic nature of humans is critical for all leaders.

If humans are basically good - then encourage others to follow their natural instincts.

If human nature is something other than *good,* then leadership requires knowledge of where we're naturally headed <u>and</u> a compass to know where we should go.

Carefully consider the nature of humans today. Are we basically good or not? Tomorrow we'll look at human nature and how it impacts a leader.

First let's review: If humans are basically good - then encourage others to follow their natural instincts. If human nature is something other than *good,* then leadership requires knowledge of where we're naturally headed <u>and</u> a compass to know where we should go.

"We were born with an evil nature, and we were under God's anger ..." Ephesians 2:3.

Man was created to have fellowship with God and with a free will. We used that free will and turned away from God. That tendency, or nature, is now passed on from one generation to another. We were born with a nature that is not good. We tend to turn away from God and go our own independent ways. A leader must recognize this and be prepared to take a naturally rebellious, selfish group of people and help them achieve things together that are good and beneficial.

"Lying is not exceptional; it is normal, and more often spontaneous and unconscious than cynical and coldly analytical. Our minds and bodies secrete deceit."
- D. L. Smith.

Understanding the make-up of your team is a fundamental of leadership. Many leaders never take into consideration our basic nature. Consider: Is our nature good, or not?

A simple observation of the human race finds mixed messages. We see great acts of courage and kindness. We also see humans can be incredibly cruel and commit horrific acts against one another. We experience tension in our own lives between selfishness and charity. So what is at our core? Today's entry takes a look at God's perspective of our core. We were created with a free will and good nature, but it was corrupted and the Bible teaches we inherit the corrupted nature. It usually shows up in selfishness.

Knowing this, a leader must realize his job (getting people moving in a positive, team orientated direction) is against basic human nature. Most of us want to achieve great things, but wanting and doing are two different things.

"I want to do what is good, but I don't. I don't want to do what is wrong, but I do it anyway. Who will free me from this life that is dominated by sin and death? Thank God! The answer is in Jesus Christ our Lord." Romans 7: 19, 24b, and 25.

Stress is why you get paid the big bucks.

Big decisions, big stakes, big wins *and* losses. The **Busy SportsLeader** is scrutinized, analyzed, and editorialized in a very public forum.

Every word can be caught on tape, misquoted or misunderstood, thus everything said in the open becomes measured and carefully crafted. Let the pressure show "out there" and everyone will see it tonight at 10.

In contrast to a broadcasted slip, a private showing of the blockbuster movie, *"Anger Mismanagement"* at home will probably go unnoticed...professionally. BUT, it isn't missed by those in the front row seats.

"Husbands, love your wives and do not be harsh with them."
Colossians 3:19.

Give the stress to God, He'll give you love for your wife.

"Negotiating…is an everyday part of life." - Leigh Steinberg.

"(A rich young ruler) came to Jesus with this question: 'Teacher, what good things must I do to have eternal life?'….Jesus told him, 'go and sell all you have and give the money to the poor, and you will have treasure in heaven. Then come, follow me.'" Matthew 19: 16, 21.

Busy SportsLeaders do a lot of negotiating. We like to negotiate with God too: *"When my family's needs are met, I'll consider giving." "I'll spend time with you when I'm not so busy." "Let me finish this job, and then I can follow you."*

Negotiating is good in business, but with God it's about surrender.

"I have never been lost, but I will admit to being confused for several weeks." - Daniel Boone.

Ever feel like Daniel Boone? Plenty of us have.

Lost – but not showing it on the outside.
Confused – and quietly looking for clues to get out of the woods.

Part of this is spiritual. Because of our sin, God created a world that would frustrate our pride and cause reliance on Him. *"Therefore its name was called Babel, because there the Lord confused the language of the whole earth; and from there the Lord scattered them abroad over the face of the whole earth." Genesis 11:9.*

In order for a *Busy SportsLeader* to get to where he is trying to go - ask for directions. Just know where to ask.

Even the *Busy SportsLeader* who loves his work can have tasks that bring him no joy and appear to be without meaning. Time spent in other areas may *seem* more profitable. Projects *could* be delegated to capable subordinates. But there are jobs that God intends for the leader to do personally.

During biblical times, travel over dirt roads was easier in the spring. Kings would lead their armies to secure the kingdom by driving off foreign forces that had encroached on the land over the winter. But the battlefield is never as comfortable as the palace.

"In the spring, at the time when kings go off to war, David sent Joab out with the king's men and the whole Israelite army... but David remained in Jerusalem." II Samuel 11:1.

When King David assigned Joab the task of protecting the kingdom, he set in motion a series of events that would destroy his throne. God intended David to do this work personally, not the capable Joab. God has work intended only for you; He has chosen **you** to do it. As *Sir Josiah Stamp* said in The English Digest, *"It is easy to dodge our responsibilities, but we cannot dodge the consequences of dodging our responsibilities."*

"The man who wants to lead the orchestra must turn his back on the crowd." - James Crook.

Perhaps the thorniest piece of leadership, especially for the young, is dealing with occasional disapproval. I have yet to meet a great leader who has been popular with everyone all the time.

Tough decisions have to be made, truth spoken, hard action taken. An increasing confusion about right and wrong only make these aspects of leadership more difficult.

The crowd isn't a good place for a *Busy SportsLeader* to look for answers.

"Don't be impressed with your own wisdom. Instead, fear the Lord and turn your back on evil." Proverbs 3:7.

"Every man is his own chief enemy." - Anacharsis, Philosopher 600 B.C.

In the midst of work and competition it is natural, and necessary, to focus on challenges before us. That focus, over time, can lead the **Busy SportsLeader** to draw false conclusions about the true enemy. Throwing all available resources into defeating an external opponent leaves us open to defeat. We as individual leaders, and our organizations, need to keep our discipline intact, and build our internal strength in order to first conquer ourselves; the rest, next.

"Like a city whose walls are broken down, is a man who lacks self-control." Proverbs 25:28.

Partial-season tickets are a popular way to entice fans to move up from day of game sales. They don't cost as much as season tickets and they usually come with the option to buy post-season seats.

Ironically the ***Busy SportsMarketingLeader*** who developed this concept may have influenced the dedication level of many Christian ***SportsLeaders***. There is a temptation to buy the *partial-commitment plan* when it comes to working in sports business and being a disciple of Christ. The partial-commitment plan allows you to walk faithfully with Christ *most* of the time, with the **hope** of great rewards in heaven. The tempting part of this plan is it still allows you a lot of "flexibility" in the tough areas of: words chosen to motivate players, honesty in negotiations, and the ever-popular temper control.

In ***Luke 9:62*** a potential disciple suggests his own plan to follow the Lord. ***"But Jesus said to him, 'No one, after putting his hand o the plow and looking back, is fit for the kingdom of God.'"***

Never one for clever marketing techniques, Jesus offers a different plan: Total commitment. This commitment doesn't mean we will never fail. Nor does it mean we will be perfect immediately. What it does mean is a whole-hearted, permanent commitment to honor God every moment of our life. He asks us to trust Him with the results of our obedience.

"If you get too far ahead of the army, your soldiers may mistake you for the enemy." - Warren W. Wiersbe.

I work with many leaders whose people have become so discouraged and confused, that they feel the biggest challenge they face is their boss. The *Busy SportsLeader* who leads from too great a distance will almost certainly lose touch with those fighting the battles.

"Perspective" is a good thing, but if it's always from 30,000 feet you might not know who's on your side. It is essential that leaders regularly get close enough to those they lead to find out.

"As Joshua approached the city of Jericho, he saw a man facing him with a sword in hand. Joshua went up to him and asked, 'Are you friend or foe?'" Joshua 5:13.

"We thought, because we had power, we had wisdom."
- Stephen Vincent Benet.

Today, at a very early age, people can acquire the three jewels of earthly glory: *wealth, fame, and power.*

The young *Busy SportsLeader* must never be fooled that any of these jewels bestow wisdom. Wisdom does not come by accomplishment. It doesn't even come from external means like reading great books. True wisdom comes from God, for He is the fountainhead. Be not fooled by what you have; look to what He has.

"Praise the name of God forever and ever, for He alone has wisdom and power." Daniel 2:20.

Over time the ***Busy SportsLeader*** will see many Christian athletes that have lived lives of admirable consistency throughout their college days. Then something startling happens. After they cash their first checks, their attitudes change, their friends seem shady, and the player becomes distracted. The same athlete you may have imagined growing into a team leader has become stunted and self-centered.

Unfortunately the weeds of fame and fortune have also strangled the spiritual effectiveness of many ***Busy SportsLeaders***.

"The seed that fell among thorns stands for those who hear, but as they go on their way they are choked by life's worries, riches and pleasures, and they do not mature." Luke 8:14.

Regularly weed the garden of your spiritual life to keep yourself growing in Christ.

"Our character is what we do when we think no one is looking." - H. Jackson Brown, Jr.

Visits to the local children's hospital with a press core on hand, a personal foundation that hosts a charity golf tournament and smiling more often when the beat writer comes around are all very nice. But looks can be deceiving.

Every *Busy SportsLeader* wants a core of players that are **"character guys"**, but finding them can be harder than it looks. Agents, PR firms and image consultants know how to put plenty of "glossy" on an 8" by 10". But how do you *really* find out? (Hold on, I know some of you are thinking, "*We have a great private detective here.*") There may be a more direct way. Let the player talk to you. Listen to his heart. *Proverbs 18:4* says, **"The words of a man's mouth are deep waters."**

This may take some time. The conversation might have to be off-site. It will have to be private, no handlers to frame the discussion.

But the trickiest part, by far, is that you have to be a **"character guy"** yourself to hear those that aren't.

Nearly a century ago Ambrose Bierce, in his satirical Devil's Dictionary, defined patience as "a minor form of despair, disguised as a virtue."

Today the **Busy SportsLeader** can find patience a crisis of faith. He is a leader because he is pro-active, yet he knows God is sovereign in His timing of events.

"The patient in spirit is better than the proud in spirit. Be not hasty in your spirit to be angry; for anger rests in the heart of fools." Ecclesiastes 7:8- 9.

Always seek the Lord's wisdom first in the decision making and then listen to His answer. Decisions need to be timely, not hasty.

The **Busy SportsLeader** needs wisdom to make decisions. A careful calculation of all factors is the "due diligence" expected from any leader before good choices are made. So how can it be that even with thoughtful analysis, seemingly good choices turn out very badly?

Good choices are built on wisdom. Wisdom stands on truth. Truth is not just facts but honest character: *the decision maker's character.* Genuine wisdom, deepest truth, and unadulterated character are unquestionably bound together.

King David understood this when he cried to God, *"Surely you desire truth in the inner parts; you teach me wisdom in the inmost place." Psalms 51:6.*

Unfortunately King David's understanding came after the two worst decisions of his life. Fortunately for us, we can learn this lesson prior to calamity.

"Never throughout history has a man who lived a life of ease left a name worth remembering." - Theodore Roosevelt.

Suffering, set-backs, struggle and sacrifice are all common threads in the lives of those who made a difference in this world.

Security, serenity, and self-fulfillment are fine for now, but will it mean anything in a hundred years?   Even the *Busiest SportsLeader* should ask that hard question every now and then.

"Consider him who endured such opposition from sinful men, so that you will not grow weary and lose heart." Hebrews 12:3.

Imagine the heavy load carried by those oppressed in an evil kingdom. Imagine the years of hoping a liberator would come. Imagine the day of fulfillment: singing, dancing, shouting, thanking.

The few that were there in person to see the fall of the dictator must have run home to tell the good news. Some who heard wouldn't believe it until they saw it for themselves. Others would be set free immediately by accepting the truth on the spot. The freedom won didn't guarantee people would chose to live differently. It simply offered the freedom to choose. It was a historic spring day that very first Easter.

"It is for freedom that Christ has set us free. Stand firm, then, and do not let yourselves be burdened again by a yoke of slavery." Galatians 5:1.

The ***Busy SportsLeader*** faces the death of dreams; passed over for promotions deserved, bonuses not paid, championship games lost.

To many of **His** followers it was the death of **their** dreams; dreams of freedom from an oppressive Roman government, dreams of self-rule and personal prosperity, dreams of glory and power. But on that cold Friday afternoon something much more died. The death of death itself! Eternal life was now offered for free. Free, but not cheap!

"And this is eternal life that they may know Thee, the only true God, and Jesus Christ whom thou hast sent." John 17:3.

Today is the day for you to ask yourself a tough question, and give yourself an honest answer. Ask this, "Do I know God and Jesus Christ whom He sent?" The question is NOT; do I know *about* God and Jesus the **historical figure**? But do you know Him **personally**? You can know Jesus by asking Him to forgive your sins and inviting Him to come into your life. He desires you to open your heart, and in an act of faith, exchange your efforts to reach God in your own strength, for His death and resurrection on your behalf so that you can know Him and eternal life.

"Expert analysts" offer commentary on everything from the hiring or firing of a coach, to ticket prices, to salaries paid to players. Many, many times these *shrewd* observers will refer to a ***Busy SportsLeader*** and say, "Well, it's his team and he has the right to do whatever he wants!" This kind of statement reflects the popular notion that **if a decision is lawful it is also proper,** whether or not it's the *best* decision, a *moral* decision, or even a *wise* decision.

The standards of God are far above an individual's legal rights.

For any decision to be truly right it **first** has to be right with the Author of right and wrong. ***II Chronicles 14:2*** is God's expert commentary on King Asa of the Old Testament. ***"Asa did what was good and <u>right</u> in the eyes of the Lord his God."*** If a decision is right in His eyes you don't have to wonder if it is indeed right.

"Our greatest glory is not in never failing, but in rising up every time we fail." - Ralph Waldo Emerson.

Failure in business is frustrating, so often it is caused by stiff competition or market changes.

Failure in our personal and spiritual lives is more than frustrating, it is agonizing. Often it simply comes down to choices we freely make. If transgression and sin have become the norm, don't give up. God hasn't. Be honest with Him about your weaknesses. Ask for strength and for a trusted friend to hold you accountable.

"Let us not lose heart in doing good, for in due time we will reap if we do not grow weary." Galatians 6:9.

"You and I have need of the strongest spell that can be found to wake us from the evil enchantment of worldliness."
- C. S. Lewis.

Worldliness has long been a beautiful distraction, diverting our attention from godliness. Godliness isn't nearly as sexy.

A *Busy SportsLeader* with a humble walk with God, accepting His direction and discipline, OR, howling laughter while sprinting toward instant pleasure. Doesn't seem like much of a choice…if all you can see are the material things of this place. Be still and consider God's Word. There is much more here, and much more to come.

"For the grace of God has appeared, bringing salvation to all men, instructing us to deny ungodliness and worldly desires and to live sensibly, righteously and godly in the present age". Titus 2:11-12.

"You may say to yourself, 'My power and the strength of my hands have produced this wealth for me.' But remember the LORD your God, for it is he who gives you the ability to produce wealth." Deuteronomy 8:17, 18.

Almost everyone in sports knows athletes with bloated egos that are the result of their wealth. It is just as tempting for the *Busy SportsLeader* to look at success, accolades and riches with the same self-centered pride in which many athletes indulge.

Perhaps the most dangerous trap for Christians is to measure their spiritual maturity by the accumulation of wealth. Churches and faith-based organizations often reinforce this fallacy when they seek leadership from individuals with great financial resources, but little Biblical wisdom.

Wealth can be a great blessing, but it is not an accurate measure of a man's walk with God.

"Who likes not his business, his business likes not him." -William Hazlitt.

Passion has been the watchword for about a decade. Every company looks for people that are passionate about their work. It's the reason so many want a career in sports or entertainment.

Feeding the poor, relieving suffering, sharing Christ with others, prayer – those things are hard for a *Busy SportsLeader* to schedule. But these things are what God looks for, what He wants us to be passionate about. A love for these won't come overnight, but start, your love will grow, not only for the work, but for your Boss.

"He gave his life to free us from every kind of sin...totally committed to doing good deeds". Titus 2:14.

"(The Pharisees) were looking for a reason to accuse Jesus and asked him, 'Is it lawful to heal on the Sabbath?'" *Matthew 12:10.*

Have you slowly become a modern day Pharisee, assuring yourself that you are a godly *Busy SportsLeader* while quietly looking for excuses not to completely follow Christ?

Reflect on the questions you ask, are they: *"Will this action honor God?"* and *"Could this cause others to stumble?"* Or are they more like: *"What are the chances anyone will find out?"* and *"Is it legal?"*

"The most serious mistakes are not being made as a result of wrong answers. The truly dangerous thing is asking the wrong questions." *- Peter Drucker.*

"Nothing is more grievous than the disappointment of a raised expectation...and the more high the expectation was raised the more cutting is the frustration of it."
-Matthew Henry, Bible Commentator, 1662-1714.

Expectation, anticipation, and hope are in abundance this time of year for the *Busy SportsLeader*. Baseball opens, football drafts, and high flying basketball teams have visions of a championship a few weeks away.

For some, shattered dreams cause them to walk away: away from their hopes, their career, their marriage, and most dreadfully - their God.

An answered prayer doesn't always mean the answer is a "yes". Sometimes the answer is "no", but it's still an answer to your prayer. And sometimes the answer is "not today". Those are the ones that someday will be the sweetest. Always hold on one more day.

"Weeping may last for the night, but a shout of joy (comes) in the morning." Psalm 30: 5b.

A friend of mine, who has led large companies and organizations, now serves as a consultant to CEO's on leadership. He regularly asks them, "Do you understand the nature of your suffering?" He tells me the CEO's are surprised and relieved by the question. They're glad to know someone else comprehends the pains of leadership.

The *Busy SportsLeader* can carry only a limited amount of burdens by himself. You need not be crushed under the weight of the load.

David, one of the great leaders in human history wrote these words, *"Hear my cry, O God, listen to my prayer. From the ends of the earth I call to you, I call as my heart grows faint; lead me to the rock that is higher than I." Psalm 61:1, 2.*

He wasn't alone through his sufferings. You need not be either.

"The ancient Romans had a tradition: whenever one of their engineers constructed an arch, as the capstone was hoisted into place, the engineer assumed accountability for his work in the most profound way possible: he stood under the arch."
- Michael Armstrong, Author.

Last week NFL teams selected the most talented young football players in the country to be part of their team. This weekend coaches will look those young men in the eye and ask, "will he be accountable to me and this team or become a loose cannon?" General Managers will ask themselves if the money they pay these gifted athletes will come back to be the team's undoing.

For the *Busy SportsLeader*, accountability of players to a higher authority becomes of paramount importance. We would all do well to remember: *"Nothing in all creation is hidden from God's sight. Everything is uncovered and laid bare before the eyes of him to whom we must give account."*
Hebrews 4:13.

Superior talent builds confidence in an athlete. Great players make a coach feel better. Excellent coaches cause a general manager to be optimistic. But job security, and sports, seems to be mutually exclusive.

The *Busy SportsLeader,* and others in high pressure jobs, can try to find rest in their superior abilities, but that comfort is tenuous at best. Change is inevitable in this world; personal circumstances, people, the game, the market can all shake you like a phone call in the middle of a good night's sleep. Great faith in fragile objects is still fragile.

Strong faith DOES NOT make a person strong; the OBJECT of their faith DOES.

"...the rock of my strength...is in God." Psalm 62:7.

"A lie told often enough becomes the truth."
- Vladimir Lenin.

"Destruction is certain for those who say evil is good, and good is evil; that dark is light and light is dark; that bitter is sweet and sweet is bitter." Isaiah 5:20.

The party ended before it started; a college football player sits alone waiting for a call that won't come until late tomorrow. A salesman and his family look for the commission check that was "mailed a week ago". An executive feels like he's the only one who ever honors a contract.

The *Busy SportsLeader* with integrity will not cave to the convenient nor manipulate to mislead. Some may call it "competitive advantage" but God calls it as He sees it, and He sees it all. Lies are not truth, bitter is not sweet, and destruction can't be good for business.

Busy SportsLeaders don't candy-coat bad news. Coaches give it straight; executives tell it like it is. Even when it comes to speaking about their careers, sports leaders openly talk of the times they have been "fired". No spin needed.

Honest evaluation of our own personal, spiritual life is not as easy. Most people want to feel good about themselves, and that is why nearly everyone considers them self to be a "basically good person".

"The Passion of the Christ" was criticized for its graphic brutality. It was not "the feel-good movie of the year", because it did not candy-coat the suffering of Jesus. The scourging, beating and crucifixion is powerful because the spin is gone. It strips away the veneer from the belief that our sin "isn't all that bad". It is that bad.

"Then Pilate took Jesus and had him flogged. The soldiers twisted together a crown of thorns and put it on his head. They clothed him in a purple robe and went up to him again and again saying, 'Hail, king of the Jews!' And they struck him in the face." Matthew 27: 26-30.

"God proved His love on the Cross. When Christ hung, and bled, and died, it was God saying to the world, 'I love you.'" - Billy Graham.

Love is not absent in the world of sports. In fact, any *Busy SportsLeader* who has been part of a great team says "love" was part of the experience. Isn't it amazing how the greatest sacrifice made for us can pale in our remembrance of a great team? Today remember the greatest sacrifice of all.

"For God so loved the world that He gave His only begotten Son, that whoever believes in Him shall not perish, but have eternal life." John 3:16.

The **Busy SportsLeader** is often in a high profile position in his community. His job can bring him respect and reward. It's easy to get used to privilege, it's also dangerous. No matter how successful or honored a person becomes, they still need to keep the perspective of a Christian servant. Those who serve God should never expect a letter of thanks or an award dinner. It is just service, which is due God.

Jesus said in *Luke 17:10 "So you, when you do all the things which are commanded you, say, 'We are unworthy slaves; we have done only that which we ought to have done.'"*

"To think creatively, we must be able to look afresh at what we normally take for granted." - George Kneller.

The **Busy SportsLeader** has to be scheduled to get everything done. Routines can be helpful. A short read of the Bible and a quick prayer of, "Bless my family, my work, and help the team win." The same basic prayer everyday with a sprinkling of urgent requests seems so efficient...and disciplined!

But God is not static. He is dynamic and He wants your relationship with Him to be dynamic also. Ask for new insights, revelations, and challenges. Grow.

"Hear, you deaf! Look, you blind, and see!" Isaiah 42:18.

"Men create the gods in their own image." - Xenophanes 520 B.C.

Xenophanes is right in one sense. If we don't like the God of the universe, a *Busy SportsLeaders* can just give himself a promotion. We'll be convinced that we're powerful enough to control things we can't; intelligent enough to explain the miraculous; enlightened enough to take away the sins of the world by redefining sin or getting rid of the "s" word completely.

It's a simple re-org.

"...do not act corruptly and make a graven image for yourselves in the form of any figure, the likeness of male or female". Deuteronomy 4:16.

Who can discern his *(own)* **errors?** This rhetorical question is asked in the book of Psalms. Ask yourself, "Can I discern my errors?"

The *Busy SportsLeader* has many people other than himself he can blame for the missteps of the organization.
Compounding this problem is a group of advisors who <u>won't</u> tell him the truth because it might put their job on the line.
The personal life of the *Busy SportsLeader* can be in obvious sin, and NO ONE will tell him THAT because it might put their *life* **and job** on the line.

If you're willing, take a hard look in the mirror today consider this: *"The fear of the LORD is pure, enduring forever. The judgments of the LORD are true and altogether righteous. They warn your servant; in keeping them there is great reward." Psalm 19:9, 11.*

Want some honesty? Ask God, and listen to His judgments.

"If fear is cultivated it will become stronger, if faith is cultivated it will achieve mastery." - John Paul Jones.

There is an old saying that goes: "Faith is like a muscle, it gets stronger when it's exercised."

Busy SportsLeaders make a living by preparation. They work long hours to assure success. There are times though, when God calls us to do things, or pray for things, that seem impossible. These are uncomfortable moments. Only by trusting that there is a God, and that He can and will work in specific situations, is our faith strengthened. As He works, we draw closer to knowing Him more fully.

"…come to the unity of the faith … the fullness of Christ." *Ephesians 4:13.*

"No temptation has seized you except what is common to man. And God is faithful; he will not let you be tempted beyond what you can bear." I Corinthians 10:13.

God tests us knowing what we can achieve if we rely fully on Him. He does not tempt us, as temptation is from Satan and meant to harm us. Even there God intervenes so that we can win if we rely on Him. In both cases success involves a partnership between us and God.

What kind of target should a *Busy SportsLeader* set for their team? Some are big on *"stretch goals"* hoping to maximize performance but risk demoralization. Some prefer *"small steps"* to build confidence but they risk mediocrity. Goals are too small if we can do them on our own. Look for objectives that **can** be achieved by a team working well together.

"Never give an order that can't be obeyed." - Douglas MacArthur.

Division, rancor and mistrust will kill any team. Often the root of the problem can be traced back to one person.

Dealing with difficult athletes is one of the greatest challenges for the *Busy SportsLeader.* Many experienced coaches would agree that, "coaching-up" someone's attitude is easier said than done.

First the leader must make clear the team standards for attitude and relationships. Then the athlete must be held accountable for their actions. If both are not in place then the leader is at fault. If both steps have been followed, along with some patience, understanding, and open communication, and no changes result - then change may have to be forced.

"Throw out the mocker, and fighting, quarrels, and insults will disappear." Proverbs 22:10.

She earned her doctorate at Columbia, taught at Georgetown, has written more than a dozen books, and served as the US Ambassador to the UN, yet I remember Jean Kirkpatrick crediting much of her success to the fact that "she just showed up every day".

As my wife and I celebrated our 25th wedding anniversary yesterday it occurred to me that much of what we call success is a result of never giving up, despite set-backs and disappointments. That's true in a marriage as well as for the *Busy SportsLeader*.

"That is why we never give up. Though our bodies are dying, our spirits are being renewed every day. For our present troubles are quite small and won't last very long. Yet they produce for us an immeasurably great glory that will last forever. So we don't look at the troubles we can see right now; rather, we look forward to what we have not yet seen. For the troubles we see will soon be over, but the joys to come will last forever." II Corinthians 4:16-18.

"In times of rapid change, experience could be your worst enemy." – J. Paul Getty.

God expects us to use our experiences and learnings when it comes to decision making in the fast paced world of the *Busy SportsLeader*. But He does not want us to lean, or rely primarily on that knowledge. Our experiences may not serve us well in all situations, especially new ones. He wants our faith to be in Him, not in our own limited capabilities.

"Trust in the LORD with all your heart and do not lean on your own understanding." Proverbs 3:5.

Re-entry to family life can be turbulent. After months of focus on professional goals this time of year brings a new focus: **family**. Jan Dravecky, wife of former major league baseball player Dave Dravecky, was once asked if the long trips baseball players took during the season had any adverse effects on family life. She said that while Dave was away she handled everything just fine: the kids, the schedule, paying the bills, and doctors' appointments. The problem came when he returned home, "He always wanted the **crown** back!"

The Bible gives us some very sound wisdom in this area. *1Peter 3:7 says, "Husbands, live with your wives in an understanding way."* Your wife is not the only one who has to make adjustments.

Here's a note to those who have kids. *Ephesians 6:4, "Fathers, do not exasperate your children; instead, bring them up in the training and instruction of the Lord."* Gary Smalley, a noted writer and speaker on family relationships once said, "Children need love and discipline, but if you err, **err on the side of love.**"

The *Busy SportsLeader* should refocus on family life with **love and understanding.**

"Management is doing things right; leadership is doing the right things." – Peter Drucker.

Organizations need leaders that dearly hold values that are clear and timeless, that behave in a way consistent with their high values.

It may seem shrewd for a *Busy SportsLeader* to say or do almost anything to gain short term achievements. But to have sustained success it is wise to remember that others might not see every step you take, but they know the path you walked. It's commonly called – REPUTATION.

"Even children are known by the way they act, whether their conduct is pure, and whether it is right". Proverbs 20:11.

"A decline in courage may be the most striking feature which an outside observer notices in the West in our days." - Aleksandr Solzhenitsyn.

Some say they must wait until they get a promotion. Others say they must wait until they are successful. And then there are some *Busy SportsLeaders* who say, "I have a great job and I don't want to lose it". Faint-hearted Christians in positions of leadership never feel the heat for their hidden convictions, but they also never fulfill their purpose.

Queen Esther could lose her job, but also much more if she took the **action** for which God positioned her. The action she needed to take was unlawful, *(approaching the king without being summoned),* but God placed her as Queen to do just that. She risked **everything,** her wealth, position, comfort, and even her life, to serve God. Her **purpose** was greater than her **privilege.**

She said, *"...and so I will go to the king, which is against the law; and if I perish, I perish"! Esther 4:16.*

Working families endeavor to reduce tension between priorities. Diplomats strive to settle conflict between peoples. Business leaders look to resolve division and strife in their organizations before the very fabric of the organization is torn apart. This is especially true of the *Busy SportsLeader*. The trick is finding a solution.

Ephesians 2:14 provides an incredible insight. *"For He Himself is our peace, who made both groups into one, and broke down the barrier of the dividing wall."*

The verse's main point refers to an actual wall that separated Jews and Gentile in their place of worship. But what is most interesting to me about this reference to Christ is that *"HE HIMSELF"* is our peace. Modernism often wants to that imply His teachings, His ideals or His love is what will bring peace. But the Bible says peace is in HIM.

"The first duty of a university is to teach wisdom not a trade; character not technicalities." - Winston Churchill.

Recruiting materials are packed with stories and photos of past players who are now pros. The lightly veiled promise is that this university is a young athlete's best chance to hit it big.

The **Busy SportsLeader** of faith has a sacred duty to pass on wisdom for a life, not just for a job.

"...train me well in Your deep wisdom. Help me understand these things..." Psalm 119:25.

Obstacles can be so tall, difficulties so overwhelming and pressure so great, it seems there is no way to win. Sometimes the more we look at a problem the larger it gets.

Read these incredible words from *I Samuel 17:45-46, "Then David said to the Philistine, 'You come to me with a sword, with a spear, and with a javelin. But I come to you in the name of the Lord of hosts, the God of the armies of Israel, whom you have defied. This day the Lord will deliver you into my hand.'"*

David was completely aware of the problem; he could clearly see the "pointed details" and yet he was confident. Not in himself per se, but in God who had called him to do this tough job.

This week you, as a *Busy SportsLeader*, may face some big problems, you may see some complicated details, but don't lose your focus on the One who put you in your position. He desires to work through you. Take a long look at Him too. Your "Goliaths" just might be cut down to size!

"Without execution, vision is just another word for hallucinations." - Mark Hurd.

Many of us have learned a great amount about living a Christian life. Surprisingly, few of us ever apply that information. We seem to feel that the *data* is the life. It makes little difference whether or not we act on the knowledge. This behavior is not uncommon in communities where there is a strong Christian culture.

Busy SportsLeaders must take care to not put on the trappings of the Life without the transformation of it.

"...not having become a forgetful hearer but an effectual doer, this man will be blessed in what he does." James 1:25.

"No man was ever wise by chance." - Seneca.

Take apart an old fashioned pocket watch. Put the hundreds of individual pieces into a bag. How many times do you have to shake the bag to have the pocket watch reassemble? It won't happen in a million lifetimes.

To assemble the watch will take time, purpose, and skill. To build wisdom in your life will take time, purpose and teachability.

"How much better to get wisdom than gold, to choose understanding rather than silver!" Proverbs 16:16.

How many voices have called you today? Ten, fifty, a hundred? They've called the *Busy SportsLeader* with worthy causes, "opportunities of a lifetime", and demands from fans and media, not to mention the constant call of family and friends. So many directions offered; some good, some exciting, and some even godly.

Jesus knew this would happen to you today. He used a familiar scene from His culture to illustrate this point.

Occasionally the sheep of many shepherds were penned together for their protection. When it was time to move a particular herd of sheep out of the pen the shepherd would simply, *"call his own sheep by name, and lead them out...the sheep follow him because they know his voice. And a stranger they simply will not follow, but will flee from him, because they do not know the voice of strangers."* *Luke10:3-5.*

Listen carefully when you're called today. Is it the voice of the Holy Spirit or a stranger? Is the call drawing you closer to God, or further away? You can't help but HEAR many voices, but you can choose who you FOLLOW.

"My advice to you is get married; if you find a good wife you'll be happy; if not, you'll become a philosopher." - Socrates.

High profile leadership is tough. Bruising by the press, pressure to win, and the lure of fame and success takes its toll.

A godly spouse is like a wellspring to the *Busy SportsLeader*. They are a salve for the hurts, an anchor for strength, and not afraid to make you take out the garbage.

Many feel they are too busy to build a marriage, but countless leaders have managed their time skillfully to flourish in leadership and matrimony. It can be done.

"He who finds a wife finds a good thing and obtains favor from the Lord." Proverbs 18:22.

"Tomorrow is often the busiest day of the week."
- Spanish proverb.

Busy SportsLeaders are good at getting work done, and on time. It's a little harder to get to the other stuff. Like…the Bible…some prayer….the family. Ask God to give you diligence in all areas of importance, not just a few.

"How long will you lie down, O sluggard? When will you arise from your sleep?" Proverbs 6:9.

"...for man looks at the outward appearance, but the Lord looks at the heart." I Samuel 16:7.

The "spotlight" on a *Busy SportsLeader* is often blinding. Attention for what a sports leader does, keeps most people from knowing who the leader really is. Sometimes it's convenient to turn the glare up to purposely keep others out. By being too busy for transparent Christian relationships, we can blind others and live in a comfortable, yet dangerous, place.

Making the time to open our heart to God daily, and to reveal our heart to trustworthy godly friends weekly, we can let others see who we really are...and are becoming. Purposely, proactively open your heart to the Lord regularly, for He cares for YOU, not just what you DO.

"Perhaps in time the so-called Dark Ages will be thought of as including our own." - Georg Lichtenberg, 1780.

If the world seems darker than ever there is good reason. The world loves it.

If you as a *Busy SportLeader* desire to be loved by the world, expect your deeds to reflect the darkness. If your desire is to have your deeds reflect the light, don't expect much love from this world.

"Light has come into the world, but men loved darkness instead of light because their deeds were evil." John 3:19.

"Nothing ever comes to one that is worth having, except as a result of hard work." - Booker T. Washington.

At the end of a life, when the **Busy SportsLeader** stands before the Heavenly Judge, He will not ask to look at your championship rings or your bank account. But He will want an accounting of your ability in regards to the Bible.

"Be diligent to present yourself approved to God as a workman who does not need to be ashamed, accurately handling the word of truth." II Timothy 2:15.

Sports management professionals in successful teams can gain a reputation for being brilliant. Their organization may be marked with sell-outs, championships, and media attention. You may not look as smart or hard working as the leader of another team. The really difficult part can be the knowledge that another organization's success isn't based on your counterpart's brilliance, but the fact that the best player in the sport happens to play for his team.

The *Busy SportsLeader's* road to success may not be super charged with great players. Perhaps your team's talent level isn't star quality - yet, or you may not have the budget of your competitor. But you can still move forward in a profound way.

"A highway will be there; it will be called the <u>Highway of Holiness</u>. The unclean will not journey on it; it will be for those who walk in that Way; wicked fools will not go about on it." Isaiah 35:8.

In Isaiah's prophetic vision we can see **God's** measure of success: upright living. No star can give *that* to us, it is our moment-by-moment choice.

127

"Be courteous to all, but intimate with few, and let those few be well tried before you give them your confidence." - George Washington.

Busy SportsLeaders have oodles of people who will do loads of stuff for them. These "friends" will provide goods and services, take an interest in you and your family, and all for a chance to experience your reflective glory. Always ask yourself, "Would these people do things and act this way if I didn't do what I do?" If you think all of them would, think again.

"A man of too many friends comes to ruin, but there is a friend who sticks closer than a brother." Proverbs 18:24.

Every academic and professional discipline has a vocabulary peculiar to that discipline. It is necessary to be versed in that language to work effectively in the related industry. In addition, there is terminology, which is not professional in nature but has common usage. An example of this is from the late great Chick Hearn who coined the term, "slam-dunk".

Many *Busy SportsLeaders* are burdened with language that was taught from past mentors that doesn't reflect who they really are. The battle for control of our words is more important than most people think and cannot be done on our own power, we need God's help.

"All kinds of animals, birds, reptiles and creatures of the sea are being tamed and have been tamed by man, but no man can tame the tongue. It is restless evil, full of deadly poison." James 3:7, 8.

Ask God to give you a new, more powerful language.

"Whether you think you can or whether you think you can't, you're right!" - Henry Ford.

Instilling confidence in a team or individual is one of the great gifts a *Busy SportsLeader* can give. Investing your trust and faith in someone can change their life. Many people look back on their years and point to the moment when a leader believed in them. It was then, they could believe in themselves.

"For as a man thinks within himself, so he is". Proverbs 23:7.

Have you ever wondered why God gave you, a *Busy SportsLeader*, the position of influence you have? Perhaps your personal goals and prayers have been answered in your current place of work, but is there a greater purpose as you lead, as you make decisions that impact your community, and as you live your public life?

God is not surprised you made it this far. He knows you're there. He put you there for a reason, for a season. A young woman named Esther was thrust into an influential position, and at critical time. But she was afraid to use her influence until Mordecai (her uncle) sent these words to her; *"Who knows but that you have come to royal position for such a time as this?" Esther 4:14.*

Take a look. God has a purpose for you being where you are today. You probably already know why you're there. He asks you to fulfill your purpose.

Rarely does the ***Busy SportsLeader*** have to face the **sudden death of an active team member**. But it does happen. His players and their **families will measure how he handles** the terrible news and the days immediately after the tragedy, very carefully.

The situation can be so uncomfortable that the ***Busy SportsLeader*** will abdicate his direct involvement and turn the whole situation over to someone else. There is no substitute for personal involvement. Phone calls and a visit to the family are a must. An outside grief counselor or famous pastor can be a mistake. A team chaplain who is regularly with the team should be a great asset and a source of wisdom for next steps.

When the ***Busy SportsLeader*** is a person who walks with God regularly he will be greatly used in these difficult moments.

"But God, who comforts the downcast, comforted us..."
II Corinthians 7:6.

"I have a dream that my four little children will one day live in a nation where they will not be judged by the color of their skin but by the content of their character." - Martin Luther King, Jr.

I have heard complaints of discrimination and reverse-discrimination from those who have been hurt by both. I know it exists and have seen it firsthand. But as Dr. King believed, character should be the standard we consider most.

For the *Busy SportsLeader* of faith, it is important to put a stake in the ground on standards and expectations for character in current employees and new hires and then maintain a consistency with those standards.

There will be times when circumstances or expediency will tempt you to waiver for short term gain, but this is a long term investment that will benefit all.

"My dear brothers and sisters, how can you claim to have faith in our glorious Lord Jesus Christ if you favor some people over others?" James 2:1.

"If you believe what you like in the gospels, and reject what you don't like, it is not the gospel you believe, but yourself." - Saint Augustine.

It has been said that "leaders are readers". I believe "**great** leaders are learners". This requires teachability, and for a *Busy SportsLeader* to be successful over the long haul, they must continue to be open and desire to grow.

I have watched many people move through their career in a predictable pattern. Early they were like a sponge learning everything they could. Next they practiced what they learned, still remaining teachable and refining their ability. Eventually they became hard, too tired or proud to learn. At this point success usually became elusive.

"As the sower was scattering the seed, some fell along the path, and the birds came and ate it up...when anyone hears the word of the kingdom and does not understand it, the evil one comes and snatches away what was sown in his heart." Matthew 13:4, 19.

One of the most influential men in the land, Job, began to suffer great affliction. His senior counselors gave him advice, but their knowledge was weak. It wasn't the "old hands" that could help Job, instead it was a **young man** named Elihu who spoke these words:

"...it is the spirit in a man, the breath of the Almighty that gives him understanding. It is not only the old who are wise, not only the aged who understand what is right."
Job 32:8-9.

Elihu promised Job he would not flatter him or show partiality to him; instead he would only speak what God had laid on his heart. He would tell it straight: **eternal values and truth**. Job didn't need answers from yes-men, focus groups or market research. Every *Busy SportsLeader* needs a godly man like Elihu, who will tell them what they need to hear, not just what they want to hear.

When the Pearl Harbor survivors marched past us last Thursday, the crowd duly honored them. They paid a very high price to keep America **free** that December morning over **60** years ago. As I looked at their faces I wondered if they were proud of how we have used that freedom.

The *Busy SportsLeader* doesn't have to look into the face of the Savior and guess how He wants us to use the **freedom** He gave us, since He arrived on earth, in the flesh, that December morning **2000** years ago.

"You, my brothers, were called to be free. But do not use your freedom to indulge the sinful nature; rather, serve one another in love." Galatians 5:13.

Summer

At this time of year champions are crowned, students graduate, and activities conclude for the summer. Many **Busy SportsLeaders** are about to enter a period of rest after another season. As you head into some precious moments of relaxation remember that rest too, is ordained by God. It has a sacred element to it. Cherish it, honor it, and be refreshed by it.

"Six days you shall do your work, and on the seventh day you shall rest, that your ox and your donkey may rest, and the son of your female servant and the stranger may be refreshed." Exodus 23:12.

Inspiration. Motivation. Stimulation.

Busy SportsLeaders are always looking for ways to take their team to a higher level. Compelling stories of those who overcome enormous adversity, or those who display great courage lift our spirits and move us to excellence.

But no book contains any story as persuasive as the one you tell everyday about yourself. The revelation of your character, commitments, and values moves others to action like nothing else. The apostle Paul realized this when he wrote, ***"Whatever you have learned or received or heard from me, or seen in me--put it into practice." Philippians 4:9.***

Paul knew he was not perfect but he didn't use that as an excuse to abdicate leadership. He knew His own example would be the standard that others would emulate. Look closely, your character is likely reflected in those you lead.

"True silence is the rest of the mind, and is to the spirit what sleep is to the body, nourishment and refreshment." - William Penn.

The *Busy SportsLeader* doesn't easily find rest. Long seasons, high demands, crucial decisions all scream for attention, crowding out the quiet. Summer can provide time for reflection, meditation, and listening.

It is wise to purposely set aside time for quietness. It's tempting to pack fun and activities into every free moment, but rest is crucial to the soul and mind.

"Rest in the Lord, and wait patiently for him." Psalm 37:7.

"Character is what you are in the dark." - D.L.Moody.

Rookies in professional sports are highly susceptible to character corruption. Not only do they now have money, but they are away from the natural support groups they've previously formed. The same is true for the whole new crop of college graduates heading into the workforce this summer.

The Busy SportsLeader can spend a lot of money and effort on programs designed to keep athletes out of trouble. These programs often fail. The key is to shine light in the dark places through relationships with teammates of strong character. Build an environment where the mature members of the team are clearly seen early in the season, in fact - the first day. Many of the destructive relationships players form are begun within 24 hours of joining the team. By-the-way, keeping good company is as important to the old as it is to the young!

"Do not be deceived: Bad company corrupts good morals."
I Corinthians 15:33.

Notice the insignia of military rank. Enlisted men wear Chevrons on their sleeves. Officers wear Stars, Eagles, Oak Leaf Clusters, or Bars on their shoulders. The Chevron is on the sleeve because these men and women are the arms and strength of the force. Officers' rank is on their shoulders to represent the burden of responsibility they carry.

Thankfully the *Busy SportsLeader* doesn't usually carry the day-to-day responsibility for the lives of those they lead, but they still bear much responsibility for them.

In the parable of the lost sheep Jesus tells how the Shepherd *(read "Leader")* takes personal responsibility for one under his care. (When the Shepherd recovers the lost sheep notice how he carries it.)

"Then Jesus told them this parable: 'Suppose one of you has a hundred sheep and loses one of them. Does he not leave the ninety-nine in the open country and go after the lost sheep until he finds it? And when he finds it, he joyfully puts it on his shoulders and goes home. Then he calls his friends and neighbors together and says, Rejoice with me; I have found my lost sheep.'" Luke 15:3-6.

"I just know I'm a better manager when I have Joe DiMaggio in center field." - Casey Stengel.

Ever wonder how many *Busy SportsLeaders* took credit for DiMaggio's play? How about Jordan, Woods, or Jack Welsh for that matter? Somewhere a coach, scout or management professor is making a living off of one student's success.

Stengel, one of the greats in his own right, was able to give credit where credit was due.

"Let another praise you, and not your own mouth; a stranger, and not your own lips." Proverbs 27:2.

"The difference between a boss and a leader: a boss says, 'Go!' - a leader says, 'Let's go!'" - **E.M. Kelley.**

There are far more managers than true leaders. Giving directions to others is easier than showing the way.

When the *Busy SportsLeader* is truly leading, he is in a position of vulnerability. He takes shots from the opposition, removes obstacles, and his mistakes are clearly seen by those following him. In a world where managing from the rear is considered good enough, few are brave enough to take on the role of leader.

Occasionally, God does ask people to manage, but when great things are to be done, He calls leaders.

"And Moses said, 'We will go with our young and our old; we will go with our sons and daughters and with our flocks and herds, for we must hold a feast to the Lord.'" Exodus 10:9.

"A real leader faces the music, even if he doesn't like the tune." - Anonymous.

One of the most difficult challenges for a *Busy SportsLeader* is the responsibility of making decisions that he knows will be unpopular. Everyone likes to be liked, and it is easier to lead when others are in hearty agreement. But eventually every leader will have to make difficult choices. Sometimes the unpopular choice is the right one.

Retaining the confidence of an organization doesn't come from your ability to use persuasive reasoning to win them to your side but instead comes from the assurance they have in your previously demonstrated character.

Most people know the mistake of putting trust in something that is untrustworthy. If your character has been proven prior to difficult decisions, your credibility will remain even though your decisions may not make the majority of the people happy.

"Confidence in an unfaithful man in time of trouble is like a bad tooth and a foot out of joint." Proverbs 25:19.

"Fear is the sand in the machinery of life". - E. Stanley Jones.

How often have you seen a Little League baseball game or a youth basketball game come down to its final moments and every kid on the team, *(and their mom),* hopes they don't have to be the one to decide the contest. When called on to win a game, the fear of failure can paralyze an athlete.

Oddly, another kind of fear has derailed many gifted athletes and leaders: the fear of *success*. Success brings expectations of more success, and for many, the pressures of living up to those expectations are too great to bear. It's just easier to be "average". Finding the key that unlocks the handcuffs of fear is a precious treasure that too few **Busy SportsLeaders** have found.

"There is no fear in love. But perfect love drives out fear". I John 4:18.

Perfect love is only found in the Heavenly Father. It is not a love based on performance or even reciprocation. It is a love unconditional. Experiencing this kind of love puts *the "oil" in the machinery of life.*

"You shall know the truth, and the truth shall make you mad." - Aldous Huxley, English novelist.

For the *Busy SportsLeader* discovering hidden realities about his organization can be painful. It can be more comfortable to pay attention to other, less difficult issues, but big problems are rarely self-correcting. The true leader must take a discerning, careful look at the thorniest problems in the clear light of the truth. Only in this setting can he make a truly sound decision.

The temptation NOT look at the hard truth can be strong, but it will eventually lead to failure. We must seek, find, and deal in the truth – even when it doesn't make us look good.

God commanded the prophet Jeremiah to warn to His people about their trust in lies:
"Say to them, 'This is the nation whose people will not obey the LORD their God and who refuse to be taught. Truth has vanished from among them; it is no longer heard on their lips.'" Jeremiah 7:28.

"We find greatest joy, not in getting, but expressing what we are. Men do not really live for honors or for pay; their gladness is not in the taking and holding, but in the doing, the striving, the building, and the living." - R. J. Baughan.

The thrill of competition motivates millions of leaders every day. Awards, rewards, and honors are given to those who perform above the rest. The results are greater financial compensation, expanded power and new levels of influence.

The public may not always honor the *Busy SportsLeader* for his contributions, but there is a way to secure the rewards of God. It comes by obtaining wisdom.

Wisdom isn't handed to us gift-wrapped with a bow on top. It is to be purposefully sought. The paradox is that it's not all that hard to find. The key is to look in the right spot and with the right motive.

"So shall the knowledge of wisdom be unto thy soul: when thou hast found it, then there shall be a reward, and thy expectation shall not be cut off." Proverbs 24:14.

I spent a week serving desperately poor children that live in and around the dumps of Mexico City and Oaxaca through the work of Northwest Medical Teams. I attempted to send an edition of *"Wisdom"* from Oaxaca but was unable to make an internet connection.

"The rich and the poor have a common bond; The Lord is the maker of them all." Proverbs 22:2.

The Busy SportsLeader provides guidance and direction to many who are highly skilled and well paid. It is not unusual for the great to become far removed from the rest of the world. In fact, sometimes we provide that distance so the skilled can hone their talents. In the course of leading the talented, it is a wise leader who reminds us we are not self-made men, but the Lord is the maker of us all.

Joe Forehand sounds like a *"Busy <u>Tennis</u>Leader"* but in fact he is CEO of Accenture, one of the world's leading consulting firms. The importance of building future leaders has moved him to create a new position at Accenture: Chief Leadership Officer. He was quoted in *American Way* magazine recently saying, *"Many CEO's focus a great deal of their time on management development and yet they tell me it is their company's "most significant weakness."*

Leadership development in any organization will take something much more costly than time and effort. Jesus warned that even a good program would fail if the people in the program were not of the highest character.

"He also told them this parable: 'Can a blind man lead a blind man? Will they not both fall into a pit? A student is not above his teacher, but everyone who is fully trained will be like his teacher.'" Luke 6:39-40.

The "All-Access" pass is a valuable possession; two kinds of people get them: those who want access because it's **fun** to be where the action is, and those who have **work** to do. The *Busy SportsLeader* often makes decisions on who will receive these valuable passes at games. God decides who gets these passes in life. Since God has no sponsors, no owners' kids, or a commissioner to whom he's beholden, He gives His people "access" for work purposes.

He has put you in places and in relationships for a purpose. Privilege and responsibility always go together. There are people that you have access to that others don't. There are places that you have access to that others don't. Your access pass has not been given for your edification and pleasure but for **His work**. The privilege of your relationships is tied to your responsibility to be an instrument of reconciliation between your heavenly Father and those who have not entered into relationship with Him. He has given you the access, made you the gatekeeper to those in your circle of influence; they are your privilege and responsibility.

"...four principal gatekeepers...were entrusted with the responsibility for the rooms and treasuries in the house of God." I Chronicles 9:26.

"There are very honest people who do not think that they have had a bargain unless they have cheated a merchant." - Anatole France, Nobel Prize winner for Literature in 1921.

An integral part of a *Busy SportsLeader's* job is deal-making. It is in this area that a significant part of his reputation is built and two important facets of a leader are revealed: personal character and business sense.

Much of the Biblical teaching on business can be summed up in one word: honesty. Not misrepresentation or under-representation, but dealing in the truth; over and over again, both New Testament and Old Testament. God will inspect the way deals are made.

"The Lord despises double standards; he is not pleased by dishonest scales." Proverbs 20:23.

One morning the eyes of the sports world turned toward a golf tournament in Texas. An outstanding woman golfer competed against men for a large sum of money. The money was secondary to those who were looking for one gender to gain an advantage over the other.

The *Busy SportsLeader* can personally and professionally hold the values taught in *Galatians 3:28: "There is neither Jew nor Greek, slave nor free, male nor female, for you are all one in Christ Jesus."*

"He leads me beside still waters". Psalm 23:2.

The *Busy SportsLeader* may be tempted to **drive** his team forward, or **push** them to advance at all costs, but the wise leader will **lead** the entire organization to places of refreshment along the way.

"Still waters" doesn't mean a place of *endless* rest, but instead a place where the group can be strengthened and invigorated in a secure setting *for a while*. To guide others to still waters means: 1. The leader knows how to get there. 2. Others trust him enough to follow. And 3. It is a safe place.

Summer can be a good time to re-energize your business and team. Wisdom from God can show you the still waters for your team.

"Most of the important things in the world have been accomplished by people who have kept on trying when there seemed to be no hope at all." - Dale Carnegie.

Leadership through great adversity takes courage, skill and *hope*. To instill hope in others you must have hope truly in your own heart. Hope is not foreknowledge. Instead the New Testament illustrates it as a *"favorable and confident expectation"*. It is one of the three main elements of a Christian's character along with faith and love.

For the *Busy SportsLeader* then, to have and infuse hope means he must develop a personal core of faith, hope, and love. That comes through time spent with God, trusting in Him and His Word, and living a life believing that His plan for us is good.

"Hope deferred makes the heart sick, but when dreams come true, there is life and joy." Proverbs 13:12.

I love summer camp, but I hate the first few nights. It always seems that getting from the main meetings back to my cabin is an unwelcome adventure. I don't know the route. I get confused as to where I am. And worst of all, I can't see the path.

Leadership can be like that, only others are following you and you're lost. The *Busy SportsLeader* faces changes in their organizations that can easily make the trail hard to see. How do you get yourself, (and everyone else), to where they want to be? First, get your bearings. Know where you are, and where you need to go. Then make sure you stay on the right trail.

"Direct my footsteps according to Your Word". Psalm 119:133.

"Seed fell among thorns, which grew up and chocked the plants...so is the man who hears the Word, but the worries of this life and the deceitfulness of wealth choke it, making it unfruitful." Matthew 12:7, 22.

Peace: a rarity in leadership. Panic: is more common. Pride: for those who look peaceful while disguising their panic.

The *Busy SportsLeader* must be in close relationship with God to truly experience peace. Then peace comes naturally, supernaturally.

"The branch of the vine does not worry and toil and rush here and there for sunshine and rain. No, it rests in union and communion with the vine; and at the right time and way the fruit comes." - Hudson Taylor.

"Can we follow the Savior far, who have no wound or scar?"
- Amy Carmichael.

The leader in battle is likely to take the most hits. The leader in exploration will have the most barriers to overcome. The leader in faith will face persecution. In today's our society it is as minor as a comment of criticism or as major as a lawsuit. In ages past it cost people their life. It's hard to tell what the future will bring. Whatever it is the *Busy SportsLeader* will need to be well grounded to endure it.

"Some seed fell on rocky places, where it did not have much soil and the plant came up quickly, when sun came up the plants were scorched and they withered because they had no root...So is a person with no (spiritual roots), they can grow quickly but when trouble and persecution come, they quickly fall away." Mathew 13:5, 21.

"The trees of the garden should bear more fruit than the trees of the forest." - Christopher Love.

Four soils: hard, rocky, thorny, or good. Four results: No growth, burned up, choked-out, or fruitful. The *Busy SportsLeader* makes many choices a day. This is perhaps the most important one they make. The first three are easy and fast; they can happen without even taking the time to think about it.

To be good soil requires a gardener's attention, water, sun, weeding, and care. It doesn't take all your time and attention, but it does take some. Even when you're *Busy!* But this is the only one with a happy ending.

"The one who received the seed that fell on the good soil is the man who hears the Word and understands it. He produces a crop, yielding a hundred, sixty or thirty times what was sown." Matthew 12:23.

"Problems are only opportunities in work clothes."
- Henry Kaiser.

Like a summer thunderstorm that builds and explodes on the plains, so is the tumult that comes upon a sports leader and his organization in rapid change. What was normal is not. What was routine is lost. Uncertainty rules, confusion reigns.

It's not really a complete surprise, the clouds have been gathering. The *Busy SportsLeader* could see it coming, unless they <u>chose</u> not to.

When the storm hits; the weak run for cover. The strong lead through the darkness and the rain to the place they know the organization should go. It takes strength and courage to lead through trouble. That kind of character is rooted deep, deep in the soul of a leader. It is cultivated from consistently seeking the heart of God, and grows in disciplined decisions. All of that preparation begins long before the storm hits.

"If you faint in the day of adversity, your strength is small."
Proverbs 24:10.

"Babe Ruth made a big mistake when he gave up pitching."
- Tris Speaker.

Even Hall of Famer's are wrong some of the time;
occasionally REALLY wrong.

The sooner a *Busy SportsLeader* can openly admit he is
sometimes wrong and realize he will be wrong again, the
wiser he'll be.

"You find mercy by admitting (your sins) and leaving them."
Proverbs 28:13.

"The unexamined life is not worth living." - Socrates.

One of the great moments in sports is baseball's All-Star break, not because of the tradition, the talent or the spectacle, but because of rest and reflection. This time of year most other team sports have the precious luxury of "time". God wants you to take advantage of these moments. The *Busy SportsLeader* requires time to seek God to have Him meet his deepest personal needs. This summer commit sacred time to quietly search the Person and will of God in your life.

"And He said, My presence shall go with you and I will give you rest." Exodus 33:14.

"For (the wicked) brag about their evil desires; they praise the greedy and curse the Lord." Psalm 10: 3.

It doesn't seem fair when success comes to those who lie, cheat, and are unethical. At the same time, many *Busy SportsLeaders* who are honest, ethical and work hard can struggle to achieve their goals.

Does God bless the scrupulous businessman who wants to honor God? Yes, but not always in the areas we expect. God is far more concerned with our character than our trophy case. There are no short cuts to godly character and no greater reward.

"I have written to you, young men, because you are strong, and the word of God abides in you, and you have overcome the wicked one." I John 2:14.

"I know what enthusiasm they have for God, but it is misdirected zeal." Romans 10:2.

One of the thorniest issues a *Busy SportsLeader* will ever deal with is the behavior of some athletes just after they come to faith. Occasionally a new Christian will become divisive on a team. He doesn't mean to be, but his zeal to convert others can result in deep fissures where unity was once the norm.

The natural reaction is usually to isolate the problem and reprimand the problem maker. But for a player who sees his relationship with God as far more important than his relationship with man, direction may be more effective than correction.

Encourage his personal growth, share your personal journey, and connect him with the other players of faith and your team chaplain. Then in this context, teach him the best ways to be a light while still being a team builder.

"...words are capable of shaking the entire structure of government (or team), words can prove mightier than ten military divisions." – Vaclav Havel, Former President of Czechoslovakia.

There are two great challenges in identifying emerging leaders. The first obstacle is to know the right qualities to look for in leadership candidates. There is not a standard set of traits that all *Busy SportsLeaders* use to measure leadership potential. Some look for behaviors that the organization needs at the moment; others want future leaders to be versions of themselves. St. Paul defines several key qualities to look for in *Titus 1:8: "hospitality, lovers of good, sober-minded, just, holy, self-controlled."* These are the same qualities God wants us to possess.

The second obstacle is discerning the true character of a person. Times of difficulty and testing are one place where the core of a person is revealed. The other is in the private places out of sight of the public. Don't expect formal interviews to expose leadership potential. Good leaders are good all the time, not just when on display.

"Surely what a man does when he is taken off his guard is the best evidence for what sort of man he is". - C. S. Lewis.

Leaders love blueprints. They give a vision of the future, guide construction, and expedite completion. *Busy SportsLeaders* are often the architect of their own blueprints, designing the organization just as they picture it.

Organizations, houses and people are very much alike in one way. The foundation has to be rock solid or, no matter how good they look, they will eventually crumble. Building on strong character is building on rock.

"But anyone who hears my teaching and ignores it is foolish, like a person who builds a house on sand. When the rains and floods come and the winds beat against that house, it will fall with a mighty crash." Matthew 7:26, 27.

"Never mind your happiness; do your duty." – Peter Drucker.

Personal fulfillment is not the chief aim of man. Nor is it of a **Busy SportsLeader.** Leadership is a duty to serve others by guidance, wisdom and inspiration for collective good. Managing others for selfish goals is manipulation.

A relationship with God is not to own a celestial Genie in a bottle for our three wishes, but to experience God's love and forgiveness, and to share that with others.

"Fear God and keep his commandments, for this is the whole duty of man." Ecclesiastes 12:13.

"The first and best victory is to conquer self." - Plato.

No one likes the bony finger of righteous indignation and judgment pointed at himself. Christianity has been called *"the religion of the second chance"*. In fact, forgiveness in Christ is available more than once or twice. While forgiveness remains available, consequences of immoral actions are still inevitable.

The **Busy SportsLeader** who thinks actions and consequences can be separated by crafty planning to hide his indiscretions is mistaken. A leader leads. Where he goes, others, *at least some of the others*, will follow. If he travels the low road, he and others will eventually suffer for it.

"In everything set them an example by doing what is good." **Titus 2:7.**

As **Busy SportsLeaders** gain success people tell them they are "right" more often, they are invited to lunch almost every day, and their jokes are funnier.

But in the midst of your popularity it's wise to seek a few Christian friends who are willing to be honest with you about your spiritual health. The more success you have experienced the more you will have to intentionally solicit this kind of frank input.

The apostle Paul was a change agent in the lives of many; he did that by speaking the truth in love. He and those that brought the gospel with him, *"never came with flattering speech". I Thessalonians 2:5.*

If you don't have someone who can be straight with you, find someone this week.

"Avarice. Envy. Pride. Three fatal sparks, have set the hearts of all on fire." - Dante Alighieri from The Divine Comedy.

The fire of pride and envy drives many to achievement. Since the appearance of modesty is prerequisite for any man to be considered "a good Christian", a humble exterior is a "must". Cloaking the pride of the heart in a humble exterior is a constant struggle for many who have had success.

The ***Busy SportsLeader*** must expose and confess the hidden sins in his own heart to God or face the consequences of his arrogance.

"He has scattered those who are proud in their inmost thoughts." Luke 1:51.

The first step is to ask God to reveal our pride to us, because in our efforts to cover it, we may have even fooled ourselves.

"To say the things he truly feels; and not the words of one who kneels. The record shows I took the blows - And did it my way!" Sinatra 3:16.

Doing what "feels right" can be deceiving. The standard by which a *Busy SportsLeader* measures their actions is important. If it is based on our feelings, how do we know everyone else feels the same way? Or more importantly, how do we know God feels the same?

"Then the LORD said to Cain... 'If you do what is right, will you not be accepted? But if you do not do what is right, <u>sin is crouching at your door; it desires to have you</u>, but you must master it.'" Genesis 4:6-7.

Doing things our own way again and again is a little like breaking-in new blue jeans; it feels better and gets easier every time we slip into them. After a while it's all you want to wear.

For over a year I raised funds for a wonderful international relief agency. The most difficult part of the job was receiving the reports of vast numbers of people in great need and suffering from around the world.

Suffering is a difficult subject. We wonder who is responsible. Why doesn't God intervene? Rarely does a *Busy SportsLeader* face the magnitude of suffering that many do around the world, but when anyone faces great difficulty it can be a severe test of faith. As we trust God today through our temporal struggles, our leadership tomorrow will bring glory to Him.

"These trials are only to test your faith, to show that it is strong and pure. It is being tested as fire tests and purifies gold--and your faith is far more precious to God than mere gold. So if your faith remains strong after being tried by fiery trials, it will bring you much praise and glory and honor on the day when Jesus Christ is revealed to the whole world." I Peter 1:7.

"Every man has his follies -- and often they are the most interesting thing he has got." - Josh Billings.

Lies and litigation, rape and murder, have permeated the coverage of sports over the last few months; if only "fan interference" was our biggest problem.

To combat the negative exposure, a warm and fuzzy commercial is shot, a charity golf tournament is attended, or a foundation is formed. The *Busy SportsLeader* shouldn't fall into the trap of putting make-up on a corpse.

Cultivate and demonstrate the love of Christ to a needy world. When that love comes from deep inside the athlete, coach, or executive and from a pure heart it is very powerful. It has to be intrinsically motivated, not created by the PR department.

"The goal of this command is love, which comes from a pure heart and a good conscience and a sincere faith." I Timothy 1:5.

"No one looks forward to being tested by God. When you are tested, you have no choice as to whether it will be the Job or Noah type." - Walter A Henrichsen, <u>Thoughts from the Diary of a Desperate Man.</u>

Henrichsen, in this excellent work, reminds us that God spoke to Noah and told him that he would be tested and what Noah needed to do to prepare for the test. Noah obeyed and God delivered him *from* his problem. On the other hand, God was silent as Job suffered. All Job could do was hold tightly to the goodness of God. God then delivered Job *through* his problem.

The *Busy SportsLeader* will face tests of his faith. Tests are not sent so that God can determine how strong you are, He already knows. He tests us to strengthen our trust in Him. When your next test comes, listen closely for instruction and be careful to do as He leads. If instead you hear nothing, remember He is still there, and He is still good.

"Blessed is a man who perseveres under trial; for once he has been approved, he will receive the crown of life which {the Lord} has promised to those who love Him." James 1:12.

He wasn't very big, but he was always very confident. A friend from my youth never worried about the size of someone he would tangle with in a fight. He felt he could take anyone if he could just reach their head with a few good blows. "If you kill the head, you kill the body", he loved to say. Now, he never did kill anyone, but he knew an important strategy to win. He also knew he needed to protect his own head in a scuffle.

The *Busy SportsLeader*, as the head of a family or anyone who influences others, has to be aware of the disaster that awaits others if they themselves become corrupt. A weakened leader will become an ineffective and possibly dangerous leader.

"Like a muddied spring or a polluted well is a righteous man who gives way to the wicked." Proverbs 25:26.

"I didn't begin cheating until late in my career, when I needed something to help me survive. I didn't cheat when I won the twenty-five games in 1961. I don't want anybody to get any ideas and take my Cy Young Award away. And I didn't cheat in 1963 when I won twenty-four games. Well, maybe a little." - Whitey Ford.

If the rules don't explicitly prohibit it, can you do it? Steroids, testosterone, speed, and HGH are the daily temptations of the athlete. Under-the-table cash, bending cap rules, posturing to the point of lying are the daily temptations of the *Busy SportsLeader.*

A study of the New Testament reveals God's directions to *"be above reproach"* and to, *"have no appearance of evil"*. These standards of behavior will stand the test of time.

"...so that no one can speak a word of blame against you. You are to live clean, innocent lives as children of God in a dark world full of crooked and perverse people. Let your lives shine brightly before them." Philippians 2:15.

"An inability to stay quiet is one of the conspicuous failings of mankind." - Walter Bagehot, Ninetieth century English journalist.

The problem with **Busy SportsLeaders** is that they are...well...busy. Busy usually means noisy, at least on the inside: lots of things to think through, decisions to be made, and actions to be taken.

Amid all the internal and external clatter, God gives a very counter-intuitive command: STOP!! He wants to remind us that He has a job, and has not turned it over to us. Sometimes it's easy to forget that.

"Be still, and know that I am God." Psalm 46:10.

"The whole world steps aside for the man who knows where he is going." - Anonymous.

As pro and college football practices start, the average fan is unaware of the *Busy SportsLeader's* detailed planning that has gone into making each day as productive as possible. Even though the entire camp may last five or more weeks, every MINUTE has been scheduled. In fact, back in May if you had asked a coach what he would be doing at 8:57 pm on August 12th, he would have told you. The schedule has become a road map to follow.

God has given us a road map that is just as thought out as any team could ever imagine. Two things are required of us. Read the directions and follow them; two simple, but often ignored steps.

"Your word is a lamp to my feet and a light to my path." Psalm 119:105.

Frustration, backstabbing, and mistrust describe the attitude of the employees at his company today. Eighteen months ago the atmosphere was arrogant, boastful, and invincible. The young executive was stunned as he shared with me the dramatic turn of events at one of America's most respected companies. Was it just the economy, or was there more to the fall of this modern icon?

"The Lord will tear down the house of the proud." **Proverbs 15:25.**

Winning is at the core of competition. Nothing can lead to pride faster than winning, especially in sports. The *Busy SportsLeader's* job is to build winning organizations. To successfully develop champions without the haughty type of pride referred to in Proverbs takes a *SportsLeader* who sees himself and his position in the right way.

Many look at the pyramid shape formed by the corporate chart, turn it upside down and look through it like a magnifying glass, designed to make the point look larger than life. The danger is that the heat of pride often shines through the glass and burns the focal point.

The wise *SportsLeader* sees the pyramid as a megaphone. His voice at the top can resonate honor and humility to the whole.

"Follow effective action with quiet reflection. From the quiet reflection will come even more effective action." - Peter Drucker.

Whether he has enjoyed success or frustration over the past few months the *Busy SportsLeader* is wise to take some time to quietly review his efforts.

This is best done away from the crowd and at an unhurried pace. Paper and pencil are essential to capture thoughts and ideas. Taking time to read the Bible will give perspective to temporal victories and defeats. It will also provide a reminder of the things that are most important.

Building separate times for reflection with family and with colleagues will also lead to insights that can be truly life changing. These times of reflection are as much a part of leadership as times of busyness, and may be more important because they inform and remind leaders where they are going.

"I will study your commandments and reflect on your ways." Psalm 119:15.

Last week a friend of mine got something he's never gotten before; *no, not a rare disease*, **an apology from a coach**. For over a decade he's worked closely with pro coaches during games. During the heat of battle he's occasionally been cussed at for mistakes he **didn't** make. Being an old player himself, he understood the fire of competition and didn't hold a grudge. This scene was replayed a few days ago. He didn't think much of it until after the game when the angry coach **apologized** for the criticism and then took rightful personal responsibility for the mistake. What an impact he had on this man's opinion of coaches.

Almost extinct though is an apology for an action that should have been taken, but wasn't. These are the mistakes of omission; the times a staff member should have been recognized, but wasn't; promotions rightly earned, but not given; misplaced praise.

Is an apology appropriate in these cases? No one was hurt, just **not** helped. God's word is clear on this subject: *"Do not withhold good from those to whom it is due, when it is in your power to do it." Proverbs 3:27.*

It takes courage for a *Busy SportsLeader* to shed light on his own mistakes. It might take more courage to face the consequences of hiding them.

"Things alter for the worse spontaneously, if they be not altered for the better designedly." - Francis Bacon.

Intelligent design is not just a phrase for use in place of creationism. Intelligent design is the forethought and implementation the *Busy SportsLeader* needs to build a champion.

Teams don't form cohesively by accident. Cohesion doesn't happen by selection of the most gifted of individuals. Cohesion is primarily a discipline once the team is selected, but it is greatly helped by choosing individuals who are inclined to work together.

Many leaders are evaluating talent for their team this very day. The wise ones will be doing that in context of intelligent design.

"Under His direction, the whole body is fitted together perfectly. As each part does its own special work, it helps the other parts grow, so that the whole body is healthy and growing." Ephesians 4:16.

"The confession of evil works is the first beginning of good works." - Saint Augustine.

Performing a system scan of a computer is a disturbing experience. All kinds of bad electronic bugs are hidden in your system. The number of items found can be astonishing. It's wise to regularly run these checks or else face a reduction in performance.

The *Busy SportsLeader* is wise to run a regular system scan on his life. It is in those times when God is invited to look into our personal lives, and we are willing to hear His report, that we can be "debugged".

It really doesn't take that long. Just a few quiet moments of honest reflection daily to acknowledge shortcomings and resolve to change them will not only greatly enhance your relationship with God, but improve your leadership.

"Finally, I confessed all my sins to you and stopped trying to hide them. I said to myself, 'I will confess my rebellion to the LORD.' And you forgave me! All my guilt is gone." Psalm 32:5.

"No one can be happy who has been thrust outside the pale of truth. And there are two ways that one can be removed from this realm: by lying, or by being lied to." - Seneca.

Even the most virtuous athlete will be tempted to lie or cheat if it is the difference between winning and losing, or the difference between performing at a hall of fame level versus struggling to survive.

The *Busy SportsLeader* can also benefit from an athlete who has gained an unethical edge. The temptation to turn a blind eye to cheating can be very strong; partly because the leader is not directly engaging in the deceit. Leadership means tough choices. When a leader ignores the weeds in the garden, it's not long before it's hard to find the fruit among the thistles.

"The wicked conceive evil; they are pregnant with trouble and give birth to lies." Psalm 7:14.

Decisive change. Radical transformation. New régime. The *Busy SportsLeader* is sometimes required to make very big decisions. These decisions are open to public debate and controversy. The big changes are never a secret.

Usually a polite, "I've decided to go in a different direction", is the line of choice.

Ever think maybe God looks at you and says, "I've decided to go in a different direction: in your very character." For anyone who has put their faith in Christ, God has said just that!

II Corinthians 5:17 states, "Therefore if any man is in Christ, he is a new creature; the old things passed away; behold new things have come."

When the *Busy SportsLeader* puts faith in Christ, God makes a radical transformation. If you haven't seen the changes you know should have happened, first make sure you have unequivocally put your faith in Christ. If you have done that, then second, let the new man live, new things have come.

In times of crisis and confusion a ***Busy SportsLeader's*** character is his greatest asset.

"For God has not given us a spirit of timidity, but of power and love and discipline." II Timothy 1:7.

Many will be in fear, but God has given to you a different spirit. The spirit that God has placed in the faithful leader's heart is one of authority and strength. The leader's confidence comes from a belief that he doesn't have to lean on his own understanding. He knows how to receive God's wisdom.

The spirit that God has placed in the faithful leader's heart is one of love. Love for those who God has put under your care reflects His care for us.

The spirit that God has placed in the faithful leader's heart is one of discipline. Your steady hand through rough seas will empower others to move forward, not just hold on for dear life.

As you consider the many trials you will face today ask God to lead you in your decision making. Keep an eye open for those who are shaken and need the love of a strong leader, and continue to move toward fulfilling your mission in life.

He was keenly aware that people out there were sick and dying. The ship in the harbor was the fastest way to the needy. Unfortunately, the ship didn't deliver medicine, only temporal comfort. He had the cure in his possession and was compelled to take action. Eventually he took command of the ship with the desire to do everything he could to save the dying. Soon he found the business of running the ship, keeping it afloat, and making it profitable took all of his attention. He would have to develop a plan to accomplish both the business of shipping and the mission of mercy.

The *Busy SportsLeader* often has a great desire to be used of God in his work, but it just doesn't happen by chance.

"We continually remember before our God and Father your work produced by faith, your labor prompted by love, and your endurance inspired by hope in our Lord Jesus Christ." I Thessalonians 1:3.

You need friends to pray for you. You need to step out in faith. The powerful medium the *Busy SportsLeader* works in takes great skill to manage, and can deliver an eternal message of hope in Christ.

"They're only truly great who are truly good."
- George Chapman.

One of the most inspiring characteristics of high performers is that they often want to do great things for God: start philanthropic foundations, speak to large crowds, help build great buildings. Their efforts can accomplish large scale results. *Busy SportsLeaders* and the people they lead are often in this category of achievers.

In the book of 1st Kings, God speaks to Solomon as he prepares to build a grand temple. God warns that a tremendous project does not give Him pleasure. What truly pleases God is faithfulness (something the PR department will *not* cover): just quiet, honest, difficult obedience. But is this inspiring? If you're one of the fortunate few who have seen this kind of rare faithfulness...you've been inspired.

"...if you walk in My statutes, execute My judgments, keep all My commandments, and walk in them, then I will perform My word with you". I Kings 6:12.

The ***Busy SportsLeader*** often faces disappointment. The team loses more than it should. Players don't play well. Financial goals aren't met. Dreams fade.

A stiff upper lip and a commitment to re-double efforts is the common response from a person who doesn't quit. There isn't time to take it too personally.

But what if more than disappointment comes the way of the ***Very Busy SportsLeader***? What if heartbreak befalls him right in the middle of a season, something truly and personally dreadful? What is a godly leader to do in the face of that? Stiff upper lip, *again?*

"When Jesus saw her weeping, and the Jews who had come along with her also weeping, he was deeply moved in spirit and troubled...and <u>Jesus wept</u>." John 11:33, 35.

He was busy. He was a leader. He had <u>*really*</u> important work to do. Yet He felt *and* expressed His sorrow in the middle of a busy season of His life. A leader <u>can</u> lead through sorrow, but he shouldn't ignore the pain.

"Is man one of God's blunders? Or is God one of man's blunders?" - Friedrich Nietzsche.

God is commonly seen by modern man as a fuzzy, warm, cuddly old man who winks and smiles at sin, possessing a "boys will be boys" attitude. It is as if the well publicized resurrection of Christ has made everything "cool" between the Big Man upstairs and us.

It is folly to think that God is made in *man's* image. It takes humility to understand the true nature of God: His wisdom, power, holiness, love, justice, omnipresence, and immutability. The *Busy SportsLeader* and the people he leads are constantly tempted by pride. Demonstrating a humble attitude toward your personal relationship with God will have a powerful influence on those around you.

"Say to God, 'How awesome are Your works! Through the greatness of Your power Your enemies shall submit themselves to You.'" Psalm 66:3.

"Maturity: Able to stick with a job until it is finished. Able to bear an injustice without having to get even. Able to carry money without spending it. Do your duty without being supervised." - Ann Landers.

The *Busy SportsLeader* has to deal with immature athletes almost daily. But what do you do when a team member behaves in a childish manner? Some leaders prefer to yell, others consult, some ignore. But the first question to ask is, "Have we, as a team, made our standards clear?"

Parents take time to teach, instruct and make their family norms plain. They often repeat and remind the family of ground rules. In addition, good parents "walk the talk" always reinforcing what they teach. In the same way team members must be taught and shown team standards; they need to buy-in to them, and the leaders have to demonstrate them in their own walk.

"A wise son makes a father glad, But a foolish son is a grief to his mother." Proverbs 10:1.

Sleepless nights wondering how to increase sponsorship sales, time spent on your vacation dreaming up new promotions to drive season tickets, hours of research looking for opportunities to restructure debt, endless meetings creating internal salary caps: anything to generate revenue and increase the bottom line. The *Busy SportsLeader* works hard and long to make his business as profitable as he can. It takes a tremendous amount of effort to be successful financially.

How much effort should we put into gaining God's wisdom? The Lord uses our own profit motive as the standard.

"How blessed is the man who finds wisdom, and the man who gains understanding. For its profit is better than the profit of silver, and its gain than fine gold. She is more precious than jewels; and nothing you desire compares with her." Proverbs 3:13-15.

A regular reassessment and reassignment of where our energies are invested can result in gaining God's wisdom.

"People generally quarrel because they cannot argue." -
Gilbert K. Chesterton, English Author, 1874-1936.

Dictionary.com defines arguing in the way Chesterton did in
the late 1800's, *"to attempt to prove by reasoning"*.

It is a good thing for teammates to make their opinions known
to each other by reasoning. Animated and passionate
discussion, as long as it's above board, is a very good thing.
Quarrelling on the other hand is personal sniping and quickly
becomes destructive.

For the *Busy SportsLeader,* getting teammates to talk, reason,
and let their heartfelt beliefs be known takes pro-activity.
Creating an environment where honest, open dialogue
between team members happens will radically reduce
quarrelling.

God invites His people to be honest and thoughtful with Him:
"Come now, and let us reason together, saith the Lord".
Isaiah 1:18.

"Striving for success without hard work is like trying to harvest where you haven't planted." - David Bly.

Have you ever wondered why God doesn't give us a signing bonus the day we come to faith by depositing the complete wisdom of the Bible into our minds? Or why we don't naturally overcome our sinful tendencies just because we want to?

The *Busy SportsLeader* knows that maturity comes through time and effort. The price we pay for maturity gives it value. We are far less likely to give up something that is expensive. No truly great leader is given everything; in fact, much of the trust people put in a leader is because they have paid a great price to earn their position.

"Brethren, I do not regard myself as having laid hold of it yet (spiritual maturity); but one thing I do: forgetting what lies behind and reaching forward to what lies ahead". Philippians 3:13.

The direction of your life, your family, your organization, all have a common thread: <u>you</u>. It is in the power of the ***Busy SportsLeader*** to guide, or influence, the path of those you touch today. This is an awesome responsibility that you will ultimately be accountable for in God's eyes. *(Almost makes you want to let someone else make the decisions.)* Don't be fearful. Be strong. God has put you in this position for a reason. Better yet, He has not left you on your own in these decisions. ***In Psalm 32:8 God says, "I will instruct you and teach you in the way which you should go; I will counsel you with my eye upon you."***

I like the part about *"which way you should go"*. If I am going to be accountable for my direction and those I influence, at least I can rely on <u>Him</u> for <u>His</u> counsel. Then when my day of reckoning comes, I'll have done well, **if** I have listened to and followed His instructions.

"Do not trust all men, but trust men of worth; the former course is silly, the latter a mark of prudence." - Democritus.

Are you making difficult personnel choices this week? Part of the process for the *Busy SportsLeader* should include: "Trust". Ask, "Can I trust this person every day or will I have to keep a constant eye on them?" "Can others trust him?"

"Whoever can be trusted with very little can also be trusted with much, and whoever is dishonest with very little will also be dishonest with much." Luke 16:10.

Fall

Driving through farmland in late summer / early fall brings an appreciation for the work that has been done by the farmer. The smell of the field and the height of the corn are a reminder that the reward for the labor is about to be realized. The fruit of the labor of the ***Busy SportsLeader*** during spring and summer is also revealed in the fall. Some enjoy great rewards and, unfortunately, others are disappointed.

In Psalm 1:1-3 the Psalmist teaches a simple lesson with a profound promise: *"How blessed is the man who does not walk in the counsel of the wicked, nor stand in the path of sinners, nor sit in the seat of scoffers! But his delight is in the law of the Lord, And in his law he meditates day and night. **And he will be like a tree firmly planted by streams of water, which yields its fruit in its season**, and its leaf does not wither; and in whatever he does he prospers."*

The Lord wants us to choose well the people we listen to, and He directs us to spend time dwelling on His Word. The benefit He offers is fruit at harvest time and prosperity.

"The sweetest of all sounds is praise." - Xenophon, Athenian philosopher, pupil of Socrates, born 444 B.C.

It is effortless to complain and bark. The *Busy SportsLeader* encounters so many problems, difficulties and challenges that complaining and barking seems second nature. But is it right?

God is gentle and just. Why aren't we?

"That doesn't work in leadership! You can't be gentle and motivate people", many leaders would protest.

God is not simply gentle, He is also just. Isn't that one of the keys to great leadership: being consistently just and focused, and at the same time understanding and meeting the needs of those that you lead? This combination is unbeatable.

"I will sing of loving-kindness and justice, To You, O LORD, I will sing praises." Psalm 101:1.

Psalm 101 is sort of a handbook on best practices for business and leadership. Over the next few days, we'll look at them here.

"When we quarrel, how we wish we had been blameless." -
Ralph Waldo Emerson.

The price of integrity is great. The reward is greater.

The **Busy SportsLeader** has many opportunities to cut corners,
lose his temper, bask in pride; but is it worth it? Does the
temporal pleasure outweigh the rewards?

Some might say, "No human is perfect!" So instead
of pursing righteousness they don't even try. The truth is most
would rather sweat for success than toil toward integrity.

"I will give heed to the blameless way... I will walk within
my house in the integrity of my heart." Psalm 101:2.

"The eyes like sentinel occupy the highest place in the body."
- Marcus Tullius Cicero.

Disciplining the eyes is an essential element of good character. The *Busy SportsLeader* needs that character and discipline to stay focused on the needs and direction of his organization. The well-being of his team can be adversely affected if he allows base distractions to capture his attention.

In the broad scope of concerns that leaders face, the discipline of the eyes may seem small, but lack of care in this small thing can prove disastrous.

"I will refuse to look at anything vile and vulgar. I hate all crooked dealings; I will have nothing to do with them."
Psalm 101:3.

"Associate with men of good quality if you esteem your reputation; for it is better to be alone than in bad company."
- George Washington.

Tempted to add a great performer with bad character to your company or team?

"Perverseness of heart shall be far from me; I will know nothing of evil." Psalm 101:4.

"One of the most striking differences between a cat and a lie is that a cat has only nine lives." - Mark Twain.

At the heart of sports is competition. The *Busy SportsLeader* is competitive by nature. The manner in which we live and compete is unimportant to an amazingly large number of people. The only goal is to win.

God desires us to work to be our best, honor Him, *and* win according to His rules. If we forget the manner in which we compete is important to Him, we invite disaster.

"I will not tolerate people who slander their neighbors." Proverbs 101:5a.

"Hard work spotlights the character of people: some turn up their sleeves, some turn up their noses, and some don't turn up at all." - Sam Ewig.

Building the team is most important for a *Busy SportsLeader*. Much of your success is determined by *who* you choose. It is easy to focus on speed, strength, and agility. Other qualities are not as quantifiable - like faithfulness.

Ask the same question that the Psalmist does when evaluating potential team members: "Would I want him to live with me?"

"My eyes shall be on the faithful of the land, That they may dwell with me; He who walks in a perfect way, He shall serve me." Psalm 101:6.

"The world is not fair, and often fools, cowards, liars and the selfish hide in high places." - Bryant H. McGill.

In a quest to find the characteristics of the most admired leaders in business, James Kouzes and Barry Posner surveyed people from around the world. The most important characteristic of a leader in <u>every</u> culture was: HONESTY.

Lies can get *Busy SportsLeaders* to the top, but they can't keep them there. Why? Because others won't follow. Thousands of years before scientific research was developed God clued us in to this truth through Psalm 101.

"He who works deceit shall not dwell within my house; He who tells lies shall not continue in my presence." Psalm 101:7.

The death of a sports fan sent shockwaves through the industry. It is on everyone's lips. Adding to the horror is that the victim of this accident is a young girl, with her whole life ahead of her.

It wasn't long before *Busy SportsLeaders* began to re-address issues of fan safety and corporate liability. They began to wonder how they could prevent this kind of thing from happening again. But I'm guessing many in venue management and sports leadership privately asked themselves, "How would I react to such horrible news? What if I was asked to make a statement? **What's the right thing to do?**"

Believe it or not Jesus was blamed for the death of his good friend Lazarus. He would soon raise Lazarus from the dead, and He knew he *would* do it, but still He was profoundly touched by the sorrow of this event.

"'Comfort, comfort my people,' says your God." Isaiah 40:1.

We can't give life again to those who have died. But we should weep with those who weep before we do anything else.

206

"Drink the first. Sip the second slowly. Skip the third."
- Knute Rockne.

Should I drink? Can I dance? How about "R" rated movies?

The *Busy SportsLeader* of faith is a follower of Christ and an example to others.

What activities are permissible, which are not? Follow closely and you'll know your answer.

"Don't drink too much wine. That cheapens your life. Drink the Spirit of God, huge draughts of him." Ephesians *5:18.*

During an interview last night a prominent SportsLeader spoke of his decision to trade a player to improve his team's overall character. He felt his season-ticket holders wanted more change in character and wanted it fast. He asked for patience from their fan base and promised to take action, but said it may take two years to make all the moves necessary.

In a separate interview last night a journalist explained how he tracked down a former player who had tremendous potential, but because of alcohol abuse, now bounces between jail and the minor leagues.

A few days ago I had a conversation with a SportsLeader who could see his team's difficulty in overcoming adversity because "lots of the guys here are bad characters".

Recalling years of immorality and drug use, a Hall of Famer this week acknowledged that poor performances were a direct result of his choices.

"The Lord laughs at the wicked, for he knows their day is coming." Proverbs 37:12.

The *Busy SportsLeader* with wisdom knows it too.

"You can't build a reputation on what you're going to do." - Henry Ford.

The dictionary defines reputation as: *"the general estimation in which a person is held by the public."*

Interacting with players, agents, and the media can test the mettle of even the most honorable person. Everything you say may be written, recorded, and not surprisingly, become very twisted. Even if it is not recorded it's remembered and it's in this environment that much of a *Busy SportsLeader's* reputation is formed.

Consistency, integrity, and honesty are all part of how others see you. AFTER Timothy had labored, cared, and sacrificed without guile and without looking for gain, Paul commended him to the Philippians in this way: *"I hope in the Lord Jesus to send Timothy to you soon....receive him then in the Lord with all joy, and hold men like him in high regard (reputation)." Philippians 2:19, 29.*

The **Busy SportsLeader** can be torn between two methods of leadership to maximize performance. There is the classic "push method" line coaches love: urging, berating, and exhorting the team toward the goal with doom as the result of failure. And there is the more modern "pull method": running out in front, outperforming, outworking, out-hustling the rest of the team causing them to move faster to keep up. Push or pull. You've seen both work. The Bible gives a third option: LIFT.

"When men are brought low and you say, 'Lift him up!' Then He will save the downcast." Job 22:29.

Encouragement and assistance can lift a team from burden, then they're own intrinsic motivation will move them forward. If you've picked your team well they already are motivated, they may just need a lift to get over the bumps.

"The only thing necessary for the triumph of evil is for good men to do nothing." A commentary on today's headlines? No, Edmund Burke, a British statesman spoke these timeless words in the sixteenth century!

The *Busy SportsLeader* is occasionally called by God to take a stand in the face of evil: even when the evil is profitable or popular. It is in these moments courage is tested.

"I sought for a man among them, who would build up the wall and stand in the gap before Me for the land, so that I would not destroy it; but I found none." Ezekiel 22:30.

Some will run, many will hide, but who will stand in the gap? Listen to the still, small voice of the Lord. Is He calling you to take action today?

"No coach has ever won a game by what he knows; it's what his players know that counts." - Bear Bryant.

I've told hundreds of athletes that the last thing you want your coach to say in the middle of a big game is, "Give me your helmet; I'll go do it myself."

Busy SportsLeaders must not be frustrated by the process. It is a wise leader that takes the time to teach.

"...teach and admonish one another with all wisdom." Colossians 3:16.

If you like the character of your current team, (their behavior, work ethic, and values), but feel they are under performing, take care as you make changes and additions. New talent may be needed for improved performance, but great caution should be given to how they will affect the whole.

The *Busy SportsLeader* with wisdom not only evaluates the physical and mental gifts of a potential athlete or coach, but also the impact they will have on others. This verse says it all:

"But it takes only one wrong person among you to infect all the others-a little yeast spreads quickly through the whole batch of dough." Galatians 5:9.

In the movie "Rudy" an aspiring Notre Dame football player seeks answers to difficult questions from a wise old priest. In response to his inquiry the priest answers, ***"In my 40 years of theological studies I have really only learned two things: there is a God, and I'm not Him."***

Sometimes we can be our own harshest critic. The ***Busy SportsLeader*** expects much out of his team and more out of himself. Many in leadership positions have not learned the lesson the priest has; they are not God! Neither are you. So why not admit it. By admitting your weakness and mistakes you'll only create an atmosphere of trust in your leadership and your organization.

"And (God) said to me, 'My grace is sufficient for you, for My strength is made perfect in (your) weakness.'"
II Corinthians 12:9.

Most people have heard that the greatest commandment is to "love God". But they're not sure *how* to love God. You can't really send Him a card, give Him a hug, or cut Him a nice big check. The many ways we are used to expressing love aren't sensible for the *"God Who has Everything"*.

The apostle John makes the application of how to love God practical in *I John 5:3, "For this is the love of God, that we keep His commandments; and His commandments are not burdensome."*

The *Busy SportsLeader* who carries many burdens does not carry more because he loves God. The love of God is more than emotion or sentiment; it is a choice, a choice we make every time we're confronted with temptation.

"Leadership is a combination of strategy and character. If you must be without one, be without the strategy."
- Gen. H. Norman Schwarzkopf.

Sixty years ago the UK endured bombings, terror, and was brought to the brink of annihilation. A leader arose among them with passion, vision and the ability to speak to the heart of the British people. He had a strategy *and* character.

Five hundred and seventy-seven miles to the southeast of London, in Germany, another leader came forward. He, too, was a man of passion, vision and possessed the ability to speak to the heart of his people. He promised to take his nation to the pinnacle of world greatness. Like the leader in England, he had a strategy to get his people where he was leading.

One helped define a generation as great. The other shattered his very own country.

The *Busy SportsLeader* is always looking for others to put into a position of leadership. Just because a person can get others to follow, doesn't mean you want them in a position of leadership. Unfortunately all too often we look at the strategy of a man, and not at his character.

"For the leaders of the people have led them down the path of destruction". Isaiah 9:16.

216

"He is no fool who gives up that which he cannot keep in order to gain that which he cannot lose." - Jim Elliott, martyred missionary to Ecuador.

Millions aspire to play or work in professional and college sports, few achieve it. Millions more climb the ladder of success, only to get to the top of the ladder and find it was placed against the wrong wall.

On those rare occasions when the *Busy SportsLeader* comes across an athlete who has a higher calling, he should be very careful to not try to persuade the athlete away from the calling.

Do sports and leadership give a powerful platform to impact our world? Absolutely. Is it the best way? Not for everybody. Even the gifted athlete or businessman may be asked to serve from a different platform.

Moreover, consider yourself. Your gifts, talents, and hard work may have put you in an enviable position, but maybe you too have a different mission from above.

"For the gifts and the calling of God are irrevocable." Romans 11:29.

My computer has a cool thesaurus that gives me a list of synonyms for almost every word I know. The list usually concludes with an antonym. A check of the word wise brings up synonyms like, "intelligent" and "astute". It also offers one antonym for the word wise: "fool".

The *Busy SportsLeader* can gain wisdom by avoiding the characteristics the Bible assigns to a "**fool**". God's Word makes many references to different types of fools, here is just one: *"The fool says in his heart, there is no God." Psalm 14:1.*

A leader may say with his mouth and think in his mind that there is a God, but how a life is led reveals what is said in the deepest parts of the heart. To live every moment experiencing the presence of God reveals a heart that says, "There is a God, and I know He is near".

"Character cannot be developed in ease and quiet. Only through experience of trial and suffering can the soul be strengthened, ambition inspired, and success achieved." - *Helen Keller.*

Strong leadership through disappointment is a hallmark of a wise *Busy SportsLeader*. In the midst of dismay and discouragement people seek a strong leader. Reassurance, direction, and the knowledge that a steady hand is at the helm are the immediate needs of the organization; but much more is possible!

The fires of failure can produce the steel of success. The key is the leader. His vision, courage, and strength create the possibility of accomplishment through adversity.

"I command you--be strong and courageous! Do not be afraid or discouraged. For the LORD your God is with you wherever you go." Joshua 1:9.

A gentleman sits down to dine at his favorite restaurant.
Eventually his meal arrives, he picks up his fork and before he
begins to cut his food he notices the fork has little pieces of
old fish on it. Oh sure it's not real chunky, but he can tell it's
there. Now he faces a terrible decision. What should he do?
If he rejects the utensil it could hurt the fork's feelings.
The fork does look **sorry** and embarrassed and the gentleman
can tell the fork still wants to be used. Unfortunately, it does
have to be sent back to the kitchen. The fork hates that. The
dishwater is so hot and the scrubbing so thorough, and well,
the fork doesn't really feel all that cleaning is necessary
anyhow.

God wants to use us. But He doesn't use dirty forks either.
*"Therefore, if a man cleanses himself from these things, he
will be a vessel for honor, sanctified, useful to the Master,
prepared for every good work." II Timothy 2: 21.*

It's not enough to just want to be used by God, or look sorry
for messes we make. The *Busy SportsLeader* has to be
diligent to stay away from sin, and present himself to God
regularly for cleansing.

"The credit belongs to the man who is actually in the arena, whose face is marred by dust and sweat and blood; who strives valiantly; who errs and comes short again and again, who knows the great enthusiasms, the great devotions, and spends himself in a worthy cause; who at best, knows the triumph of high achievement; and who, at the worst, if he fails, at least fails while daring greatly, so that his place shall never be with those cold and timid souls who know neither victory nor defeat." - Theodore Roosevelt, "Citizen in a Republic", April 23, 1910.

Buried in Roosevelt's famous quote is the key to great leadership. It's not simply: *"If at first you don't succeed, try, try again."* Look closer; it's, "great devotions", or the daily exercise of discipline that unlocks success. For the *Very Busy SportsLeader* it is easy to pass up daily study of God's Word and time in prayer, but in that attention to detail the character of a leader is forged.

"Be diligent to present yourself approved to God as a workman who does not need to be ashamed, accurately handling the word of truth." II Timothy 2:15.

221

Twenty, fifty, maybe more? How many "bosses" have you had over the course of your life? What number was truly life-changing? One or two? Every boss wants to get the most production possible out of their employees, but the *"Busy SportsLeader"* can do much more. They can be life-changers. They can be one of the few who make a difference. More than simply managing others' work, they can be **life leaders by showing love for spouse and children, care for others, honesty, integrity and faithfulness to God.** To be this kind of leader, you have to be this kind of person. Few are.

Gideon once had 82,000 soldiers; God led him to choose only 300 to take into battle. Even this elite group was to do more than follow instructions; they were to follow Gideon's **actions**.

"'Watch me,' he told them. 'Follow my lead…do exactly as I do.'" Judges 7:17.

"I do not think much of a man who is not wiser today than he was yesterday." – Abraham Lincoln.

Many things in the business of sports are elusive. Financial success, continued winning, and championships are all difficult to grasp. It can seem that every time the *Busy SportsLeader* closes in on a goal, someone moves it out from under them.

What a miracle to find something that is valuable that won't run away. Imagine something wonderful that wants YOU. No chasing, no hunting, no striving, in fact – just listen and it will tell you right where to find it.

"Does not wisdom call, And understanding lift up her voice?...Beside the gates, at the opening to the city, at the entrance of the doors, she cries out".
Proverbs 8:1, 3.

"First talk to God about your children - Then talk to your children about God." - Anonymous.

The **Busy SportsLeader** carries many burdens. A leader's spouse often carries extra burdens at home. One responsibility that must never be totally delegated to a mate is teaching your children about how to have a vital relationship with God.

No matter how busy you get, or how inadequate you feel, it is your duty to instruct your children about God. <u>This will always be your primary leadership role in life</u>. That's how God designed it. Leaders must take valuable time to pray for, and teach their own children in this most important area. It is so important that God promises a great return on this investment of your valuable time and effort.

"Train up a child in the way he should go; and when he is old, he will not depart from it." Proverbs 22:6.

224

Developing leaders and building a team is a little like going into a gold mine. It has always taken skill to extract the gold from the ore; but today the gold doesn't want miners digging around until they're sure the miners are NOT thieves in disguise. The miners don't know it, but the gold is running a background check every day.

If the *Busy SportsLeader* wants to effect change in his organization in today's world, he must accept that **HE IS THE MESSAGE**. No longer will fines or psychology influence today's athletes. They are looking for authentic people to follow.

Paul set the model for the modern influencer when he wrote, *"...in all things show yourself to be an example of good deeds". Titus 2:7.*

"The ultimate measure of a man is not where he stands in moments of comfort, but where he stands at times of challenge and controversy." - Martin Luther King, Jr.

The **Busy SportsLeader** is called on to do many things for those who follow him. One of the most difficult duties of a leader is providing comfort to those who suffer loss. Suffering people will look to a leader for direction, certainty and solace, even when the leader suffers the same loss. Giving comfort is a tall order for someone who needs comfort themselves.

It is crucial for a leader to seek the peace of God in the midst of difficulty, without it, those he leads are sailing on a rudderless ship.

"He comforts us in all our troubles so that we can comfort others. When others are troubled, we will be able to give them the same comfort God has given us."
II Corinthians 1:4.

"Success on any major scale requires you to accept responsibility... in the final analysis, the one quality that all successful people have... is the ability to take on responsibility." - Michael Korda, Editor-in-Chief, Simon & Schuster.

The president of a pro sports team once told me to always avoid jobs that, if you disappeared, you wouldn't be missed. He said, *"Always look to be a weight-bearing wall."*

Bearing weight and responsibility requires strength. To increase responsibility requires you to increase your strength. *The Busy SportsLeader* can find what he needs in an ever growing knowledge of God.

"A wise man is strong, yes, a man of knowledge increases strength." Proverbs 24:5.

227

Business is competitive. Sports are competitive. The battle for the entertainment dollar is growing fiercer by the year. Interest in NASCAR, X-games, and women's sports is gaining among fans. To grow market-share means hustle, skill, and the ability to fight off the competition, even if that competition is from the inside.

The *Busy SportsLeader* can be in the battle 14 hours a day: a scrapper for customers, a combatant against challengers to his position. It's a small move to go from being a hard worker to becoming what old timers call a "pug". The word is from pugilist. It means a person who's ready to jump into a fistfight, and fast. It has to do with losing your temper.

Paul qualifies a Christian leader as one who *"is not pugnacious" in Titus 1:7.* Be smart, hustle, and grow, but don't be quick tempered.

"Self-justification is a treacherous servant." - Wellington Mara.

When the **Busy SportsLeader** quietly reflects on his or her leadership, execution of responsibilities, and the quality of their relationship with God, they must be honest. Now is the time to make the brutal truth the only standard by which you judge your work and relationships.

Take the time while on vacation to stand before God and say, *"show me the truth - about ME !"*

"If you need wisdom--if you want to know what God wants you to do--ask him, and he will gladly tell you. He will not resent your asking." James 1:5.

Things always change. Deals seem to be moving targets. What you thought was done, is not. The *Busy SportsLeader* is like the high school algebra student: always battling variables.

For the *Busy SportsLeader* who was an athlete or a coach, these constant changes can be tough. Athletes and coaches use discipline and planning to prepare for the ebbs and flows of a sporting contest. But the business of sports is not as easily programmable.

In the winds of change that life brings, there is One who never changes. He never asks to re-negotiate a deal. Never fails to make His deliverables, and shows up more faithfully than you best season ticket holder. You can always rely on Him.

Why did you read this page today? Maybe God wanted to remind you that *"Every good thing bestowed and every perfect gift is from above, coming down from the Father of lights, with whom there is no variation, or shifting shadow." James 1:17.*

The *Busy SportsLeader* doesn't have much time to think creatively about improving and advancing his organization. Yet he does it regularly. He has too. Usually improvements are a result of solving a problem. The scope of innovation can tend to be narrow and in the area of the leader's greatest concern. To broaden the scope of his organization's advancements, experts and consultants are hired. People who have been successful leaders in the past may offer opinions. The *Busy SportsLeader* will weigh the advice he's given and decide if it's worthy of implementation.

There is another, often untapped source of profound analysis: lower level employees. They're the foot soldiers of your operations. They see things you don't have time to. Worldly wisdom suggests that the only opinions worth listening to are from the powerful, not the weak.

Solomon writes in *Ecclesiastes 9:16, "Wisdom is better than strength. But the wisdom of the poor man is despised and his words are not heeded."*

Think back a few years. You were one once, too. I'll bet you had some wisdom that was ignored by your leaders, and you still remember.

"Bad habits are like a comfortable bed, easy to get into, but hard to get out of." - Anonymous.

It's a common problem for every type of leader, **"What do I do about our BBHP?"** Whether it's your top salesman, wide-receiver, financial analyst or star-slugger, Bad Behaving High Performers pose a dilemma. They're seemingly too valuable to manage off the team *and* too much of a liability to keep on the team.

For the ***Busy SportsLeader*** this is particularly troublesome because the BBHP can easily become the "face" of your organization.

The biggest reason for keeping the BBHP is their numbers; easy to track, obvious to compare, this guy is the best.

Much harder to quantify is the BBHP's negative impact on the team. Here it takes wisdom to make a tough decision. One question to consider is, "Are we reaching our ultimate <u>TEAM</u> goals with him on the team? If not, it may be time for a change.

"So give Your servant an understanding heart to judge Your people to discern between good and evil." I Kings 3:9.

Leadership, by definition, means someone must follow. But what motivates a person to follow another? Is it money, or wisdom, or the opportunities a leader offers that causes others to follow? If so, then the followers are only "temps". When someone else can offer more, they'll move on.

Nothing engenders a more passionate follower than a leader who has some personal touch in their life. A leader who has taken time, made sacrifice, and gotten their hands dirty for others will eventually hold the greatest loyalties.

In II Corinthians chapters 11 & 12, the apostle Paul recounts how he suffered shipwrecks, dangerous journeys, hunger and thirst, all because he wanted to personally minister to others. He crystallizes his commitment to them in *II Corinthians 12:15, "and I will most gladly spend and be personally expended for your spiritual well-being."*

The *Busy SportsLeader* may be tempted to take short cuts. A gift bought by an administrative assistant on your behalf or free merchandise redirected to staff may be nice, but it lacks the personal touch people need. God wants to use us as an instrument in His hands. The primary need of people is spiritual. Take the opportunity today to touch those you lead in a personal and spiritual way.

The **Busy SportsLeader** tries to anticipate the needs of his organization. Planning and preparation is an important facet of future success. It is a wise, but rare, SportsLeader who anticipates the needs of his community. Widespread tragedy and disaster could affect the community at large at any time. The response of a sports organization can be a catalyst to the business community and the community at large. God has instructed us to be an instrument of comfort to those around us. Plan ahead as to how you can use your influence as a leader to show the love of God to those in need.

"But whoever has the world's goods, and beholds his brother in need and closes his heart against him, how does the love of God abide in him?" I John 3:17.

"Leadership is a matter of having people look at you and gain confidence, seeing how you react. If you're in control, they're in control." - Tom Landry.

In the midst of difficulty people look to their leaders for guidance. How leaders react, respond and navigate disturbing times gives cues to others as to how well challenges will be handled. In small problems, as well as tragedies on a worldwide scale, leaders make a difference.

When dealing with trouble, taking some sort of action is almost always the right thing; fortunately for most leaders it is also natural. For the Christian who is also a *Busy SportsLeader*, action that reflects his faith and values is the right thing; unfortunately this may <u>not</u> be natural. Faith and values are the core of a leader. A leader's action should be the outward expression of his inward nature.

"Therefore we do not lose heart, but though our outer man is decaying, yet our inner man is being renewed day by day." II Corinthians 4:16.

Imagine God personally sending an angel ahead of you and your team to make sure you're always a winner; every goal achieved, every game won. How often have we heard an athlete or coach thank God for the blessings of success and thought to ourselves, "God really did bless him, he must be a great Christian. *I wonder if I can get him to speak to our men's group at church.*"

God once promised an angel to go ahead of His people. The angel would assure victory in battle and secure the Promised Land. But He didn't make the offer because of their faith; instead He made the offer because they were "a stiff-necked people", and He did not want to go with them personally. **God would give them presents, but not His presence.**

Moses knew blessings are not confirmation that all is right between God and His people. He said to Him, *"If your Presence does not go with us, do not bring us up from here." Exodus 33:15.*

The *Busy SportsLeader* should judge his walk with God, not by achievement, but by doing His will.

Got a tough boss? How does he handle it when an assignment you're responsible for doesn't go very well? Has he ever said anything like this: *"throw that worthless servant outside, into the darkness, where there will be weeping and gnashing of teeth"? Matthew 25:30.*

Would it surprise you to discover the *"Boss"* speaking in Matthew 25:30 represents God? Yes! The same loving, patient God with whom we've become very comfortable. In this parable Jesus teaches that God the Father has given us responsibility in His work. If that responsibility in not taken seriously, or put off until later, He is not pleased.

God has given the *Busy SportsLeader* great and powerful responsibilities. If we are not faithful to make the most out of what He has given us, He may very well take it away and give to someone else who **will** be faithful.

"They say that football builds character. But I don't really think it does. If anything, football <u>reveals</u> character. Character is the sum of the internal (moral) decisions you have made in your life." - Bob Ladouceur, five-time high school football national champion head coach.

For a *Busy SportsLeader* the playing days may be long gone, but the revelation of true character can still become evident in the competition of business and during interpersonal conflict.

When difficulty comes upon us like a flood, and emotions run high, it's too late to develop character. If you're not satisfied with the character you see in yourself during difficult times you <u>can</u> change. To change, decisions need to be made immediately which are difficult and life-altering. Usually each individual is keenly aware of what those decisions are; if anyone is uncertain, a trusted friend can help. Fortunately we don't have to build our moral fiber by ourselves.

"What this means is that those who become Christians become new persons. They are not the same anymore, for the old life is gone. A new life has begun!" II Corinthians 5:17.

"Long is the road to learning by precepts, but short and successful by examples." - Latin proverb.

Many universities offer a Masters Degree in Sports Administration, but nothing teaches more than the example of a real live leader. Day in and day out, the *Busy SportsLeader* interacts with others. Each point of contact makes a difference. The way a leader responds to difficulties, enjoys success, and carries out his responsibilities has an impact on the future of those around him.

Your values, attitudes, and language will most likely be reproduced in the leadership style of those near you. Someone is always watching and learning.

"I have given you an example to follow. Do as I have done to you." John 13:15.

"Either this man is dead..........or my watch has stopped!" - **Groucho Marx**

A long time veteran of the NFL, Charle Young, used to often quote the verse, *"We are but a vapor"*. He was one of a few that truly understood the brevity of life. Only within the context of this brevity can a **Busy SportsLeader's** depth of wisdom be judged.

"Show me O Lord, my life's end and the number of my days; let me know how fleeting my life is." Psalm 39:4.

"A life of frustration is inevitable for any coach whose main enjoyment is winning." - Chuck Noll.

A *Busy SportsLeader* once told me he felt fine the evening of a win. He felt desperately depressed for days after a loss. And the rest of the time he was kind of nervous. So, he concluded, "Last year was a great year for us. I only felt badly 245 days."

In a competitive world, the only prospect for lasting joy is in God.

"Why am I discouraged? Why is my heart so sad? I will put my hope in God! I will praise Him again." Psalm 42:5.

"Academe, n.: An ancient school where morality and philosophy were taught.
Academy, n.: A modern school where football is taught." -
Ambrose Bierce, 1842-1914.

Bierce's observation is as true today as it was a hundred years ago.

Busy SportsLeaders often try to solve this problem with *programs* on character. What are really needed are mature *people* with character - to lead young people who are willing to learn character.

"Moral dropouts won't listen to their elders: welcoming correction is a mark of good sense." Proverbs 15:5.

Several years ago former Atlanta Falcons quarterback Steve Bartkowski and I were playing golf on a course surrounded by million dollar mansions. I was awed by the luxury and comfort so many people enjoyed. My running commentary on the lavish houses must have gone on for several holes when Steve flatly stated, "Pat, there are a lot of heartbreaking stories in those homes. Just because the residence is big doesn't mean the people are happy."

"Better is a little with the fear of the Lord, than great wealth with turmoil." Proverbs 15:16.

The *Busy SportsLeader* can pay extraordinary amounts of money to talented athletes and coaches, but that is no guarantee of a contented home life for those in your organization. Creating an environment where God is honored and faith encouraged can be more valuable that gold.

Solving complicated ethical dilemmas is difficult for an experienced **Busy SportsLeader** or business leader.

This week I posed a very thorny problem to several groups of high school students. Their values became evident as they waded through the moral decision making process. The most striking shift in thought came when I asked them to, "Pretend for a moment that there is a God and that He is not silent. Pretend, that He is all powerful, all knowing, ever present, not restricted by time or circumstance. Pretend He knows your needs, your words and your actions. Pretend He has given you a personal letter outlining the things you must avoid in your solution, such as lying and deception. Now under those circumstances, does it change your decision?"

Almost to a student they answered, "Well, if that were true, sure it would make a big difference in my decision making!"

"Who has measured the waters in the hollow of His hand, and marked off the heavens by the span, and calculated the dust of the earth by the measure, and weighed the mountains in a balance, and the hills in a pair of scales?" Isaiah 40:12.

Imagine, what kind of difference it would make in our ethics if there really **were such a God?**

"Our young boys in this country, they need to hear from you. Our boys are getting a lot of the wrong messages about what it means to be a man in this world. About how you should act, and how you should dress, and how you should talk, and how you should treat people. They don't always get the right message, but you guys have the right messages. You know it. You live it." - Tony Dungy.

Is it proper for a *Busy SportsLeader* to use his position to exhort others in sports to be an influence in our world? **IT IS!**

In this day when it seems so many people are offended so easily, and the fear of offending others has caused the good to say so little, it is time to be courageous. God puts us in positions of influence, not so we can enjoy the comfort of fame, but so we can face the challenge of change.

"Why are you silent while the wicked swallow up those more righteous than themselves?" Habakkuk 1:13.

Diligent study, years of experience and gifted teachers; that is where most find the knowledge to lead. Reliance on this map of knowledge has long been accepted as the way to find the road to success.

To find your road to success, you must **first** know where to start. For the *Busy SportsLeader* the starting point is found in the map called The Book of Proverbs.

"The fear of the LORD is the beginning of wisdom, and knowledge of the Holy One is understanding." Proverbs 9:10.

Theologian Charles Ryrie defines *fear of the Lord* to be: *"a reverence for God expressed in submission to His will."* He further says, *"Wisdom is not acquired by a mechanical formula but through a right relationship with God."*

The *Busy SportsLeader* can begin a relationship with God through faith in Christ. The road to wisdom is a long one. He is ready for you to start down that path with Him right now.

Delegation is undoubtedly one of the characteristics of a great leader. The **Busy SportsLeader** gives oversight, yes, but doesn't do others' jobs for them. Assistant coaches prepare a segment of the team. The CFO takes care of the finances and the VP of Sales gets people in the stadium. That's the way it works.

It is a mistake though to believe you have delegated your personal spiritual maturity to a pastor, priest or chaplain. You may be thinking, *"Isn't that kinda their job?"* It is NOT. Your spiritual maturity is your responsibility.

"Therefore let us leave the elementary teachings about Christ and go on to maturity." Hebrews 6:1.

If you desire to grow in your faith it is your task to spend time studying the Bible and talking to God *(prayer)*. Most importantly it is on your shoulders to choose to be obedient to God: outwardly and inwardly. Your pastor can teach and guide you but he can't MAKE you grow.

Twenty years ago Notre Dame hired a new football coach. Gerry Faust succeeded Dan Devine; they had very different backgrounds. Faust was the most successful high school coach in the country and had no college or pro experience. Dan Devine had been a professional coach and won a national championship while at Notre Dame. In a private moment, Devine asked Faust to write the most important quality of an assistant coach on a piece of paper, and then fold the paper. Devine wrote on a separate piece of paper what he felt was the most important quality, folded it, then the two exchanged papers.

Two very different men; two very different backgrounds; hundreds of qualities to choose from. Amazingly they both wrote the same thing: **LOYALTY**.

As an experienced leader Paul advised the young leader Titus, *"Reject a factious man after a first and second warning".* *Titus 3:10.*

Paul didn't fear disagreement. But he wouldn't take on a man who **divided the group into contentious parts.**

If you were asked, *"Who has had the greatest influence in your professional life?"* you probably wouldn't have to think long. One, two and sometimes three people really stand out. Sport writers love to trace lineages like these with head football coaches. These "trees" are less obvious in other sports and positions, yet the truth remains; **someone has made their mark on your life.** How you make decisions, hire people, handle conflict and even your language are often a reflection of your mentors.

Have the courage to look around today. **Your mark is being left in the lives of those around you.** Your strengths are being passed on; so are your faults. It's the undeniable curse and blessing of leadership.

Stadiums built and championships won are the legacy most *Busy SportsLeaders* wish to leave; neither is permanent. It's often said the only things that are eternal on this earth are God's Word and people. You're making a mark already. You decide if it's for now or forever.

"For I gave you an example that you should do as I did..."
John 13:15.

The **Busy SportsLeader** might attend a church service, or squeeze some time into his schedule to read his Bible and pray a little. Pregame chapels are often packed. Players and executives alike tend to keep track of how well they perform professionally as it correlates to the amount of "God stuff" they do. The more stuff the better, they hope.

It doesn't always work out that way. Sometimes the bad guys win, sometimes the good guys win. And from time to time, the guys who do all the stuff they can - get ticked off at God. They don't get the return on investment they expected.

Job had been keeping track. He did lots of "God stuff" and when things didn't go his way he started to give God a piece of his mind. I love God's response when He says to Job, *"Now gird up your loins like a man. And I will ask you, and you instruct me! Where were you when I laid the foundation of the earth?" Job 38:3, 4.*

God has much more for us than simple professional success when we seek Him. When we don't get what we want, we should remember He made us in His image; we didn't make Him to be our lucky charm.

Every day the letters in my mail proclaim that I am "Pre-Qualified". Cool! I haven't even tried and yet somehow I'm "Pre-Qualified" for credit cards, loans, and memberships.

Salesmen talk about potential customers that are "Pre-Qualified". It means they know that people they take the time to call on can afford their product.

When the *Busy SportsLeader* looks for someone to bring into his organization, it is a very good idea to "Pre-Qualify" the candidate before they get an interview. The first item that they should pre-qualify isn't their resume, but their character, and character is far harder to determine than just reputation.

The turn of the century author Elbert Hubbard once said, *"Many a man's reputation would not know his character if they met on the street."*

Character is a costly quality. Job's wife advised him to curse God and be free of suffering. When Job refused she asked, *"What price will you pay for character?" Job 2:9.*

When you find a candidate who has been willing to pay the price for his character, then you have found someone who is truly "Pre-Qualified" for your organization.

The **Busy SportsLeader** often finds himself on a long plane ride. Before notebook computers and air phones this was frequently the only place many could find to think. Even with the distractions of work, the road trip is still often the place where our imaginations are most active. It's in moments like these that our mind and heart stop just long enough to dream and desire. The thoughts that occupy us in these times can become the map we set our course upon. The trip we plot may take us to ports of joy or rocks of destruction.

Proverbs 4:23 admonishes, **"Watch over your heart with all diligence, for from it flow the springs of life."**

The word "heart" means our mind or inner being, and from that flows our spiritual vitality. It is so very important to discipline our thoughts and desires to what we know are good and right before God.

Next time your work takes you on the road, choose to make it a *"Bon Voyage"*.

"Courage is not the absence of fear, but rather the judgment that something else is more important than fear." - Ambrose Redmoon.

Lots of motivations push *The Busy SportsLeader.* The core incentive is often a person. People are tangible and in your face. Being pushed through life by others gives control where it doesn't belong.

God created us not to be pushed, but to be led: by Him. His leadership supersedes man's. Following His lead is a willful choice we make. It's not as easy or convenient as being pushed by someone else, but following His lead has eternal value. Before decisions, actions, and plans are executed we should ask, "Is the Lord leading me this way, or is someone else?"

"The fear of man brings a snare, But whoever trusts in the Lord shall be safe." Proverbs 29:25.

"The death of God means the death of morality", wrote Charles Colson in his modern classic, *How Now Shall We Live?* Colson also asserts, **"...traditional notions of morality and social order are largely derived from Christianity, these moral conventions likewise crumble when God is dismissed as irrelevant or nonexistent."**

The ***Busy SportsLeader*** has to ask himself, "Is God irrelevant in my professional life? Is my faith in God clearly apparent in my words, deeds, and values?" When God "dies" in the personal <u>or</u> professional life of a leader, morality "dies" in the arena they lead.

"Let your light so shine before men, that they may see your good works, and glorify your Father which is in heaven." *Matthew 5:16.*

"Cultivate an attitude of gratitude." - Jim Stephens.

We know that Thanksgiving is intended to give thanks to God. But some of the gifts that God gives are people. A principle of great leadership is letting people know *"why"* you're glad they are on your team.

For the *Busy SportsLeader* it is easy to be so busy that we forget to let others know the qualities we are thankful for in them. Find time today to let those around you know "why" you thank God for them.

"Every time I think of you, I give thanks to my God." Philippians 1:3.

The ability to deal with problems, plot a course for the future, and make decisions usually develops from experience. Some *Busy SportsLeaders* use statistical analysis to lead, while others work from a gut feeling. But whatever means a leader uses to make a conclusion, it is hampered by their personal limitations.

To ignore God's help in your leading is foolish. Read *I Kings 4:29* and imagine what you'd have to pay a consultant to get these results.

"God gave Solomon wisdom and very great insight, and a breadth of understanding as measureless as the sand on the seashore."

Logic. Experience. Gut-feeling. The *Busy SportsLeader* may be guided in his decision-making by many factors. But who he is, and how he sees the world, is the foundation for all of his personal and professional decisions.

Professor J.I. Packer proclaims, *"Disregard the study of God and you sentence yourself to stumble and bumble through life, blindfolded as it were, with no sense of direction and no understanding of what surrounds you."*

Out of eternity and into the moment cuts God's truth, bringing wisdom to every leader who will hear it.

" the word of God is living and active. Sharper than any double-edged sword, it penetrates even to dividing soul and spirit, joints and marrow; it judges the thoughts and attitudes of the heart." Hebrews 4:12.

The **Busy SportsLeader** has so much to offer those who work for him: expertise on business, advice on management, knowledge of the industry. Most leaders take the mentoring role seriously, with the hope of helping others. But mentorship is often lacking an important element, spiritual values.

It's a common misconception that people have little interest in learning about God and how He relates to all aspects of their life. A deep need is present in those around you, deeper than you can imagine. The prophet Amos vividly describes what is all around us.

" *'The days are coming,' declares the Sovereign Lord, 'when I will send a famine through the land -- not a famine of food or a thirst for water, but a famine of hearing the words of the LORD. Men will stagger from sea to sea and wander from north to east, searching for the word of the LORD, but they will not find it. In that day the lovely young women and strong young men will faint because of thirst.'" Amos 8:11-13.*

A great leader can nourish the starving by sharing his relationship with God.

"Life without thankfulness is devoid of love and passion. Hope without thankfulness is lacking in fine perception. Faith without thankfulness lacks strength and fortitude. Every virtue divorced from thankfulness is maimed and limps along the spiritual road." - Jim Stevens.

The *Busy SportsLeader* faces incredible demands on his time. It's easy to take some things for granted when the urgent closes in. One thing we should never take for granted is giving thanks, especially when someone does something for our children.

I am humbled by what Christ did on the cross for me, but to imagine He has made that sacrifice on behalf of my children almost takes my breath away. I daily thank Him for His grace in their lives. As a leader, your responsibilities begin at home. One of those responsibilities is to pray for those in your care and to thank God for His Gift to them.

"I thank my God always on your behalf, for the grace of God which is given you by Jesus Christ." I Corinthians 1:4.

The long anticipated moment arrives. The family sits around the table and reaches for each other's hands. The smell of turkey, potatoes, and pie fills the air. Someone begins to speak to God on behalf of this little group. For many children this is the only time in a year they ever hear their father pray. Usually heartfelt, often awkward, the words come forth. As the family listens each has a thought in mind of their own, a thing or person for whom they are personally thankful.

If your name came across the mind of those you lead, would they thank God for you? In moments like these it's not your acumen, intelligence, or even the pay scale you provide they would be truly, deeply thankful for. Thankfulness is a response to God's love and grace. If you are an instrument of God's grace and love in the lives of others then you will be paid the highest compliment of all, one you'll probably never hear: someone thanking God for you.

"We give thanks to God always for all of you, making mention of you in our prayers; constantly bearing in mind, your work of faith and labor of love and steadfastness of hope in our Lord Jesus Christ in the presence of our God and Father." I Thessalonians 1: 2-3.

"We can try to avoid making choices by doing nothing, but even that is a decision." - Gary Collins Ph.D.

You make countless choices every day. Some are comfortable choices, others are not. Your choices influence others as they decide which choices they will make. In essence this defines who you are and the quality of your leadership.

A *Busy SportsLeader* may feel more comfortable keeping his values and his faith to himself, avoiding scrutiny and accountability. But this choice cheats those he leads. If they endeavor to lead in the same way, they are ill-equipped for the task, for they have only seen the product, not the blueprints.

"...choose for yourselves today whom you will serve...as for me and my house, we will serve the Lord." Joshua 24:15.

"The first responsibility of a leader is to define reality. The last is to say thank you. In between, the leader is a servant." - Max De Pree, Fortune Magazine Business Hall of Fame.

Responsibilities can be threatening or rewarding; the year-end review goes a long way to determine which one it is.

The *Busy SportsLeader* should first, as De Pree suggests, define reality. But remember reality is both temporal and eternal. Leaders should also give thanks, including to God, who ultimately gave the responsibility. And yes, in between, leaders are servants. Who is served, and how well He is served will be revealed in a "year-end review" of sorts.

"So then each one of us will give an account of himself to God." Romans 14:12.

Acknowledgements

To the mentors who have built into my life:

Jim Keller who refused to let me be mediocre.

Mike Ryan who built me up when I was down.

Earl Smith who educated me in the things I need to know about other cultures and has faithfully ministered to the 49'ers after my departure.

Jeff Farrar who has often brought me into the presence of God with his gift of teaching.

To the old friends who helped shape my faith:

Sam Ashkar – for demonstrating leadership *(two sixteen yr. olds being co-captains of a HS football team was tough).*

Rick Faust – for your gentle walk with God and tenacity on the football field.

Craig McCullum – for challenging me to grow and go anywhere God called.

David Robinson – for your fire for Christ, success at reaching Eastern Europe *and* for introducing me to Nico.

To Board Members and Advisors for their wise counsel:

Greg Jamison, Bob Rittenhouse, the late Roger Post, Don Broesamle, Bill Russ, John Choma, Brent Jones, Bill Decker, Don Wood, the late Skip Williams, John Morris, Bill Hargis, Ken Allen, Billy and Laurel Shields, Hank Gay, Chuck Collings

Acknowledgements

To the Players who have been co-laborers:

Brent Jones who has been my best friend in California in-spite of the fact I never thought he'd make it in the NFL because he was too good to be true.

Darin Jordan whose passion for life and God has been a light of joy to my family.

John Choma who has become a Redwood of faith from humble beginnings.

Steve Wallace who defied the threat of a $75,000. fine in 1991 to continue the 50 yard prayer for years to come.

Guy McIntyre, the late Dave Waymer, Bubba Paris, and Ron Lewis who, along with Brent and Steve - as well as members of the New York Giants , who knelt for the first post-game prayer on the night of December 3rd 1990.

Charle Young, Bill Ring, Willie Harper, Dwaine Board, Milt McColl, Manu Tuiasosopo, Wendell Tyler, Tom Holmoe, Ron Ferrari, Jeff Kemp, Mike Moroski, Atlee Hammaker, Scott Garrelts, Darren Lewis, Mark Davis, Dave Dravecky, Tom Cousineau, Merton Hanks, Brian Bollinger, Sanjay Beach, Kevin Greene, William Floyd, Steve Young, Kevin Gogan, Jeff Brantley, Candy Maldonaldo, Arturs Irbe, Igor Larionov, Bart Oats, Orel Hershiser, Billy Shields, Gary Carter, Brett Butler, Royce Clayton, Bill Mueller, Mark Dewey, Ron Hadley, Antionio Goss, Craig Awbry, Rich Branning, Mike Cofer, Derrick Deese, Tommy Vardell, Mark Harris, Marc Logan, Ken Norton Jr., Jesse Sapolu, Nate Singleton, Dana Stubblefield, Bryant Young, Kevin Lewis, Ronnie Lott, Anthony Lynn, Ray Brown, Jeff Odgers, Doug Zmoleck, Bob Breuning, and the dozens more who were so important to me in my 18 yrs. as a team chaplain.

Acknowledgements

To the Coaches and Administrators who have been co-laborers and helped advance Godly Wisdom:

Mike Holmgren whose friendship began the day we met.

Dusty Baker, a great natural leader, of whom I've often said could take over an NHL team and make them better because he's so good with people.

Greg Jamison, the late Bobb McKittrick, Sam Wyche, Chuck Studley *(the greatest name any coach ever had!),* the late Bill Walsh and John McVay, *(two men who opened doors for a 24 yr. old chaplain),* Ed DeBartolo *(for trusting Bill and John),* Mike Solari, Allen Lowrey, Ned Colletti, George Seifert and Steve Mariucci, Marc Trestman, Ricky Sandoval, Dave Wannstedt, Norv Turner, Kevin Constantine, Wayne Thomas, Tony Dungy, Jon Richardson, Phil Savage, Marvin Lewis, Neal Dahlen, John Marshall, Jim Mora Jr., John Fox, Herm Edwards, Jack Del Rio, Bill Brooks, Kevin Warren, Larry MacDuff, Larry Kerr, Ray Rhodes *(I'll tell Dave Bratton you went to chapel).*

To those who have labored in sports ministry with me:

Dave Bratton former Chaplain of the New York Giants who I first shared the vision of two teams praying together and his guts to lead Giants players to join us.

Steve DeBardelaben, John Weber, Mike Bunkley, Hollis Haff, Steve Newman, the late Dave Swanson, Wendell Deyo, Dave Hannah, Dave Wilson, Tom Petersburg, Bill Rader, Dave Deal, Tom Lamphere, Mike Sigfrids, Andy Stewart, Jim Stump, Msg. Peter Armstrong, Norm Evans, Corwin Anthony, Charles Collins, Vince Nauss

About the Author: Pat Richie

Pat Richie is a speaker and consultant in the areas of teamwork and leadership to Fortune 500 companies, professional and college sports organizations, and government agencies.

His work in the area of teamwork and leadership has made an impact all across America.

From 1981-1998 he served as team chaplain of the San Francisco Forty-Niners. Three times he was awarded Super Bowl Rings for his contributions to the team.

In 1990 he was inspired to encourage NFL players to pray on the 50 yard line at the conclusion of the game. This prayer has become a tradition across football and today every NFL, major college, and many high school games end in prayer between opponents.

He also served as team chaplain to the San Francisco Giants, San Jose Sharks, and Stanford University football. Before that he worked on the campus of the University of Notre Dame developing the personal and spiritual lives of student-athletes.

More information on Pat Richie's work can be found at:

www.sports-leadership.com

Pat can be reached at:

pat@sports-leadership.com

Special thanks to my wife Nico who did so much to edit this book, and to my daughter Angelica who took time from a hectic schedule to assist in the editing also.

TABLE OF CONTENTS

How beautiful it is to do nothing, and then rest afterwards.
– Spanish Proverb

PREFACE

Cruising is among the most affordable and comfortable ways to travel. The Panama Canal (one of the greatest engineering feats of the 20th century) embodies the allure of history with the adventure of sailing through the Continental Divide. So, why not combine the two experiences and make life-long memories to treasure and share?

This is our experience (the good, the not-so-great, and the unforgettable) during a 17-day cruise from San Francisco to Fort Lauderdale, Florida, by way of the Panama Canal. While it is specific to the Holland American Cruise Line (since that's the line we were on), we've included enough general information to give you an idea of the cruise experience.

One caveat, though. Each cruise line has its own personality, and each cruise is unique. Our Holland America cruise appealed mostly to an older (I'd say over-50) crowd. So if you want more youthful activities than we describe here, check out other cruise lines – such as Carnival, Celebrity, Cunard, Crystal, Disney, Norwegian, Princess, Regent Seven Seas or Royal Caribbean.

We've written this book with you in mind. We hope to both inform and entertain you as we share this once-in-a-lifetime trip.

INTRODUCTION

Between the two of us, Al and I have made 137 trips around the sun. That clearly qualifies us as a "senior" couple. Whatever is the current term for those who qualify for Medicare and Social Security (*senior, elder* or *old*), it applies to us even though we see ourselves as just slightly post-middle-age, still full of curiosity and enthusiasm.

Yet, we've both chalked up long and varied careers.

Al is a retired Silicon Valley engineer (electrical/mechanical). He has traveled through many spiritual traditions, including ordination as a Methodist minister, and has settled as a Roman Catholic. In recent years he's been a licensed general contractor. His greatest love, however, is film photography. And he speaks passable Spanish, a small plus for this trip.

I've been a newspaper editor, magazine editor, daily newspaper reporter, university news director, owner of a PR/marketing business, and most recently, a newspaper columnist.

And here we are, on the cusp of genuine retirement, facing that great unknown: what to do after we quit working.

Since we both like to work, and suspect that we'll find plenty to do once we end the officially employed years, we decided to herald our coming retirement with this long-dreamed-about trip.

HOW THIS CRUISE BEGAN

Actually, this cruise started with a car wreck.

An irresponsible female, driving an SUV while texting, upended our lives on July 8, 2012.

We were sitting at a red light, just outside of Napa, California. A large silver van sat in the lane next to us, waiting for the light to turn green. Then the texting driver slammed full speed (60 mph) into us both, totaling all three vehicles in an explosion of metal and glass.

The rest of our summer filled up with doctor appointments, wrangling with insurance companies, complaining loudly and often about irresponsible drivers, and declaring that people who fool with their phones while driving should be jailed promptly and have their driver's license revoked.

The wreck also brought home to us how quickly the lovely life we share could end. How in a moment, one or both of us could be lying in a morgue or hooked up to monitors in a hospital.

The wreck, and its unpleasant aftermath, made us realize it's time to do some of the things we've talked about doing "someday."

We decided to make "someday" today.

Al has always dreamed of sailing through the Panama Canal – so we started researching Panama Canal cruises.

WHAT'S SO GREAT ABOUT CRUISING?

There are many good reasons to travel by cruise ship. Here are five that resonate with us:

1. **Value.** For the price of a cruise, you'll get lodging, all the meals and snacks you desire, entertainment from movies to Broadway-style musicals and other live performances

and an array of onboard and off-ship activities. Plus all your transportation, from one port to another throughout the entire trip.

2. **Convenience.** You unpack once. Someone else does all the "driving" from port to port. You never have to check a map or double check a GPS. You're just along for a lovely ride.

3. **Comfort.** Cruise lines aim to pamper. No matter what the cost of your stateroom – from suites to inside cabins – you'll find luxurious bedding, fluffy towels and washcloths and very nice soaps, shampoos and body lotions. In addition, there are many spa and sport offerings. Room service is included in the price of the cruise, as is daily room cleaning.

4. **Social life.** Cruising offers opportunities to meet others who share your interests. Sharing travel experiences can form the basis of lifelong friendships.

5. **Togetherness.** There's nothing like carefree travel together to renew or deepen romance. Cruising is the "together travel"

style for making a lot of great memories –
without stress.

In my early adulthood, I loved the thrill of the
road, jumping into my car and heading across the
state or across the nation. Staying in a different
hotel room every night or camping out on friends'
couches, I'd explore the wonders of DC or LA, New
Orleans or Taos, NM.

In those days, I was as apt to sleep in my car
on the way to some desired destination as I was to
pitch a tent and camp a few days beside a mountain trail or ocean beach.

But somewhere past 50, after marrying Al
Lockwood, I discovered that exploration doesn't
have to be made at breakneck speed. It's more civ-
ilized to sleep in the same comfortable bed each
night, while the ship's captain guides our vessel to
new ports.

On a cruise, I awaken to a new place, enjoy
breakfast in the dining room and head out at an
easy pace to discover new ports of call. No grocery
shopping necessary, no cooking, no cleaning up
after the meal.

It feels like you have your own little home, and yet the ship comes with a variety of restaurants, coffee shops and lounges. Each evening there are entertaining acts in the main theater and live music to enjoy in the various bars. Days are filled with onboard activities ranging from history and ecology lectures to cooking and computer classes, bingo and other games and even dancing lessons.

WE FIND A PANAMA CANAL CRUISE LEAVING FROM SAN FRANCISCO

We found a reasonably priced Panama Canal cruise leaving from San Francisco (just 45 minutes south of us). We called our travel agent – Maureen Dinnocenzo at Above & Beyond Travel – and we were on our way.

Only two major decisions to make: what kind of stateroom and what kind of dining arrangements we wanted. The *Zuiderdam* (rhymes with "cider dam") has four types of staterooms: interior, ocean-view, verandah and suite. Other cruise lines offer similar accommodations.

We chose the least expensive: an interior stateroom. Interior rooms are smaller and have no windows. We reasoned that we'd spend most of our time outside the room, so why pay more for a place where we're just going to sleep and change clothes?

We selected dine-around dining. On a cruise, you can choose to eat at a specific time each evening in the main dining room, or you can eat whenever you wish in a second dining room. The more casual, anytime dining arrangement is called dine-around. This is just what we wanted.

Each cruise has a certain number of formal nights when men are expected to wear tuxedoes or handsome suits and women wear evening gowns or cocktail dresses. Dine-around dining frees us from this requirement (another plus for those who don't wish to do the traditional formal nights).

Since we both had up-to-date passports, we were set. Our agent took care of all the details.

On board ship, all charges are made directly to the credit card you use when you sign up for the cruise. You only need cash for trips ashore.

WHAT'S INCLUDED IN THE PRICE OF A CRUISE (AND WHAT ISN'T)

Cruising can be a wonderfully affordable way to travel in comfort. If you are not careful, however, you can easily add thousands to your travel costs.

Here is what the price of your cruise includes:

- Stateroom or suite accommodations
- Ocean transportation
- Gourmet dining
- Buffet dining (often round the clock)
- Supervised kids' programs
- Entertainment (Vegas- or Broadway-style shows each evening, and live music in the various bars on board)
- Entrée to onboard clubs, piano bars and more
- Activities like yoga and basketball
- Gym, pool and hot tubs
- Noncommissionable fares and taxes.

Here's what is not included:

- Gratuities (you can ask what your daily gratuity charge will be)

- Spa treatments
- Alcoholic beverages
- Soft drinks and designer coffees (sometimes)
- Casino gambling
- Shopping
- Shore excursions
- Babysitting
- Laundry and dry cleaning
- Some onboard specialty restaurants

LET'S WRITE A BOOK ABOUT OUR PANAMA CANAL CRUISE

Al and I began reading books and articles on the building of the Canal in preparation for our cruise, and the more we read about it, and the more we researched Holland America's *Zuiderdam*, the more excited we became.

"Let's write a book about our cruise," I suggested one day over breakfast. "I'll bet people would be interested."

"Great!" Al said. "I'll cover desserts and you can cover healthy stuff."

We both laughed, but the more we mulled the idea over, the better it seemed. I could write about all the cruise offered apart from fattening fare, and Al could cover the mouthwatering sweets. I emailed Holland America, asking for contacts I could interview, and Al began thinking about how he'd describe the delicious and fattening goodies onboard.

I must confess that my sweetheart has a rich and crazy sense of humor. While I struggle to get every fact correct, he loves to dip and soar in the literary universe of hyperbole. To give you an idea of what you'll read from him in this book, here's his introduction:

Dear Reader:

In the pages that follow, you and I will embark on a journey of thousands of miles and tens of thousands of calories. We will travel from California to Florida by way of the Panama Canal on Holland America's MS Zuiderdam, *a Dutch word that means "chocolate extravaganza" (at least in my copy of* Fodor's*).*

It is, as you may now suspect, the objective of both trip and writing to fully explore the joys of cruise sweets

– the desserts, the pastries, the chocolates, the little midnight dulces, those tender bits of sucrose that bring joy to the heart (and girth to the waist, but we won't go there).

Yes, it is true: sugar in its myriad of forms is, for me, a food group. My dear spouse, on the other hand, envisions broccoli at the summit of the food pyramid. The mere sight of a freshly harvested, organically grown summer squash easily raises her blood pressure 20 points. To each his – or her – own, I say. Vive la différence! Bring on the raspberry mousse!

A bit more about me. I'm a senior citizen (i.e., old). I'm mobility impaired (i.e., gimpy). I'm six-feet-one (down from six-feet-four) and weigh 172 (or 185 cm and 78 kilos for the metric minded). In former lives I've been a pilot, an engineer, a minister, a contractor and a photographer, not necessarily in that order or at the same time. I may be in the autumn of my years, but I think of life as an adventure to be lived as God gives me opportunity, which gets back to the subject at hand. Nowhere on earth is there such opportunity to eat desserts 24/7 than on a cruise! Bring the fork and napkin, Ma; we're off!

In preparation for this journey, I've read every possible review of onboard fare. I've all but memorized the ship's deck plan, locating every spot where food is served, and noting the hours they're open. In the event that an uncontrolled desire for crème brûlée strikes at 2 a.m., I'm prepared.

It is of note that cruising, like flying, isn't quite as free as it once was (yes, my age is showing). As numerous online reviews stated, "Main dining room food quality is ... good." In an era of gastronomic exceptionalism, "good" is a code word that often means "edible." The really good stuff, however, costs extra. C'est la vie. I am not deterred by cost barriers: a truly magnificent Strawberries Arnaud knows no class distinction. Thus the pages which follow will rate the great and the not-quite-great, wherever they may be found aboard. (And a disclaimer: Like Sesame Street's Cookie Monster, I never met a cookie I didn't like.)

OUR ANTICIPATION

Al and I think one of the best things about travel is the pre-trip state of anticipation – planning, dreaming and looking forward to the journey.

In preparation, we read books on the building of the Panama Canal, and we went shopping: new clothes, a wheeled suitcase for Al, a digital camera, prescription sunglasses for me. Lots of fun!

And I researched the *MS Zuiderdam*. One reason I wanted to sail on this ship is its extensive art collection.

The descriptions of the copper and cast-aluminum elevator doors, inspired by the art deco work of New York's Chrysler Building, enthralled me. I was eager to see the 6,000-pound Waterford Crystal Seahorse suspended in a three-story atrium near the front desk, as well as Andy Warhol's painting of HRH Queen Beatrix of the Netherlands and medallions by Frank Lloyd Wright. I learned that the ship is full of antiques and centuries-old paintings, as well as more modern sculptures. I wanted to see them all.

I kept thinking, it's going to be wonderful living in a floating art gallery for 17 days.

AL'S ANTICIPATION OF 24/7 DESSERT INDULGENCE

It was summer when I first discovered that we could get to the Panama Canal by sailing directly from San Francisco. I headed for the medicine cabinet and doubled-down on my blood-pressure-management meds. Cruising! On Holland America! Seventeen days! The Canal! And no TSA airline hassles (or at least at one end). Did I say I was excited?

I first discovered cruising more than 20 years ago, beginning with a voyage in the Caribbean that edged into a hurricane. Everyone else on board was seasick, but I kept working the buffet line night and day. All that food, all that entertainment, all those never-before-seen vistas. I had arrived. Gatsby, move over. My life-path was forever set.

The Zuiderdam looked to far exceed those early experiences. A whole ship full of art, from steerage to bridge. A floating luxury hotel, catering to my every need, if not whim. A wonderfully stocked library. Days spent stretched out in a deck chair, lazing in the Baja sun. The soft motion of the sea, rocking me to sleep at night. Every other day, an interesting port of call. Leisurely morning Mass. Interesting companions to be met.

And food. Just think of it: two dining rooms below, six buffet lines above, a hamburger stand, three fancy restaurants. Mid-ship cookie stops. Healthy eating for the wife; dulces (sweets) for me. After all, why should dessert be confined to the evening meal? Doesn't the ship have a pastry chef? I need to seriously investigate. Bring on the apple crisp.

Thus the days wound down to our departure, and finally the time came to shut off the computer and pack the fork. Ready for the buffet, I planned to visit it within 30 minutes of dropping my suitcase in our cabin. As it turned out, I would not be disappointed.

DAY 1
Tuesday, October 2, 2012

DEPARTING FROM SAN FRANCISCO

Leaving San Francisco. The city's skyline was spectacular.

We arrive at Pier 35 about 11:30 a.m. It's an unusually warm, clear day in San Francisco, the deep blue bay aglitter with sun splash, white gulls wheeling overhead.

Crowds fill the sidewalk. Taxicabs drive up to the curb in an almost rhythmical cadence, depositing people and luggage like musical notes, then easing away as new taxis pull up, deposit their passengers and drive away.

A friend from church has driven us to the pier. As soon as we climb out of his car, a young woman with a luggage cart approaches and takes our bags. We keep our laptop and two small carry-ons with us.

As we weave our way to the pier entrance, moving among the sidewalk crowds, I feel buoyed with joy. All these cheerful people on this stunning, sunny day and we're all about to take an incredible journey!

After showing ship personnel our passports and boarding documents, we walk to an inside counter where we're quickly and courteously checked in. Our cabin keys will also serve as cruise credit cards during the 17 days we'll be on board.

A nice thing about cruising is once onboard you never need cash. You can walk about purse-free. Just slip your credit-card-sized room key in a pocket and you're set to go.

Along with our room key, we are given a "*Zuiderdam* Deck Plan," which folds to credit card size and opens to show each deck in detail. Since I lack a good sense of direction, this most-welcome map will be my lifesaver around our floating resort.

OUR FIRST SURPRISE

The ease of boarding is our first, and very pleasant, surprise. Less than 30 minutes after checking in at the pier, we are in our stateroom (#5005).

"This is the smoothest boarding experience I've ever had," Al says. He has been on more cruises than I have. All I know is that moving from sidewalk to cabin was incredibly easy.

"Now let's go see what's for lunch," Al says.

I know his heart and mind are focused on desserts – pie and cake and cookies. He and several of our friends have been teasing me about my goal of staying healthy (and not gaining weight) on our cruise.

"Who wants to travel with you?" one friend emailed me. "I want to cruise with Al!"

But I have a plan. And it does not include self-denial. I plan to relish all that this cruise has to offer, not just the palate-pleasing aspects. I'll take classes, go to lectures, use the gym, enjoy the artwork and (in general) fill my days with fun and enjoyable activities. I'll also delight in the wonderful meals available to me. I simply won't make a pig of myself and gain a lot of weight on this cruise.

Here's my three-point personal plan:

1. Eat only when I'm hungry.
2. Survey everything available and choose only those things to eat that are spectacular. (Skip the hamburgers, pizza, French fries, hot dogs. We're paying for a special, gourmet-type journey, so I shall choose only those offerings that are fresh, delightful to eye and tongue, delicious and gourmet. As to rich desserts, I plan to go easy on them.)
3. Use the stairs instead of the elevator.

We head to Deck 9. The mesmerizing beauty of the elevator doors immediately grabs my attention. When have I ever noticed elevator doors? These freeze me in wonder, with their stunning swirls of aluminum and copper. They open and we step inside.

On Deck 9, we walk past the spa where you can pay for hair and nail appointments, massages and other pampering treatments. We pass the large swimming pool with its huge *Mama Polar Bear with Cub* sculpture, the Lido Bar and its whimsical sea-creature seats, and enter the Lido (the cafeteria-style buffet). The fragrant tang of spaghetti welcomes us.

I head for the salad aisle, where I fill my plate with apple, pear and roast-pecan salad and Sonoma chicken salad.

Since we're from Sonoma County, I like the idea of eating Sonoma chicken salad as part of my first meal onboard. As I indulge in a generous helping, I hope the chicken is truly from Sonoma County. Why? Because most Sonoma chickens are free range. They lead the good life, with plenty of outdoor grass and bugs and sunshine and no antibiotics or added hormones. How nice to have this "Sonoma connection" first thing on our cruise.

Al finds a window table and fetches lemonade for us.

After I finish the salads, I return to the buffet for a small portion of curry chicken and freshly steamed green beans.

Al completes his lunch with, of course, a dessert, but I'm fully satisfied with what I've eaten.

What we discover, and come to love, at the Lido buffet is an Asian stir-fry area complete with freshly made sushi. At breakfast, the Lido staff makes to-order omelets.

Following lunch, we explore what will be our floating home for the next 17 days. This 935-foot-long, 82,000-ton ship can carry 1,936 guests. The crew of 823 works in an array of restaurants and bars, a series of shops, an art gallery, a casino, a Vegas-style theater, a spa, and on numerous events that are held every day. Our ship resembles a small city.

It's time to find our way around.

We locate the coffee shop (the Explorations Café) on Deck 10. This busy counter, with its espresso machines and pastry display shelves, fills a wall in the ship's library.

About 1,000 books stand proudly on the library's light oak shelves, displayed according to genre. Floor-to-ceiling windows keep the entire area well lit.

Being enthusiastic bookworms, we immediately begin to peruse the biographies, history books, best sellers, travel books, science books, fiction and nonfiction.

There is also a nook, or side room, displaying magazines and a large reading table. And there are plenty of comfortable chairs and tables throughout the entire library where you can sit while you read. No doubt the Explorations Café will become a regular hangout for us.

Just beyond the coffee shop and library, the Crow's Nest Lounge gives a grand view of where our ship is headed. Situated above the ship's bow, the Crow's Nest hosts games during the day and live music and dancing at night.

After our brief exploration of Deck 9, we ride the elevator all the way down to Deck 1 (Main Deck) and locate the front desk, the shore excursions reservations counter and a desk where we can get information about our various ports of call.

At the front desk we sign up for a cooking class. I'm not a cook, but I think it will be fun for us to take a class together with one of the ship's chefs. So, come Sunday, we'll be in the Culinary Arts Center learning to make something scrumptious.

We also make a Friday night dinner reservations at the Pinnacle Grill – one of the two specialty restaurants aboard described as "exceptional" in Holland America promotional material. Unlike the ship's dining rooms, the Lido and other eating areas, the Pinnacle Grill charges 25 dollars for its dinners.

Back to our room, where our bags have been delivered, we unpack and settle in.

As on most cruise ships, our room's twin beds have been pushed together to form a very comfortable queen bed. Its pillow top and elegant linens will make sleeping a pleasure.

The towels and washcloths in the bath are fat and fluffy.

Al points out the useful laundry line in the shower. We can wash our undies and hang them on the line to dry, thus saving a steep laundry charge.

Although the room is small – about 145 square feet – it's comfortably adequate for us. There are two sizeable closets, a third closet-like storage area with shelves for folded items, two generous cubbies under the bed, a small desk, a table and chair and a flatscreen TV with a DVD player for in-room movies.

We each have a bedside table with two shallow drawers and, below them, additional storage space for shoes or purses or backpacks or books.

Large mirrors add a spacious feeling to our room.

The bathroom is modestly sized, but there's plenty of room for our toiletries, along with the soaps and lotions provided by the ship. It would feel crowded if we were both combing our hair in the bathroom at the same time. But taking turns works fine.

As we place clothes on hangers and shelves, stash notebooks and pens and cameras, we hear the announcement for the lifeboat drill. After the *Costa Concordia* cruise ship disaster off the coast of Italy, I'm glad that we'll have the lifeboat drill first thing.

When the drill begins, all passengers go to appointed lifeboat areas out on Deck 3. There, along with everyone else, Al and I learn exactly what to do in the case of an emergency.

This important exercise makes me feel secure. I'm glad to know, even before we lift anchor, what to do and where to go should we face an emergency on this cruise.

At 3 p.m. we head for the Vista Dining Room for tea. What became for us an almost daily tradition offers a great way to meet others and enjoy tea and sweets.

I have green tea, a small chocolate cream puff and a chocolate and pecan square.

The jacketed waiters come to our table often, bearing trays of finger cakes, open-faced bite-sized sandwiches and tea.

Sharing our table are a couple from New Jersey, a woman from Seattle, and three women from Australia.

Conversation is light and the nibbles are good.

At 5 p.m. the ship pulls away from the pier.

The entire ship's company makes its way to the Observation Deck railing to watch as we leave San Francisco and stand out to sea.

We travel around Alcatraz Island in the soft evening light. Triangles of white dot the blue waters of the bay as we head for the Golden Gate.

Behind us, the city recedes, stretching out in white geometric forms across the hills.

The elegant Golden Gate Bridge is just ahead. I've never sailed beneath it ... and as we approach, I feel excitement rise. Everyone on deck points cameras at the bridge, snapping away as the *Zuiderdam* sails under the iconic span and out into the Pacific.

We're on our way.

AL'S THOUGHTS ON SAILING OUT UNDER THE GOLDEN GATE BRIDGE

The first – and only other – time I'd sailed under the Golden Gate Bridge was more than 50 years ago, returning from Vietnam via Yokosuka, Japan, on the U.S.S. General W.A. Mann *(APA-112).*

The Mann was a WWII–vintage "attack transport," her holds packed with seasick Army troops cycling back from Korea. The Navy found somewhat better quarters for us returning pilots in the chief petty officer's "goat locker," but it was still a week at sea from Honolulu, juggling inedible food in stainless-steel trays on unstabilized, rolling decks. Our collective joy in seeing the Bridge knew no bounds.

Being outbound under the Bridge on the Zuiderdam on this beautiful October evening is a decidedly different experience. The sky is blue, the sea is smooth and none of the passengers is in desperate need of a shower.

Once we've looked at the underside of the Bridge as we pass beneath, it is mutually agreed that yes, we are underway, and it is time to head for the Vista Dining Room. There, sumptuous five-course meals await, served by attentive Indonesian waitstaff on real china atop beautiful linen-covered tables. Life has definitely changed since those days of yesteryear... and much for the better.

DINNER AT SEA

Al and I dress for dinner and make our way to the Vista Dining Room on Deck 2. Although the dine-around option we chose is less formal than the regular dining room – no tuxedoes or evening gowns required – it is still dressier than the Lido buffet. One does not wear jeans or shorts to dinner.

Doors open at 5:30 p.m. and we want to be there when they open so we'll have plenty of time for a leisurely dinner before the 8 p.m. evening show in the Vista Show Lounge at the bow end of the ship. (The dining rooms are at the stern of the ship, according to Al. I call it the front and the back. The dining rooms are at the back, the theater at the front of the ship.)

Evening entertainers perform at 8 and 10 p.m. in the Vista Show Lounge. And since we're early-to-bed-early-to-rise types, we want to watch the 8 p.m. show. By 10 p.m., we'll most likely be sleeping.

At dinner, we share our table with Bill and Connie from our own Sonoma County (a most pleasant surprise to find "neighbors" along on our cruise) and Inge and Tom from Salt Lake City.

After studying the menu, I choose an appetizer of Farmer's Veggie Puree (a puree of seasonal vegetables swirled with cream, which leaves me totally satisfied). For my main course, I choose grilled Coho Salmon, with a soy-ginger glaze, served with wasabi mashed potatoes and seasoned vegetables.

Although Al and I are teetotalers, I'm impressed that the menu includes wine recommendations, with detailed descriptions of each vintage. Clearly, the wine steward has taken pains to present the perfect pairings for those who wish them.

I'm too full for dessert, but Al orders something rich and chocolaty, so I take a generous forkful of his dessert.

EVENING ENTERTAINMENT

Once we're finished, we excuse ourselves and hurry to the Vista Show Lounge. Between the dining room and the theater, we pass the Explorer's Lounge, the Art Gallery, the Pinnacle Bar and Pinnacle Grill, the three-story Atrium (with its Waterford Crystal Seahorse suspended high above), the Culinary Arts Center, the Sports Bar and the Piano Bar, then walk through the casino into the Vista Lounge.

To our surprise, we find the 900-seat theater almost full. It's 7:45 p.m. and already the place is packed. Obviously, we're not the only early-to-bed folks aboard. Where can we sit? We scan the rows of upholstered seats.

The theater has several large posts supporting the balcony. The seats behind each post are empty, but those blocked-view seats don't appeal. Yet, almost every other seat in the whole house is already occupied. We finally sit beside one of the posts, settling for a partial view of the stage.

The performer is a Las Vegas magician named James Cielen. His show is a beautiful blend of artistry and clever illusion. He makes pretty ladies disappear inside tiny boxes. He creates colorful "snow" blizzards and silky waterfalls. He has doves appearing from nowhere.

But the part of his act that I love involves dogs. He has two darling miniature poodles that appear and disappear, and trot like old show-biz pros around the stage, never whimpering or barking, but always commanding attention. I'm not a dog person, but these two pooches won my heart.

When the show ends, Al and I wander slowly back to our room, feeling pampered and happily sleepy.

Clearly we're on a magic carpet journey. And it's only just begun.

On our turned-down bed, we find the *Explorer* newsletter, outlining tomorrow's onboard events. Al is eager to attend Mass in the morning, so we order an early room service breakfast and hang our order outside our door.

Each of our pillows holds a gold-foil-wrapped chocolate. A sweet little ending to a perfect day.

TOUCHES OF LUXURY FILL OUR ROOM

Hanging on hooks next to our bed are deluxe waffle-weave bathrobes for our use during the cruise. We can buy the robes and take them home for a mere 49 dollars each. But we have robes at home. These lovely white robes will serve us well during the cruise.

Our towels and washcloths are thick and soft.

The shower is large.

There's a magnifying makeup mirror, and salon-quality hair dryer.

Our room has a flatscreen TV and DVD player suspended from the ceiling.

And we discover a catalogue with 1,000 movies available to us. All we have to do is call the front desk, ask for a movie, and a steward will bring it to our room.

There is a programmable safe for valuables.

Beneath the TV is a makeup table, which Al immediately transforms into a computer center. Using our room's data port, Al sets up our laptop. This is where we'll download pictures from our cameras each evening, and keep notes on the cruise.

Under the makeup table is a small refrigerator filled with chilled drinks.

Our stateroom has two large and beautiful prints, both of tulips (perfect for Al, who photographs wildflowers and loves all things botanical), titled *Tulip on Parchment* by M. S. Merian (1647–1717).

DAY 2
Wednesday, October 3

AT SEA

The ship's library, one of our favorite places onboard.

Our room service breakfast is delivered at 7 a.m., just as we ordered: a veggie omelet, coffee and juice for me. Granola, an English muffin with jam, coffee and juice for Al. Oops, a second omelet! Maybe we made a mistake on our order form. In any event, this early morning surprise is not unpleasant.

We eat in our robes, watching the morning news on CNN. Our TV carries Fox and CNN news, ESPN sports and a variety of other channels, some promoting the *Zuiderdam*'s various shops and services.

A few minutes before 8 a.m. Al grabs his Bible and heads for Mass.

I head for "Morning Tai Chi with Life-Stylist Nick Reiersgard." The class will be held poolside on the Lido Deck (Deck 9).

The Lido Pool area is open to the elements, and today's gray, misty, cool air feels good.

Nick, tall, red-haired and dressed in black, stands before us, ready to guide us through the basics of this worldwide exercise style. He looks like he's in his late twenties or early thirties.

The other people gathered poolside have gray or white hair and appear to be a little older than I am. Since I work out almost every day, I assume that the gentle flowing movements of Tai Chi will be a snap.

Imagine my surprise when I discover that it takes quite some skill and concentration to complete the various movements with grace.

We start with our feet shoulder-width apart, our knees slightly bent and our back straight. Nick leads us through a deep breathing exercise and then gently introduces some basic Tai Chi movements.

When the half hour routine ends, I realize that, despite the slow and gentle movements, I've *really* had a workout. What a concept!

OUR SECOND SURPRISE: MY SWEETHEART BECOMES "FATHER AL"

Shortly after I arrive back in our clean room with its freshly made bed, Al comes in the door.

"So how was Mass?" I ask.

"Well, it was interesting to say the least," he says with a grin. I can tell a story is on its way.

"Seems that the ship's priest died unexpectedly. And the replacement priest, who was supposed to board yesterday in San Francisco, missed the ship."

"Don't tell me," I start to smile even as a mirroring grin spreads across his face. He nods as I say, "You ended up conducting the service?"

He says, "There were about 30 people there. They were happy to have someone conduct the service properly."

This is so like Al – stepping in when needed.

"Well, how about that?" I say. And we both laugh.

Then we turn to our *Explorer* newsletter to see what's on today's schedule.

A lot, as we are quick to learn. Every day, every half hour from 7 a.m. to midnight, something interesting is going on somewhere on the ship.

We each already took part in an 8 a.m. event.

At 9 a.m. there are four events: a creative crafts class in the Culinary Arts Center, Aqua Aerobics at the Lido Deck pool, an Interdenominational Religious Service in the Hudson Room, and a daily Quiz & Sudoku available at the Explorations Café.

Mention of the Explorations Café makes us both hungry for a latte and midmorning munch. So off we go to Deck 10.

The place is mobbed – people in line for designer coffees and pastries. Couples sitting at window tables with lattes and books or cappuccinos and the ship's daily condensation of the *New York Times* or the *Canadian Times*.

OUR THIRD (PLEASANT) SURPRISE: THE DAILY *NEW YORK TIMES*

To our surprise, every morning, strategically placed throughout the ship, an eight-page condensation of the *New York Times* is available. Canadian passengers can pick up a similar condensation of the *Canadian Times*.

Since Al and I love the *NYT*, we are thrilled with the Xeroxed 8½ × 11–inch copy waiting for us each day at the Explorations Café, the front desk or just outside the Lido buffet restaurant.

This condensed version includes page one stories, opinion pieces, some sports news, business news and other brief articles. Just a perfect read for breakfast, or midmorning coffee.

As we take our lattes from the counter, a couple leaves a small window table, and we claim their seats. Then Al goes back to get himself two brownies and me an open-faced salmon sandwich.

The designer coffees and teas at Explorations Café cost extra. Ours, with its 15 percent gratuity, comes to about five dollars for the two of us.

As we sip our coffee and eat our small repasts, our eyes scan nearby bookshelves, taking in titles and author names. I see a book on the Panama Canal. Although we've already read two small but thorough books on the building of the Canal, I want to learn more, so I pull this travel book from its shelf.

As I flip through the pages, I realize anew the overwhelming difficulties that had to be overcome in building the Canal. It took from 1904 to 1914 to complete it, but that was after the French had done much of the preliminary work. The French started building the Canal in 1881, but abandoned it in 1889. Fifteen years later, we Americans took up where the French left off.

In the process of building the Canal, thousands of workers died of disease and in construction accidents.

In 11 days, we'll see the Canal up close and personal, as the *Zuiderdam* transits this historic path between the oceans. We'll be one of the 30 or so ships that pass through the Canal each day.

We'll pass through the Canal by climbing up three sets of locks (rising 85 feet), sailing through the nine-mile Culebra (Gaillard) Cut, crossing Gatun Lake (formed by damming the Chagres River), then down through three sets of locks and into the Atlantic Ocean at Limon Bay.

The Canal is the magnet that drew us all to this cruise.

As I finish my latte, I gaze out the window. The sea is a bright gray – waves and swells like undulating molten pewter. Above, the light-gray sky frames gulls riding the ship's draft. A few wing flaps and then 15 minutes of gliding. Tranquility at its best.

This kind of overcast makes me want to curl up with a good book and a hot latte (or cup of tea). Obviously it's the same for all the others filling the Explorations Café.

When the librarian slides in behind her desk, several people approach her to check out books, although they don't really have to wait for her. The entire library operates on an honor system. You take the book you want, write down its title and your name and cabin number on a checkout sheet that's always at the librarian's desk and off you go.

When you are finished with your book, just bring it back and put it in the book drop beside the librarian's desk.

But people have questions, and the librarian has answers, and so people crowd around her desk.

I go from the Explorations Café to an introductory class in digital photo editing.

I arrive at the tech classroom about 10 minutes before class begins, only to find the place already packed.

There are about a dozen computers and twice that many eager students, all well past their working years. Nonetheless, I take a seat near a computer, reasoning that I can at least learn something by listening and watching.

By the time the class starts, there are 31 students, squeezing into every spare inch, even sitting on windowsills.

The onboard tech expert, Trisha, is not only a great teacher, she's also highly entertaining. There's lots of laughter in this classroom.

I learn many useful techniques, the one I'm most grateful for is how to stitch photos together to make stunning panoramic pictures.

Trish has classes every day in the small tech classroom across the hall from the Culinary Arts Center on Deck 2. Today's digital workshops include how to manage your health information, introductory photo editing, PC security, introduction to the Cloud, and an inside look at Windows 7.

I'll be taking more classes from her, but next time I'll arrive earlier so I can get a computer.

Back in our room, Al works on his homily for tomorrow's Mass. Because we'll be in port in San Diego for the day, Mass will take place at 5 p.m. tomorrow instead of the usual 8 a.m. Al wants to be prepared for those who come to worship.

Nonetheless, the two of us agree it's time to take a little nap.

✵✵

As we slowly wake up in our gently rocking room, Al says, "Our room reminds me of a camping trailer that's moving a little all the time. It's cozy in here."

It is indeed cozy.

Midafternoon we go to the Lido restaurant. The ice cream bar is open, and people have formed an eager line for cones and sundaes. In the glass display case next to it are several shelves of different desserts. I see one-inch-square servings of tiramisu. And dishes of pudding – pink, chocolate and vanilla. Al and I both take a dessert. They do not disappoint.

Later, we have dinner in the Lido: I have crab cakes and fresh asparagus. Delicious.

Then it's off to the 8 p.m. show. Tonight, entertainer Duncan Tuck performs. He's billed as a singer, guitar player and comic. We get there early enough to get a good seat.

Duncan Tuck plays a hot guitar and sings familiar and upbeat songs. Some of the tunes in his show are "California Dreamin'," "The Wind Beneath My Wings," "King of the Road" and "Daydream Believer."

In between the songs, he has one-liners and funny stories. Nothing too heavy or highbrow.

He apologizes before saying, "I probably shouldn't tell this one on a cruise ship. But, do you know the kind of coffee they served on the Titanic? Sanka."

He sprinkles his performance with "you're probably a redneck if" jokes. The only one that I can remember, is, "You're probably a redneck if you think loading the dishwasher means getting your wife drunk."

After the show we return to our cabin, feeling content and at home.

Just like last night, we're greeted with a freshly tidied room, a turned-down bed and chocolates on our pillows.

AL'S MUSINGS ON HIGH TEA

The announcement that high tea would be served in the Zuiderdam's Vista Dining Room brought back memories of long ago: of afternoon high tea in the magnificent Empress Hotel in Victoria B.C. Thus I scurried with Sunny and my fellow passengers to see if the ship's high tea was equal to the standard set in days of yore.

Once seated around our table, a be-gloved Indonesian waiter offers each of us a selection of teas. I choose herbal: something with a hint of orange and a suggestion of cinnamon. I'm not British enough for Earl Grey.

And then the goodies begin arriving – or, more formally, the petit fours. This is a French phrase that translates "I'll have several, please."

Our waitstaff brings trays of delightful little sweets in various colors and flavors. It's better than a family reunion: I never met – tasted – one I didn't like.

The unquestionable highlight, however, is the chocolate éclair. Unlike the sandal-sized treat one usually finds at the bakery, the Zuiderdam's high tea éclairs are little bite-sized morsels of flaky pastry filled with a light crème and coated with an exquisite dark chocolate.

The occupants of our table, who heretofore had been snacking on things containing raspberry and coconut, switch en masse to the éclairs. Gone in an instant, not to be seen again, the éclairs leave only sighs and wonderful new memories.

ZUIDERDAM DINING CHOICES

If you're hungry on the *Zuiderdam*, you can find plenty of places with plenty of choices:

The Vista Dining Room serves breakfast and dinner. Graced with fine art and antiques, Vista's five-course meals are served on Rosenthal china and crisp white table linens.

The Pinnacle Grill serves dinner (for 25 dollars). Holland America's Pinnacle Grill is billed as the finest in gourmet dining. Intimate dining featuring Sterling Silver Beef and fresh seafood. Luxurious appointments including Bvlgari china, Riedel stemware and Frette linens. The Pinnacle's extensive wine list features many selections rated "Excellent" by *Wine Spectator*.

The Lido Buffet Restaurant serves meals from 6 a.m. through midnight, including fresh, cooked-to-order specialties such as omelets and pastas. This buffet or cafeteria-style eating venue offers an abundance of salads, sandwiches and other deli-type items. It includes an Asian area where sushi, noodle dishes and other such specialties are available. There's also a Bistro area where we enjoyed curried dishes, crab cakes and other such hot offerings. In the afternoon, the Lido opens an ice cream bar and also offers fresh baked cookies.

The Terrace Grill is poolside and serves pizza, grilled burgers, hot dogs and gourmet sausages with all the trimmings. Sometimes the Terrace Grill is transformed into a Mexican-themed grill, with refried beans and rice and all the fixin's for tacos.

The Canaletto is a specialty Italian restaurant, serving dinner (for 10 dollars). The evening begins with the chef's selection of antipasti with a taste of the delicious fare and personal, polished service to follow. Here courses – *il primo, il secondo,* and *il dolci* – are offered.

In addition, our cruise includes

- Complimentary 24-hour in-room dining
- Hot hors d'oeuvres during cocktail hour
- The Explorations Café, with its pastries, small sandwiches, and espresso drinks
- Daily afternoon tea service
- Late-night snack: Chocolate Dessert Extravaganza.

DAY 3
Thursday, October 4
PORT OF CALL: SAN DIEGO

The historic Hotel Del Coronado, near San Diego.

Instead of a full breakfast, Al and I have coffee and fruit in the Lido.

Pete, my brother, is meeting us at the pier, and will take us to his favorite breakfast place in

La Jolla. Then we'll be off for a day of Southern California sightseeing.

Whenever we go ashore, we must take our room key and photo ID (driver's license). Using our room key, ship personnel check us out when we leave, and back in when we return.

Pete picks us up in his new car, a 2012 Hyundai Elantra. Pete and I share the genetic trait of Scottish thriftiness: we try to keep our possessions in like-new condition, and rarely spend money on items we do not need. This Elantra is the first new auto he has bought in decades. His last car, a Honda, had more than 500,000 miles on it and was so faithful that he actually sold it (had buyers standing in line) before buying the Elantra.

Now Al and I praise his new vehicle as he drives us to The Cottage for breakfast. While I'm marveling over the beautiful morning, Al's noticing other things.

AL'S TAKE ON EARLY MORNING LA JOLLA

The City of La Jolla (pronounced "La-HOY-ya"), California, is, at first glance, a typical Southern California city – palm trees, tile roofs, fabulous-looking people wearing sunglasses. So it seemed to me until, while driving through downtown, I had a Dorothy Moment (as in "Toto, I don't think we're in Kansas anymore").

As we sat waiting at a traffic light, I noted a Ferrari dealer on one side of the street, its showroom packed with svelte roadsters. Ooooh!

And then, on the opposite corner, for the somewhat-better-off, was the Maserati dealer, where a fire-engine-red GranTurismo sat, begging me to drive off into the sunset with a blonde starlet on the seat beside me. Yes, indeed: definitely not Kansas.

OFF TO CORONADO

After breakfast, Pete drives Al and me through the University of California, San Diego campus, which my nephew (Pete's son) attended before graduating last June. Then to a beautiful beach where seals and pelicans share ocean-sprayed rocks.

It's a perfect California day, drenched in sunshine and sparkling ocean waves. Although I grew up in Michigan, a beautiful state full of forests and lakes and salt-of-the-earth people, California is home to my heart. And today reminds me of that fact, with its clear blue skies, gentle surf, slim people of all ages walking their dogs energetically and shiny clean cars zipping along gleefully.

This long-coasted state has it all – the wide open ocean, craggy mountains, beautiful deserts, forests filled with giant sequoias and spectacular wildflowers, unforgettable cities like San Francisco and gentle bays like Monterey's, Gold Rush history and a string of Catholic missions, to say nothing of the people of every race and creed raising food in the Great Central Valley, creating technology to improve our world, teaching and learning on campuses from one end of the state to the other and creating art, music and literature to open the heart and flood the soul.

To me, California is a magical place that never stops surprising me with delightful discoveries.

Today, Al wants me to see the fabled Hotel Del Coronado, so Pete heads the car in that direction.

We approach Coronado by crossing the gracefully arching 2.2-mile-long San Diego–Coronado Bay Bridge. This famous resort city, filled with interesting cottages, is home to Naval Base Coronado (seven separate naval installations). The city is also one of the most expensive communities in the U.S.A.

But it's the historic Hotel Del Coronado I want to see. Featured in the movie *Some Like It Hot* (1959), the hotel has welcomed presidents, royalty and celebrities since it opened in 1888.

And when Pete pulls up to this grand old building with its many red turrets, I'm thrilled. The Coronado Hotel is designated both as a National Historic Landmark and a California Historical Landmark.

When it first opened its doors, it was the largest resort hotel in the world. The famous who have stayed here include Thomas Edison, Charles Lindbergh, Muhammad Ali, presidents William Howard Taft, Franklin D. Roosevelt, Lyndon Johnson, Richard Nixon, Gerald Ford, Jimmy Carter, Ronald Reagan, Bill Clinton, both Bushes and Barack Obama, as well as many Hollywood celebrities.

Today it's one of the few surviving examples of American wooden Victorian beach resorts.

Al and I snap photos of the fanciful architecture – elaborate white porches and towers, windows large and small, all topped off by steep red roofs or turrets.

Inside, my breath is taken away by the deep, dark wood, and a huge chandelier dripping with crystal.

In front of the hotel, one of the most beautiful white-sand beaches in America stretches out among palm trees.

Eventually, after oooohing and ahhhhing, we arrive at the Hotel's Sheerwater Restaurant for lunch. We are seated on the patio overlooking the beach. The soft afternoon breeze strokes our faces and plays with our hair. Absolutely wonderful.

One glance at the menu and I'm reminded of how different various parts of California are.

Al and I have lived for years in the rural California county of Calaveras. Despite the county's rich Gold Rush history, today Calaveras is a poor county. The average hourly wage earned by those who can find a job is 10 dollars. And few jobs include benefits. So we both are fairly conservative when it comes to spending money. Lunch in most restaurants in Calaveras County runs about eight dollars. Dinner is a tad more.

To my eyes, this lunch menu has nothing but expensive offerings.

But this is Al's party. He wants me to experience as many aspects as possible of this famous old hotel, and I can't wait. We agree to split a turkey sandwich. Pete orders a small house salad.

The food is good. The view of the beach is superb. The price of lunch is 40 dollars.

We drive back to the ship, full and happy and feeling properly introduced to the famous Hotel Del Coronado.

Mass (with Al's daily homily) takes place today at 5 p.m.

Later, following an enticing dinner in the dining room, we enjoy Fiona Jessica Wilson in the Vista Lounge. This tall soprano with the crystal-clear voice sings a variety of arias as well as popular tunes. She is elegant, with her long blonde tresses flowing down her back and her lovely voice weaving beauty in the air.

Dropping into bed after that performance was like nestling with a lullaby, the musical memory of Fiona's voice followed us "home" and tucked us in.

AL'S DESSERT EUPHORIA

High atop the Zuiderdam *on Deck 9 and encompassing a full third of it (the aft third, in nautical-speak) is the buffet court, known to the Spanish-speaking as* la Plaza de las Horquillas *(the Plaza of the Forks). Officially the "Lido Deck."*

It is here that the ship's hungry herd gathers to graze from 6 a.m., when it opens, until midnight, when it closes.

In the informality and conviviality of the Lido, there is no need to comply with the propriety of dress required of the ship's dining room, far below. Those choosing the plaza's varied fare need only throw on the most casual of attire and a pair of flip-flops and – voila! – suitable fashion.

The Lido has a long center galley with three buffet lines on each side, interspersed with beverage aisles. Each line offers an almost bewildering range of possibilities.

Take breakfast, for example. Oatmeal? Cream of wheat? Muselix? Dry cereal? Eggs? How many? How cooked? Ham, bacon, sausage patty or sausage links? Pork or turkey? Muffin? What kind? And that's only the beginning, and that's only breakfast.

Kinda puts "But wait, there's more" in a different perspective, doesn't it?

Lunch and supper, of course, are fully as ostentatious. But I'm not interested in entrées.

No, my focus is on what comes after the main course: dessert.

At the very epicenter of the Plaza of the Forks is a relatively small glass display case we shall call el Pequeño Mercado de Dulces, *the Little Market of Sweets.*

Here, on six stacked glass shelves each but a meter long, are a dazzling array of ever-changing delights promising to bring joy to the tongue and inches to the waistline. Nothing in the Little Market could be called a complete "dessert" unto itself: the portions are small, at least for those of us who consider sugar a food group. Six bites and it's gone. "Time for another, eh?" as the Canadians would put it, and right they are.

A *week of sampling the* mercadito *reveals their variety of offerings: cakes of every sort, mousses, fruit crisps, éclairs, custards, pies (the Key Lime disappeared in minutes) and, best of all, tiramisu, which only appeared once, on our second day (sigh!).*

Last night little cups of chocolate pudding appeared, each topped with shredded dark chocolate, floating on a spoonful of chocolate syrup. Never before had this inspired creation been offered, and experience suggests it won't again (in consideration of this risk, I had two). It is this, the very threat of see-it-once-and-nevermore that spurs the true dessert-eater to new (sugar) heights.

Fortunately, it is always possible to "hit the Lido" and carry back two or three of these little treasures to one's cabin for a nighttime nibble.

If you should happen to see a fellow shipmate weaving down the corridor to his stateroom, he's not been into the sherry. No, as you'll learn on closer inspection, he's juggling an armload of sweets, perhaps a petite raspberry shortcake, something lemony in layers, and a little dish of custard, chocolate perhaps.

The challenge in his exercise is avoiding dropping any of los dulces *or smearing them on his shirt while* at the same time fishing out the credit-card sized "key" from his pocket, getting it in the lock and opening the door.

This is not easily done on dry land, but in the rolling sea it's an accomplishment of the first order. I will ever remain astounded that the cruise director hasn't hosted a competition.

Thus fortified, one can endure the long night, awaiting the rise of the sun and the muezzin's call to breakfast. Life is good.

"Just one minute," you say, "I prefer my desserts refrigerated." Not to worry. Right next to those six shelves of goodies is the ice cream bar, staffed by a young lad whose only purpose in life is to meet your ice cream wishes.

Here you will find four kinds of ice cream – strawberry, chocolate, vanilla and (highly recommended) cinnamon – in hard or soft form. These flavors can be had in dish, plain cone or sugar cone form, or concocted into a variety of sundaes. And don't forget the sorbet or the sherbet.

"Dish or cone, sir?"

"Yes" is always the best response to all such queries. What's a calorie or two? I'm on vacation.

The pleasure of a bowlful of ice cream is always enhanced with a cookie. Here again, the Zuiderdam *excels. A full tray of chocolate cookies ever sits adjacent to the ice cream, each cookie baked to perfection and packed with chunks of chocolate. Take two; they're small.*

Perhaps one more for the cabin? Want something lighter? Try a sugar cookie (or two), lightly flavored with a hint of vanilla and sprinkled with crunchy sugar.

Does your taste run, instead, to peanut butter? Fear not, your wish is granted. Never did the humble peanut go to a more glorious reward than in the Z's PB cookies.

It was once said that all roads lead to Rome, but here, in the Plaza of the Forks, all roads lead to the Little Market of Sweets.

DAY 4
Friday, October 5

AT SEA

The Lido pool, overseen by a polar bear and her cub
(and no, the water was not icy cold).

Today is iPod art tour. Checking out an iPod from the librarian, I listen to the calm voice directing me to one piece of artwork after another.

This tour begins in the library/Explorations Café with two 19th-century porcelain pieces hanging behind glass among the bookshelves. The iPod narrator explains that these beautiful items, which resemble teapots, are actually Chinese characters.

From there I walk to the Crow's Nest right next door to view a maritime painting by Bonaventura Peeters (1614–1652) and, below it, a late-18th-century VOC cannon.

The tour takes me to a life-size white marble sculpture of Venus created by Jean-Baptiste Boudard, in France in 1752. This statue is located, appropriately, in the ship's spa area.

Next, the huge bronze polar bear mother and cub on an ice flow overlooking the Lido Pool, then a massive wall-sized flower painting (oil on aluminum) by Bela Bodo in the Lido Restaurant.

Outside the Vista Dining Room hang 8th-century German still lifes, and exquisite blown glass art fills shelves near the Pinnacle Grill. And on and on.

It takes a little more than an hour to follow the iPod tour. But the tour doesn't begin to reveal the array of art and antiques on this ship.

There are a series of life-sized cast-in-bronze statues by Lebigre & Roger (Italy, 2001) located on various decks close to the mid-ship elevators. The two on Deck 1 are particularly fanciful: *Pierrot*, a clown with arms spread wide in ecstasy, and *Colombina*, a woman perched on a crescent moon.

On Deck 2, the Lebigre & Roger life-sized bronze is of Bip, the pantomime character made famous by Marcel Marceau. The Bip statue wears his familiar battered opera hat and baggie trousers. I find it totally endearing.

If your artistic tastes lean more toward show biz, the Northern Lights bar on Deck 2 has a series of posters from Hollywood's golden age, adorned with autographs from long-ago movie stars

The MGM Studios poster bears the signatures of Fernando Lamas, Janet Leigh, Olivia de Havilland and Cyd Charisse among others.

A poster of the Republic Studios is signed by 38 early cowboy stars including Roy Rogers, Dale Evans and Slim Pickens.

The 20th Century Fox posters are autographed by Cesar Romero, Ernest Borgnine, Don Ameche, Anthony Quinn, Joan Collins and others.

I find the autographs themselves as fascinating as the artwork. What do these flamboyant or cramped signatures indicate about their writers?

The Sports Bar has several humorous sport figure paintings and a series of comic ceramic characters by Jan Snoeck.

Maritime art of one kind or another fills the various stairway landings throughout the ship: reproductions of weathervanes, paintings of Holland American Cruise Ships throughout the years and other nautical scenes.

The elevator areas at the rear of the ship (I believe that's called the stern) have colorful benches heavily carved with scenes and characters that remind me of Shakespeare's *A Midsummer Night's Dream*.

In the Piano Bar on Deck 2 hang five paintings by Hans Leijerzapf.

There are antiques and sculptures and clever little shadowboxes filled with touching and humorous scenes.

In short, the *Zuiderdam* is a floating art gallery with artistic delights at every turn.

And if you don't want to wander around searching for artworks tucked away in the stairwells and corners, the ship has an actual Park West art gallery filled with works by Peter Max, Thomas Kincade, Dalí, Goya, Picasso and other historic and contemporary artists.

Park West conducts art auctions during the cruise, enabling passengers to bid, buy and take home gallery works they covet.

When I tire of looking for (and at) art, I meet Al in the Explorations Café for latte and goodies. I get open-faced salmon sandwiches, which will serve as my lunch today. He gets brownies and cookies.

Back in our room, I notice on today's event schedule a knitting and quilting meeting, an Introduction to Bridge class, dancing lessons (learn to foxtrot), a cooking show in the Culinary Arts Center, a blackjack tournament in the casino, plus a lecture on Baja California.

We attend the 2 p.m. lecture in the Vista Lounge and enjoy it, learning lots we didn't know about this northernmost and westernmost state of Mexico.

The ship is presenting lectures on Baja because our next three ports of call are all in Mexico, and it's good to know a little about the places you're going to be visiting. The three Mexican ports of call are: Cabo San Lucas tomorrow, Zihuatanejo on Monday and Huatulco on Wednesday.

After a brief nap, we watch *The Natural*, one of the movies we've ordered from our in-room catalogue. I always enjoy seeing Robert Redford bring some character to life on screen.

DINNER AT THE PINNACLE GRILL

This is our first big night out. Because of our budget, we probably would not have paid for a dinner at the Pinnacle Grill. It costs about 25 dollars per person to eat there. And the dinners in the Vista Dining Room are beautifully served, and flavorful, leaving us no need to spend extra at the Pinnacle.

But when I contacted Holland America to inform them that we would be writing a book about our Panama Cruise, the company responded with several perks, among them a complimentary Pinnacle Grill dinner.

Eating at the Pinnacle gives me a chance to dress up and wear one of my new outfits.

We arrive promptly at 5:30 p.m. A young man in a tuxedo greets us and leads us to a large, luxurious window seat, where we have a grand view of the entire restaurant, and if we turn slightly to our left, a striking view of the ocean outside.

The feeling here is of relaxed elegance. Despite the dark burgundy carpets, the place is filled with light from its oceanside windows.

Overhead lights resemble large, white water lilies. Suspended from the dark ceiling, they give the impression that we're under water, looking up toward the pond's surface. It's a lovely and surreal effect.

Our waiter brings an assortment of breads and three kinds of butter: tomato, garlic and traditional. He also brings three varieties of sea salts.

The chef sends us an aperitif – a little cracker piled high with a flavor-filled sea food concoction.

For our appetizer we both order the Dungeness crab cakes. They're superb.

Although the menu holds several enticing offerings, we both choose the specialty of the house:

Sterling Silver Beef. We each order a side of fresh asparagus. Al also orders a side of sautéed button mushrooms.

My dessert is fresh berries. Al's is a tray of sumptuous crème brûlée (three kinds: chocolate, caramel and vanilla). I have a spoonful of each ... rich beyond compare!

The meal is the culinary high point of our cruise (so far): the service prompt but not hovering; the food, superb and the setting, as I've said, pure elegance.

AL'S TAKE ON THE PINNACLE GRILL

To merely describe the Pinnacle Grill's fare falls far short of adequate explanation. The very word "pinnacle" denotes the peak, the culmination, the very top and such is what we found when we came to dine there.

Rather than dwell on the outstanding service, the fresh-and-not-rock-solid rolls, the unbelievable crabcake appetizer, I will, instead, focus on the entrée: the filet mignon.

We are not beef eaters, particularly in large chunks, but this one time we thought we'd give beef a try.

I will only say that my steak came from a cow that had lived a rich and pampered life, perhaps cared for by a farmer's young daughter who wept when it was led away. The beast had surely received absolution for its sins before a significant portion of it was laid on our plates. Cooked to perfection, the outside redolent of the aroma of a red-hot grill, the steak's core was that ideal just-pink color and as juicy as a lover's tryst. Never before had I eaten as much boeuf *in one sitting, and glad I was for every bite.*

But wait: there's more!

What would a steak be without mushrooms, sautéed gently in butter, heaped alongside my magnificent mignon? Somewhere aboard, perhaps in some dark cabin, there has to be a mushroom farm: these were far too fresh to have been brought aboard and stored in the icebox. By themselves, they would have made an outstanding entrée.

And just as I was growing concerned about the security of the buttons on my trousers, the pièce de résistance appeared for dessert: crème brûlée. And not just one little ramekin of this elegant dessert – far from it. Three brûlées appeared – chocolate, vanilla, and caramel – each in its own serpentine trough in a large, white ceramic dish.

The ideal brûlée is sprinkled with sugar and then flamed to caramelize it, and so it was. We had to share, but try as we might, we couldn't get the last bite down, a regret I will carry to my dying days.

If I were to find one flaw in the evening, it would be in the name of the restaurant. "Pinnacle" needs to be replaced with "Everest" because the experience just doesn't get any higher than this.

JEFF TRACTA STARS IN THE VISTA SHOW LOUNGE

We make it to the Vista in time to get a good seat for tonight's show. Jeff Tracta ("Thorne" on CBS's *The Bold and the Beautiful*, "Danny" in Broadway's revival production of *Grease*) puts on a great and booming show that features comedy, singing, rap, impressions and lots of high-octane dancing.

Immense video screens filled with singing and dancing characters (and he is every one of those characters, thanks to some high-tech wizardry) fill the stage. The studio orchestra pounds out rousing accompaniments to the stories he tells. We find ourselves laughing, tearing up and cheering as this energetic entertainer gives his all to the performance.

It's impressive that every night in the Vista Lounge there is a different and very entertaining act. Magic, music, comedy and, tonight, a loud, enthusiastic combination of special effects and personal magnetism's power.

It's not until his second (10 p.m.) performance that we learn how truly loud it is.

OUR FOURTH SURPRISE (NOISY CABIN)

As I've mentioned before, we are early-to-bed seniors. It appears that we are not alone in this trait.

As we've noticed night after night, the 8 p.m. show in the Vista Lounge is always packed, but we've heard that there are lots of seats to choose from during the 10 p.m. show.

We chuckle, realizing that the explanation for this lies, at least in part, on the "older" clientele taking this cruise. If my nieces or nephew or any of their 20-something friends were on the cruise, they'd be preparing to go out for the evening just as we are climbing into bed.

Luckily, our comfortable bed with its tranquil linens has helped us drift "gently down the tides of sleep" as Longfellow would say. And each morning, when we wake up, we rise refreshed.

So tonight, when we're suddenly awakened shortly after 10 p.m. by the musical uproar and the accompanying clamor of applause coming from the Vista Lounge, we are shocked.

"What's all that racket?" I ask, totally irritated at being jerked from an interesting dream.

"The 10 p.m. show," Al says.

"Oh no!" I realize that we've got an hour or more of this noise before we can go back to the welcome darkness of slumber. Our room on Deck 5, which has been such a restful sanctuary, is directly above the theater. Of course, Deck 4 is between us and the theater, but it does little to muffle the enthusiastic uproar from the show. I feel sorry for the folks on Deck 4. And sorrier for myself.

While *Jeff Tracta Live!* was wonderful while we sat in the Vista Lounge; it is something quite different now that we're trying to sleep.

From now on, every time there's a loud show in the Vista Lounge, we lie sleepless and frustrated until after 11 p.m.

The lesson to be learned: If you're an early-to-bed type, check out the location of your cabin in relation to noisy areas of the ship (the theater, the casino, the shopping promenade) and come prepared with earplugs if you are anywhere near the theater.

DAY 5
Saturday, October 6

GETTING THE INSIDE SCOOP
FROM EXECUTIVE CHEF KARL ELLER

Cabo San Lucas, filled with sunshine, jet skis and pelicans.

Many passengers head for today's port of call: Cabo San Lucas. They climb aboard tenders (small boats that ferry folks from cruise ship to shore) to see the beaches and bars of this port, but Al and I stay on board.

I want to get the "inside scoop" on food from the *Zuiderdam*'s Executive Chef Karl Eller.

I meet him on Deck 1, just outside the front desk area, and am struck at what a handsome man he is. Tall and tan, with close-cropped white hair that looks almost like a halo, Karl Eller appears both wise and youthful at the same time. With a firm handshake and easy smile, he puts me immediately at ease.

Despite the fact that this man routinely works 12- to 15-hour days onboard, he graciously spends almost two full hours with me.

We climb the Atrium stairs to Deck 2, and find a table in the Pinnacle Grill where we can talk. Chef Eller has coffee brought to our table and then settles in to tell me all about food on the *Zuiderdam*.

His clear, blue eyes twinkle as he shares stories about being top chef on a cruise ship. It's obvious that he loves his work.

"I order from a list of 2,500 different items," he says. "The vendors' trucks deliver the dry food to the ship nine days in advance of the cruise. Menus vary by itinerary, season and location."

He says Holland America contracts with farmers for fresh produce. "They're close to harbor, not far away. That helps ensure quality and prices. Holland America has the highest quality food of any cruise line."

Chef Eller's enthusiasm for food preparations started early. He grew up in Germany, where his father owned a restaurant and served as its main cook.

Besides working in the family restaurant, Eller apprenticed as a cook in Germany and also attended culinary school there. He worked in hotels and restaurants in Austria and Switzerland before discovering cruise lines.

He says he loves being a cruise ship chef.

"Traditional cooking in hotels is mundane," he says. "It's the same menu year round. You're rarely challenged."

But the challenges facing an executive chef on a cruise ship can be many.

"What you order and what you receive from the vendors can be two different things, and then you have to make do with what you receive."

His dedication to his work is exemplified in a long story he tells about the beginning of a 30-day cruise to Asia. There were 17 pallets of food and produce supplies on the pier ready to be loaded aboard. But the men refused to load the goods.

"They were angry at the farmers or some such thing and they wouldn't load it. And we had to sail away without those provisions. I worked all night, figuring out (new) menus using what we had on board.

"The first 10 days, sailing to Honolulu, I switched the food all around, designed different dishes," he laughs softly to himself, recalling his efforts.

"When we got to Honolulu, I ordered what we needed flown in from Tahiti, but the pilots were on strike and only half of what I ordered was delivered."

That's when Chef Eller took matters into his own hands and found a local truck to take him to nearby farms, where he bought and helped load excellent (and much needed) produce.

"It took hours to harvest and pack the truck, and then I lay on top of the goods, holding everything down, as we drove back to the ship. I was spread-eagled on top of the produce all the way back to port and, believe me, when we finally arrived, I was sunburned. And tired. Some of the passengers saw the truck pulling up with me spread out on top. I think they were impressed that their chef would go to such lengths," he laughs heartily and takes a long drink of coffee. "I got back to the ship by 6 p.m. I was exhausted. Done for the day."

He describes how even when things go as planned – when the pallets of produce and other goods are loaded on board – he and others must fully inspect the deliveries and see what's there. If they find substandard foodstuffs, they get rid of them (they go in the ship's mulcher). And then he makes adjustments to the menus.

Chef Eller supervises a galley staff of 130 and a 150-person waiter staff.

His galley workers include the 2nd executive chef, sous chefs, chef de parties, demi chefs, kitchen helpers, kitchen assistants, assistant cooks (yet to graduate), apprentice cooks, bakers, pastry chefs, butchers and assorted attendants.

The ship also has a Cellar Master.

PROVISIONS FOR OUR CRUISE

I ask him about the provisions for our cruise. He says he ordered

- 5,000 pounds of beef tenderloin
- 2,500 pounds of prime rib
- 4,500 pounds of strip-loin
- 3,500 pounds of fresh-caught Alaskan salmon ("We use more salmon on the Alaskan cruises," he says.)
- About 10,000 pounds of chicken
- About 412,500 pounds of fresh vegetables
- About 22,250 pounds of potatoes

Since I know Sweetheart-of-the-Sweet-Tooth Al will want to know all about the dessert makings, I ask about them. Chef Eller grins and flips through a paper notebook filled with handwritten notes. "These are estimates, but they are close," he says. For each day on the cruise he orders:

- 350 pounds of sugar
- 450 pounds of flour
- 251 pounds of flour mixes (breads)

- 50 pounds of flour mixes (muffins)
- 24 pounds of white chocolate
- 24 pounds of milk chocolate
- 24 pounds of semi-sweet chocolate
- 24 pounds of chocolate for Le Cirque
- 22 pounds of dark chocolate
- 20 pounds of butter
- 4,500 to 5,000 fresh eggs
- 40 boxes of pasteurized eggs
- 26 pounds of egg whites

As we talk about food and cooking and all that goes into menu design, Chef Eller reveals more of his personal philosophy regarding food.

"The presentation is important," he says. "It needs to appeal to the eye. And the taste of things is a little more important."

He says he especially likes to work with fresh ingredients, but loves working with vegetables, potatoes and herbs.

"I love to cook using fresh, local and seasonal ingredients," he says. "It might surprise people to learn that almost everything onboard is made fresh, and in smaller batches than you might expect."

Since most of the guests on our cruise are past retirement age, I ask if he's made any special changes to his ordering and menus for this cruise.

His eyes twinkle as he nods and says, "Older people eat less salt, less fat and a lot of vegetables. They also eat smaller portions. But they usually eat everything on their plate. Younger people take more and leave more."

"I'm trying to eat well without gaining a lot of weight," I say.

"But we want you to gain," he replies with a sly chuckle.

I ask, "How much do most people gain on a cruise?"

"About a pound a day on a short cruise," he says. "But I'll tell you this, people eat less as the cruise progresses. In the beginning they gorge, but as they days go by they settle down and eat less."

I ask why he thinks that's the case, and he laughingly replies, "I think their clothes begin to shrink."

"Do you have any advice for eating well without gaining weight?" I ask.

He lists five things:

1. reduce your intake of starch
2. stay away from fried food
3. eat fish from the grill
4. increase your vegetable intake
5. stay away from butter.

As our conversation winds down and our coffee runs out, I ask what's most rewarding to him about his work.

Without hesitation, he says, "When the cruise is done and everyone's happy. That's my motivation."

Then he walks me through the galley that serves the Vista Dining Room, proudly pointing out where salads are made, desserts staged and other aspects of each dinner prepared. Photographs of how each dish is supposed to look hang above each station, so that whoever is preparing the dish will know exactly how to present it.

It is clear that this is his world, and he keeps it operating at peak performance.

"By regulation, we are required to wash and sanitize every night in preparation of the next service," he says, explaining how these stainless-steel work areas all can look so sparkling clean.

Although I will enjoy seeing Chef Karl Eller throughout the cruise – in the Culinary Arts Center, at the Chocolate Extravaganza and at other times and places – having this extended interview and galley tour has been simply wonderful.

LATER THAT AFTERNOON

It's 3 p.m. and we could be enjoying high tea in the Vista Dining Room – jacketed waiters bringing trays of small, calorie-packed finger cakes, cream-puffs and truffles to us while the others around the table introduce themselves.

Instead, however, we're sitting in the mostly deserted Lido restaurant, reading and writing. The floor-to-ceiling windows reveal the clear green waters off Cabo San Lucas.

Rock islands thrust gray brown bulges toward a pale blue sky, while jet skis and small motorboats slice white paths through the gentle waves.

Our ship is anchored a few hundred yards off beautiful white-sand beaches. One of the beaches is named "Lovers' Beach" at one end and "Divorce Beach" at the other. The sand is full of couples quite oblivious to anything other than the beauty, unremitting heat and humidity and the fun that can be had in the water.

Paddleboarding, windsurfing and parasailing fill the scene beyond our Lido table.

And the weathered tops of the rocky upthrusts are smoothed into steeply arching hills, carpeted with green. Birds and butterflies (white and yellow) flit around our windows.

The few people who didn't catch a tender and go ashore are scattered among the window tables, eating salads, sandwiches, pizza or ice cream.

A lazy afternoon.

As the sun changes position and more boats and jet skis tear up the water's surface, the rumpled liquid green turns into a glittering expanse of eye-piercing silver.

I head back to our room.

DAY 6
Sunday, October 7

COOKING CLASS

Chili-rubbed Ahi Tuna Kebabs, which we
learned to make in cooking class.

Last night, after the show (a comedian named
Dan Gabriel), we went up to the Crow's Nest,

hoping to hear classical guitar. But the music was simply a man singing and accompanying himself on the guitar, so we wandered out on deck. There we found the "classic"-ness we were seeking.

The night seemed beautiful, even enchanting. It wrapped its darkness around us with a gentle tropical breeze warm enough to lull us asleep.

What is it about a warm breeze in the dark that always make me feel so young and full of happiness? Who knows how long we stood entwined at the railing, as the ship slid through the sea and the night's black magic embraced us.

Eventually we returned to our room ... found a cute towel animal created by our stateroom attendant, and our two nighttime chocolates.

This morning we oversleep, so Al misses Mass. We blame it on the time changes (we've had to set our watches two hours ahead in the last two days). Because we overslept, we also missed breakfast in the dining room.

The Lido is packed, and all the copies of the *New York Times* are gone. I check the newspaper holder outside the Lido, at the Explorations Café and at the front desk. All empty. No morning paper with our breakfast. Nuts!

Nonetheless, I enjoy fruit, oatmeal and coffee. Al has French toast, juice and coffee.

Three times, people stop by our table to tell Al they missed his homily. I could tell their words touched Al.

"They're part of my little congregation," he whispers to me, smiling. "I can't miss Mass again."

At 10 a.m. we find a seat in the Vista Lounge for a lecture on Magellan. I love cruise ship lectures. The people who give them are usually so well-versed that I feel like I'm back in college, sitting at the feet of a world-renowned expert.

One of the most interesting aspects of the Magellan lecture is the maps he and other explorers of the era used. These various maps are projected on a huge screen. None of the maps bear any resemblance to the world we know! North America looks narrow and misshapen. California appears as a large island in the Pacific. The various continents look like a committee gerrymandered them into letters of the alphabet. Such inaccurate representations of the world – and yet people used them to navigate.

Magellan's expedition was the first to sail from the Atlantic into the Pacific, and the first to circumnavigate the earth (although he was not onboard the entire trip, having been killed in the Philippines).

But it's the maps he sailed by that evoke thoughts about our own understandings (or misunderstandings) of life – our own "inner" maps – those guides we believe in and follow and swear by.

Obviously, we can get through life believing almost anything – that the world is flat, that there is no ultimate meaning to life, that we are the creator or victim of our circumstances, that I am right and you are wrong and so on.

But I suspect life is easier (and a lot more pleasant) the closer our inner maps match with reality, just as these early explorers would have had an easier time if their maps had born some resemblance to actual geography.

Upstairs in the Explorers Café there's a large globe. Usually a group of people are standing around it, checking out our location or finding where we'll be tomorrow. I think that group of people exemplifies the human desire to know the truth, to understand the world and our place in it.

It occurs to me that this cruise is part of that desire to understand, to know. We've learned what we can about the Panama Canal, but actually going through it will give us a far more realistic understanding.

COOKING CLASS

At noon we head for the Culinary Arts Center on Deck 2. This state-of-the-art kitchen in an amphitheater setting presents gourmet cooking demonstrations throughout the cruise. In the evening, it doubles as a cabaret theater (curtains hide the kitchen area). And during the cruise, cooking classes are offered here.

We'd heard that the kitchen classes fill up quickly, so we signed up the day we boarded. Classes are limited to 12 participants. Our class has four – Al and me, and another man and woman.

Since I do not cook, I'm a little nervous, but our master chef (Shiva) puts me immediately at ease.

Each of us receives a full-length apron. The meal we'll prepare includes corn chowder; chile-rubbed ahi tuna kebabs with cucumber salad; chicken with fresh apricots, ginger and cracked almonds and for dessert, fresh berries in lemon mint syrup.

Each of us is responsible for part of the meal. We must prepare four servings of our menu item.

Al remembers the class as chaotic. "We arrived, put on our aprons, looked at our recipe cards and dove in."

I remember how amazingly Chef Shiva kept us all on track, moving among us, directing, correcting, encouraging, making us laugh with his jokes, having us taste our dish as we went along, adjusting our seasonings and always making us feel like we were true culinary artists.

I choose the soup because it consists mainly of chopping up vegetables, and one thing I can do is chop. Chef Shiva gives me an example of the size to chop each item, and I simply copy him. I chop potatoes, red peppers, onions, celery and green onions. Corn was already taken off the cob for me.

While I'm chopping veggies, the other woman (who is taking this cruise with her husband as a 50th anniversary celebration) prepares the kebabs, cutting up the tuna into large three-inch squares. For seasoning, she combines ancho powder, cumin, coriander, caraway seeds and cayenne pepper with smashed garlic cloves, mashing it all into a paste.

As the class progresses, she stirs this concoction in an oiled pan and adds the tuna, tossing it until the pink fish is well coated. Then she impales the seasoned tuna chunks, along with peppers, mushrooms and onions on eight-inch bamboo skewers.

Al and the other man prepare the chicken. First they cut up and bake the almonds. While the almonds are baking, they brown fresh apricots in melted butter. After removing the apricots, they add olive oil and the chicken breasts, and hover over their skillet like two master chefs.

Things smell delicious by now. I take my camera and snap a number of photos of us all concentrating on our part of the meal.

The other woman and I ask for help all along the way, and Chef Shiva is happy to assist us. Al and the other man figure out their dish between them, rarely asking for assistance.

When all my ingredients are chopped, I stand back and admire the bright and beautiful colors: red and green and yellow and white, a veritable cornucopia of hues and textures. My mouth waters.

Then Chef Shiva puts two large spoons full of butter in a saucepan, and when they melt and bubble has me add the onions and potatoes. When the potatoes are cooked, I put in the corn. In a moment, I add the rest of the ingredients and some chicken broth and let the beautiful mixture boil gently.

By this time, Al and his partner are cooking the chicken breasts. They add ginger, scallion whites, lime zest and chile to their skillets and stir the mixture and the chicken breasts until the chicken is cooked through. They remove the chicken and add maple syrup and the apricots to the skillet, warm the concoction through, then return the chicken to the skillet for a final heat-through.

Meanwhile, the kebab lady grills her skewers until they are lightly charred and just cooked through.

My final step is pureeing everything in a large industrial blender while adding whole milk and thick cream. Then I pour the thick, gorgeous yellow-orange chowder back into a sauce pan for another minute of gentle boiling.

Somehow the cucumber salad and the delicious lemon mint syrup were also prepared. I suspect Chef Shiva made them in between directing us as we tried to work culinary magic.

In just a little more than an hour, all our cooking is complete. Chef Shiva arranges the kebabs, chicken breasts, and cucumber salad on large white platters. Then he pours my soup into good-sized white bowls, sprinkling scallion greens on top for garnish, and places a bowl on each platter with the chicken, tuna and salad.

The dessert plates – piled with brilliantly colored blueberries, red raspberries and blackberries in a freshly cooked lemon mint syrup – have to be set on a separate tray, along with a bottle of white wine and a bottle of red wine.

Then, carrying our culinary creations, we follow the chef to a window table in the Pinnacle Grill and enjoy ourselves, eating our various dishes with gusto and delight. Just beyond our window the Pacific sparkles in gentle waves, blue and clear.

What a feast! What a thrill to be part of such an inspiring class.

In addition to our aprons, we also receive recipe cards for each of the dishes made in class.

MOVIES IN OUR ROOM

The *Zuiderdam* has a lovely little movie theater called the Screening Room. It consists of a large movie screen, about 30 big, comfortable upholstered chairs for viewing and free popcorn. Every day there's a new movie. And even though the movies show up later on the in-cabin TVs, they're fun to watch in the theater.

However, this afternoon, we decide to watch a movie in our room. We look through the catalogue, call the front desk and order *Indiana Jones and the Kingdom of the Crystal Skull* (2008) and it arrives at our door promptly. We pop it in the DVD player and recline on our bed to enjoy an old favorite.

AL'S TAKE ON CHOCOLATE BROWNIES

If you look carefully on the top shelf of the Lido buffet's dessert cabinet, you may be fortunate to find a huge chocolate brownie. If such is your luck, grab it immediately. This isn't your run-of-the-mill Safeway Aunt-Betty-mix brownie. Not by a long shot. This is the MOAB: The Mother Of All Brownies, the very standard against which all other brownies compete – and lose.

On close inspection, you will first find that the brownie is split horizontally. The gap between top and bottom layers is filled with creamy chocolate pudding. Take care when you bite in, lest you need the services of a dry cleaner.

But the delightful deliciousness doesn't stop there. This tasty little chocolate sandwich is topped with a thick, gooey layer of dark chocolate frosting. Finger-licking is permitted, even, necessary.

And you're not done yet, for atop the chocolate frosting you'll discover a liberal layer of milk chocolate sprinkles. What more could anyone ask? How about another to take back to the cabin, for starters? Or two. And don't forget the milk.

DAY 7
Monday, October 8
PORT OF CALL: ZIHUATANEJO, MEXICO

The serene scene from the fishing village of Zihuatanejo.

I really like the rhythm of this cruise ... a day at sea, a day in port, a day at sea, a day in port. Gives me breathing time to savor both the ports of call and some of the onboard activities.

We catch a tender and go ashore around 10 a.m.

Zihuatanejo is a historic fishing village on a beautiful bay ... and it still looks something like a fishing village today. Lots of small boats pulled up on shore. Fishermen working with their nets.

The village is walkable. No high-rises here. And we walk, looking at traditional buildings and enjoying the picturesque narrow lanes. We walk with our cameras at the ready, snapping shots of lovely (or crumbling) architectural details.

As we come around one corner, a man steps out from a street-side café, spreads his arms and greets us with a big smile. "Welcome home," he says.

I think it's the best hook-and-catch-and-reel-them-in line I've heard. And it works on us.

We take a seat at one of the sidewalk tables, covered in red-and-white-checked tablecloths, and begin to visit with Monk. This is his restaurant.

He brings us ice water while we scan the menu. The heat and humidity, which have increased significantly since we left the ship, are bearing down on me, causing my appetite to diminish.

Al orders fish tacos. The fish were just caught this morning in the bay out front, Monk says. And

I believe him. The grilled onions and green peppers, and the cool tomato salsa are also fresh as can be. I pick at Al's plate while he eats and talks with Monk.

After this meal, we continue meandering through the village. I take pictures of the many bronze sculptures of women and men, sculptures that illustrate the rich history of this area.

But the heat is getting to me.

We stop at a beach cabana restaurant and I order a smoothie. What I get is a cool mixture of banana, milk and ice. It's not exactly what I had in mind, but it's cold and I'm grateful. While I sip my smoothie, we enjoy the gentle background music of the surf, the palm trees, the afternoon breeze and each other.

Although the beach tempts us, I'm beginning to feel ill from the heat and humidity. "I've got to get back to the ship, back to our room where there's some air conditioning," I tell Al. He's ready to return, too.

So we head for the pier to wait for a tender.

Ship staff members greet us on the pier with ice water, lemonade and chilled washcloths. All these small efforts to assure our comfort feel like luxuries to me. The chilled washcloth refreshes my face and neck.

Back on the ship, I take a long, cool shower until I feel somewhat revived. Then slip on my comfy robe and take a nap.

Al wants to go to dinner and the show, but I'm bushed from today's heat and very content to simply stay in the cabin.

"I'll get something from room service," I say. "And there's football on the TV."

So he takes off and I make myself at home with the remote and the room service menu.

After a while, I order salmon with fresh vegetables, and for dessert (yes, I actually order a dessert), chocolate cake with raspberry sauce.

When my meal arrives, I lift the stainless-steel plate cover. It's as if I've been served a feast. The generous salmon steak is accompanied by garlic mashed potatoes and grilled zucchini, summer squash and carrots, along with broccoli florets. The fragrance alone is enough to satisfy me.

I eat slowly, enjoying each forkful. Such color. Such texture. Such taste.

And when my main meal is finished, I lift the plate cover off my dessert and am amazed. Presented there on a large white platter is a slice of three-layer chocolate cake with chocolate frosting and raspberry sauce drizzled across in sensual swirls. Way too much dessert for me. But way too delicious looking to ignore.

I can only eat half, knowing that Al will joyously consume the rest when he returns.

AL'S REVIEW OF CHOCOLATE CAKE WITH RASPBERRY SAUCE

Should you arrive at day's end, tired, sweaty and completely unable to even make it to the buffet, the Zuiderdam's helpful staff will bring supper to your stateroom.

The menu's offerings are both broad and tasty, as one might expect. Keep on reading. Nestled at the bottom of the menu, inconspicuously placed among more pedestrian desserts, is a wholly unexpected treasure: chocolate cake with raspberry sauce.

Now you might be inclined to say "What's so special about chocolate cake?"

Dear reader, this is the chocolate cake that sets the standard against which all other chocolate cakes fall short. Even your mama's, I daresay. Eat your heart out, Betty Crocker.

Let's begin with the cake itself. I have no idea how it's done, but the Z's baker manages to combine both perfect moistness with a deep, dark, smoky chocolate flavor. Then, slathered between each of the cake's three layers is a thick layer of chocolate frosting, soft, appropriately gooey, and with finger-licking temptations. The same frosting is applied to the top.

All this would be well and good unto itself, but it's the raspberry sauce that turns the corner from great to magnificent. Take just one big bite of cake, dripping with chocolate frosting, swirl it in the raspberry sauce, and your day is complete: nothing more could be added. No, not even the kiss of a fair maiden. Well, perhaps ...

In short, this is a dessert you miss at your great loss.

DAY 8
Tuesday, October 9

INTERVIEW WITH LIFESTYLE SPECIALIST NICK

One of our delicious desserts. Al had two.

It took me long enough, an entire week on board, to set up an interview with "Life-Stylist"

Nick Reiersgard. But today's the day. After his 8 a.m. Tai Chi class and his 10 a.m. Introduction to Meditation class in the Ocean Bar, he and I will chat about eating healthy while cruising and strategies for staying trim onboard.

Nick guides Tai Chi by the Lido Pool most mornings and some evenings.

This morning, while Al leads his congregation through morning Mass, I practice the age-old art of slow-motion meditative exercise.

Following Nick's directions we concentrate on our breathing and the movement of our hands. Once we get the inhaling and exhaling properly timed, we begin a series of movements involving feet, legs and arms.

The movements are gentle, graceful and not as easy as they may appear.

By the end of our half hour, I feel both relaxed and well-exercised. I can see how people could become very attached to this form of exercise.

Of course, if you want something more intense, there is the ship's fitness center with treadmills, free weights, lots of resistance machines and classes of all kinds: yoga, Pilates, spinning, stretching.

Some of these classes charge a nominal fee, but use of the gym is included in the cruise price.

Back when I was a daily newspaper reporter, working for the *Union Democrat* newspaper in Sonora, California, I'd often be assigned stories about local gyms or local health clubs. And in my research for these stories, I'd be reminded of how damaging a sedentary lifestyle is.

I'd read, repeatedly, how sitting around all day can double the risk of heart disease, diabetes, obesity and can also increase the risk of colon cancer, high blood pressure, osteoporosis, depression and anxiety.

The solution? A mere 30 minutes a day of moderate exercise. Take a walk, ride a bike, swim, work out at a local gym.

After writing enough health-and-wellness stories, after enough years of reading about the problems and solutions, I decided to get moving. I said to myself, "Why are you just sitting here year after year reading about this stuff and writing about it? You can *do* something to make sure you aren't a heart attack or diabetes statistic. Get moving."

So for nearly a decade now, I've been exercising religiously. I'm so glad that when I take a cruise, I can continue this wonderful tradition of mine. Regular exercise, even moderate exercise, helps me feel better and sleep better. I recommend it.

Nick and I meet on Deck 3 for our chat.

Turns out, it was a sports injury that got 24-year-old Nick started in lifestyle practice. While he recovered, he learned the moves that allowed him to exercise without stressing or straining his injured muscles.

A college graduate who loves hiking, Nick tells me about the advantages of regular exercise and a well-balanced diet. Although he's "preaching to the choir," I enjoy listening to his advice and insight.

I describe how impressed I am at all the fresh fruits and vegetables onboard, and how the variety of salads and entrees has kept me from getting bored with the fare.

But since I'm interested in sharing how to live and eat healthy onboard and keep from packing on the pounds, I get right to my questions for Nick.

I ask how people on a cruise can eat well while keeping the diet well-balanced and in check.

He grins, then gives me his suggestions. "Eat in the dining room, skip the buffet. The dining room portions are appropriate. Of course you can always get seconds and thirds, but that's not as likely in the dining room as overeating is at the buffet. At the buffet there's always the temptation of piling on the food."

He pauses, then adds, "And the food served in the dining room is usually a little higher quality."

His second tip is to eat slowly. "Slow down. A friend of my mom's slowed her eating by changing from a fork to chopsticks. But anything you can do to slow down your eating will help."

He also says that the healthier meals are often marked on the menu.

Third tip: limit alcohol. Although nutritionally empty, alcohol is full of calories, Nick says.

"Is there any one thing that might be most important for folks to do to stay healthy on a cruise?" I ask.

He nods and says, "Use the stairs instead of the elevator."

I feel proud of myself because I've been using the stairs almost exclusively since we got on board.

"And take advantage of the fitness classes offered in the gym."

All good advice, especially coming from someone whose business is to know about such things.

After my interview with Nick, I swing by the Culinary Arts Center and discover that there's a celebrity cook-off in progress. All the seats in this small theater are filled, and four chefs in white are trying to outdo one another. It's fun to watch ... and I know that recipe cards will be handed out at the end of the contest. With the cards, everyone will have the ability, when they return home to their own kitchens, to make what the chefs are preparing today.

Back at the room, Sweetheart and I decide to go to the Screening Room for the movie of the day, *We Bought a Zoo* (2011). Grabbing two bags of popped corn as we enter, we quickly find comfortable seats and wait for the movie to begin.

After an entire week on board, we are starting to recognize some of our fellow cruisers. It's fun to spot people as they enter the Screening Room, and give them a smile or nod. It's feeling like a "home town" crowd.

We find the movie enjoyable (we'd rate it a C+). Nothing spectacular ... but fun for a lazy afternoon on board.

The rest of our afternoon is taken up with reading, wandering to the Explorations Café for a latte and napping.

This evening, we share our dining room dinner table with two interesting Canadian couples: Jeanne and Ray Ferris, and Gloria and Tony.

Turns out Ray is a movie buff and while we eat, he and I exchange titles of our favorite movies. He agrees with three of my favorites: *Babettes gæstebud/Babette's Feast* (1987), *Il Postino/The Postman* (1994) and *La Vita è bella/Life Is Beautiful* (1997), all foreign films with deeply moving messages.

Tony, like Al, is a retired engineer. He and Al talk about engineering, while Ray and I talk movies. Tony and Gloria excuse themselves before dessert is served. They want to get a good seat for tonight's show.

But Al and I stay and visit with Ray and Jeanne, talking about movies, Canada, cruising and other topics of mutual interest. We stay so long that we actually miss the beginning of the 8 p.m. show.

We decide to visit the Crow's Nest to listen to a little gentle guitar music, then slowly walk outside and let the warm, dark night surround us.

DAY 9
Wednesday, October 10

PORT OF CALL: HUATULCO. MEXICO

This green parrot kept his eye on us as we explored
the streets of Huatulco.

Up at 7 a.m. Breakfast in the Lido (coffee and
Muselix for me. Coffee and French Toast for Al).

Al's Mass. My morning exercise in the fitness center. Then off for a morning stroll through the tiny seaside village of Huatulco.

Huatulco is nestled in the Oaxaca coastline. According to the information provided by Holland America, Huatulco enjoys average year-round temperatures in the high 80s. The nine bays comprising the tourist complex have azure waters, fine white sand and an unusual landscape that provides privacy and gives each bay a distinct personality.

Huatulco is composed of three areas: Santa Cruz is the resort area; La Crucecita is the residential, restaurant, and shopping area; Tangolunda Bay is the main beach area.

The name Huatulco comes from the Nahuatl word *cuautolco*, meaning "the place where the wood is adored." Legend has it that the great civilizing god Quetzalcoatl left the inhabitants of the bay and port of Santa Cruz a wooden cross.

No need for a tender here. The ship pulls right up to a pier, and we disembark and walk into the village.

A giant anchor stands next to the "Welcome to Huatulco" sign. Seems like everyone wants to be photographed next to the anchor and sign. Even Al and I.

As we step from the pier to the shore, the first thing that strikes me is the beautiful date palms filled with singing birds. The palms' graceful, long fronds barely move in the morning breeze, but the music coming from them, from hundreds of tiny, enthusiastic beaks, fills the air like a well-rehearsed community sing fest.

What a joyous way to start the day!

We wander among beautiful flowers and flowering shrubs.

Even the people are beautiful.

And the white-sand beach stretches out under clear green water.

We meander through the village. No crowds, no traffic snarls, just the pleasure of warm, fragrant air, the gentle shush of surf, and birdsong.

In the small harbor, dozens of boats await. A young man offers to take us in his boat to a nearby bay. He has a photo album with pictures of the bay, but we decline.

Two women, at different times, approach us with necklaces and other beadwork, asking if we'd like to buy something. We thank them, but say we are not buying today. And they move on. I wish them well in their entrepreneurial endeavors.

There are white tables with red-and-white-checkered tablecloths, sitting in the sand, waiting for tourists.

And a father-son duo plays the marimba outside a shop on one of the main walking streets.

What a beautiful and inviting village, one I wouldn't mind spending more time in. But we want to get back on the ship before the midday heat turns this pleasant excursion into an oven-like ordeal. On our way back, we notice a big-eyed parrot, all in green, watching us from a palm. The large clusters of green coconuts and this curious parrot create a joyful atmosphere as we stroll to *MS Zuiderdam* and the little room that has become our home.

Back aboard, we head straight to the Explorations Café for iced lattes. From our window table seat, we watch the gentle surf wash the sand. We can see the steep, wooded hills rising from the beach. Near their crests stand homes and condos painted white. Some have thatched roofs. Others have red tile roofs. The whole scene is serene and peaceful.

I pull *Fodor's Essential U.S.A.* off one of the library shelves and thumb through it, enjoying photos of amazing cities, neighborhoods, highways and other familiar places of my wonderful country.

I'm surprised to find that I've been to many (if not most) of the places described in this book. No doubt my age and travel-lust has much to do with this. But I love being reminded of all the wondrous places I've enjoyed, from New York City to Taos, Yellowstone to Yosemite, Puget Sound to Macinac Island to Cape Cod to New Orleans and to such small and charming places as Angels Camp, California, and Soda Springs, Idaho.

And here we are, Sweetheart and me, sailing a very pacific Pacific Ocean, heading to the Panama Canal. How wonderful is that?!

Lunch in the dining room: fresh pineapple dusted with coconut. Salmon with mango salsa and root veggies. And for dessert – banana pudding.

At 2 p.m. we find seats in the Vista Lounge for a lecture on Costa Rica, our next stop. Guest Lecturer Jim Clement discusses Costa Rica's volcanoes, jungle, beaches, handicrafts and its wondrous array of animals and birds.

He talks about the 10,000 kinds of plants, the 1,000 kinds of butterflies, 850 kinds of birds and other natural wonders of this small Central American nation. How Columbus discovered the place in 1502 and thought it was filled with gold, thus the name "rich coast." But later explorers found it to be a poor region.

The lecture is fascinating, and the slides that accompany it make me want to explore this nation further.

Back in our room, we look at the shore excursions brochure. At every stop on this cruise there have been several shore excursions available. We haven't taken one, preferring to simply wander around on our own, taking photos (and saving the shore excursion expense).

But we may never get another chance to see Costa Rica. And the lecture whetted our appetite for guided exploration. So we study their offerings, which range in price from 40 to 200 dollars per adult, less for children.

We choose an eight-hour "Discover Costa Rica" guided tour. It is described like this:

Explore firsthand Costa Rica's culture, history, architecture, flora and fauna. Visit Palmares to view the unique church made of eggs. Continue to the Historical Landmark Doka Estate and Coffee Plantation. Enjoy a guided tour and lunch at the estate. Discover the botanical garden La Garita.

There are adventure tours, shopping tours, and short picturesque tours, but this one seems to be the most all-inclusive – allowing us to see several aspects of the country.

We go to the tour reservation desk (near the front desk on Deck 1) to make our reservation. I clarify that we will have an air-conditioned bus for the day. That seals the deal for me.

Come Friday, when the ship docks in Puntarenas, we will board our tour bus at 8 a.m. for a day of discovery. The price: 90 dollars apiece.

A FEW WORDS ON SHORE EXCURSIONS

Shore excursions can be one of the best elements of a cruise. After all, cruising takes you places you wouldn't ordinarily visit on your own. And shore excursions can give you an up-close and intimate awareness of these places, whether they are tropical islands, bustling cities, exotic deserts or beaches, or exciting activities such as ziplines.

Because there are usually several shore excursions to choose from, and because the cost of shore excursions adds to the cost of your cruise, you may be wondering how to choose the right shore excursion. Here are some tips.

1. Research shore excursions before you cruise.

    Check the cruise line's website to learn about the cost and length of excursions. You can also research through the online site Cruise Critic (cruisecritic.com). Check under the port you want to visit on the "ports of call board" and read what others have experienced.

2. Find out what the shore excursion you're interested in includes.

    If it's an all-day excursion, is a meal included? If a meal is included, find out if it is a bag lunch, buffet or a barbeque. If you're choosing a snorkeling or hiking shore excursion, make sure the equipment you need is included. If you are choosing a demanding hike, check to see if drinking water will be provided or if you must bring your own.

3. Make sure the activity level suits you.

Our ship's brochure on shore excursions rates each excursion (easy activity, moderate activity, strenuous activity) and indicates if a snack or meal is included.

4. Shore excursions can be booked on board, or online beforehand.

It's all up to you. I have heard about people who schedule more than one shore excursion a day. I don't know how they do it (either financially or energy-wise).

Shore excursions are worth it if you want to venture to attractions that are far from the pier, learn more about an area through a guide or participate in physical activities that require gear (biking, diving, golf).

Some cruise lines offer free guided shore excursions in addition to the ones they charge for.

However, you do not have to take a shore excursion. You can, like Al and I often do, simply wander the village or town with a camera, recording your own discoveries. If you wish to prepare for your wandering, you might visit the local tourism bureau (if there is one) for maps and information. Often, you can do this online before you cruise, and plan your local "walking tour" yourself.

Another possibility is putting together your own excursion by hiring a private taxi to take you around. This can be quite economical if several people share the cost.

Or you can hire a local tour company. Many advertise on the Internet. However, when you are on your own, you're responsible for returning to the ship by the appointed time. If you're on a ship-related shore excursion, the captain will wait for you to return. But if you are out on your own, exploring and having a blast, the ship does not wait for you. You alone are responsible for getting yourself back in time for departure.

I would caution you, however, to be careful with do-it-yourself shore excursions in third-world countries. Unless you are familiar with the customs, the currency and the language, you could find yourself in embarrassing and/or unpleasant situations.

INDONESIAN CREW SHOW

At 3 p.m. we find seats in the Vista Lounge for the Indonesian Crew Show. We'd heard about the Indonesian and Philippine Crew Shows from those who had cruised *Zuiderdam* before, and had been looking forward to today's performance.

Since the crew (from cabin attendants to dining room waiters) is nearly 100 percent Asian and most of those cruising for pleasure are not, this performance helps us passengers see and appreciate the crew in new ways. And it also introduces us to cultures we may not encounter otherwise.

We'd learned that Holland America supplies the crew with its own staff of chefs. The crew's food is based on the traditional Asian diet of rice and fish. The crew chefs make sure crew member meals are familiarly delicious.

And during each *Zuiderdam* cruise, crew members put on a show highlighting their cultural dances and music.

Seems pretty impressive to celebrate the culture of the crew. We love the show! Everyone else seems to, too.

Following the show, we head for the Observation Deck and find window seats. The ocean is dark, covered with restless whitecaps all the way to the horizon, where the pale, overcast sky forms a long, straight line.

Al is reading his book. I'm enthralled by the big, dark waves.

SHIP SHOPS

Like all cruise ships, the *Zuiderdam* has a mall area or "Promenade" filled with shops selling jewelry, watches, blouses, jackets and liquor. It is on Deck 3.

I'm not much of a shopper, but wander the promenade to see if there's anything I might like to buy. I'm intrigued that there are no magazines for sale. There are very few books ... a couple on the Panama Canal. Since I've already read two books about the Canal, I think I know enough to feel at home as we go through.

I look for "thank you" notes or some kind of stationary I can use for them. Nothing. Nuts. I've been wanting to write brief thank-yous to several staff and crew members who have gone out of their way to make our time onboard exceptionally wonderful. But there are no such notes available.

I also look for blank-paged journals or notebooks, but there's no writing or reading material to speak of. Oh well, most people don't go through life with a notebook and pen in hand like I do.

If you like to shop, you'll no doubt find things onboard to buy. On the evening of your last day aboard, you'll receive a final bill for all the "extras" you've bought with your room key, including clothing and jewelry from the ship shops, alcohol, designer coffees and shore excursions.

Back on the observation deck, I notice the wind really whipping up the sea. Dark and heavy waves heave themselves into white-capped hills that rise, then sink and rise again.

Even this agitated, liquid world fills me with calm. It's lovely just sitting here watching the ocean and the wild wind.

What a gift – to spend an hour (or more) just staring at the ocean, or just reading, or just thinking or just daydreaming.

Having a lot of unstructured time makes me feel like a kid again.

Of course, if you grew up in a family where days and weeks were crammed with sports and club appointments, some event happening every hour or so, you can duplicate that kind of life again on board, too. It's all up to you.

Each evening, our *Explorer* newsletter describes the next day's events: classes, contests, movies, demonstrations, lectures and so on. Way too many opportunities for a mere 24-hours.

AL'S ANTICIPATION OF THE PANAMA CANAL
With only four more days before we reach the goal of this cruise – our passage through the Panama Canal - my thoughts turn to what lies ahead.

I've wondered about the Panama Canal since I was a child. What's it like? Back then, I had a vague notion of some sort of ditch in which ships floated between the Pacific and Atlantic oceans. It really didn't sound like that big a deal.

My curiosity had been piqued, however, by my father's sea stories. A steamship captain for American President Lines, he'd been on the trans-Pacific run until World War II intervened, leaving him marooned on the beach, doing paperwork in Panama City. He told tales of tropical forests, of monsoon rains, and, most of all, of the perfidy of certain locals. It sounded pretty exotic to me.

Vietnam taught me about tropical forests, monsoon rains and, yes, locals of doubtful character. Exotic, sure, but I'll take California, thank you. The Canal slipped to the bottom of my wish list, there to remain for a half-century, quietly simmering away like a crock-pot bouillabaisse.

When the opportunity to actually go to the Canal presented itself, I had no idea what I would find. Sunny and I plowed into books, discovering the history of the place and the incredible work it took to build the Canal.

Best of all, we discovered, yes, perfidy, my favorite word, in the story of the way the country of Panama was pried away from Colombia. American "gunboat diplomacy" at its finest indeed.

The very notion that something as huge as the Zuiderdam (82,000 tons, housing 1,936 guests and a crew of 823) would not only fit in the Canal's locks, but that it could and would be lifted and lowered as smoothly as a rubber ducky in a bathtub was outside my ability to imagine.

I checked the dimensions. The ship is 916 feet long; the lock, 1,000. OK. She is 106-feet wide; the lock 110. Tight, but OK. How will they keep her centered in the lock, at the same time that zillions of gallons of water are being poured in? How long will it take for the water to fill the lock and lift the ship? I have far more questions than answers.

All this is too much for a brain on vacation. It's time to head for the dessert cabinet on the Lido Deck. A dulce (or two) will calm my fevered brow. The answers will come when we reach the Canal; for now, I need sweet refreshment.

DAY 10
Thursday, October 11

AT SEA

Among the ship's considerable art collection is
this painting of a Venetian fishing village.

After Al's Mass, my morning exercises, and breakfast, we sit on the Lido Deck, right beside the pool, reading our *New York Times* and staring out at the placid, gray ocean. In the background, couples are playing ping-pong. The plunk-plunk-plunk of the white ping-pong ball forms a kind of background rhythm to my thoughts. And every so often someone jumps into the pool with a huge splash. Plunk, plunk, splash!

"How would you describe cruising? What would you say it's like?" I ask Al.

He cocks his head, thinks a moment, then says, "Cruising is like being in a good hotel with great food but very small rooms."

I laugh. "I'd say that cruising is like being at home and traveling both at the same time."

Al smiles, then says, "Cruising is like waking up in your own bed and not knowing what country you're in."

I say, "Cruising is like being at Grandma's – all the cookies and cake and pie you want – served with love. And you don't have to make your bed or hang up your towel after you shower."

He asks, "Are you saying that cruising spoils us rotten?"

"I'm just saying ..."

We return to the *New York Times*, while ping-pong balls plunk in the background.

This morning the sea is calm. Large, white clouds fluff themselves up above the blue water, and above the clouds stretches bright blue sky.

At 10 a.m. Al attends a morning "conversation/ interview" with the captain. I head to Deck 3 for a guided meditation in the Hudson Room, where Catholic and Protestant services are held each day (not at the same time, but in the same room).

As I enter, I notice a half-dozen others, most of whom I recognize. It's nice to recognize fellow cruisers.

"Lifestyle Nick" arrives just a couple minutes before 10 a.m. He's in his all-black outfit, carrying a water bottle. A handsome young man with a full head of red hair, Nick's face always looks serene.

More people arrive. When the guided meditation begins, there are about 20 people in the room.

The woman closest to me is an RN. She says she's loving the cruise, and I tell her I am too.

With a tranquil voice, Nick guides us from one closed-eye meditation to another. He instructs us to focus on our breathing. "Let noise and conversations just flow in and out of your mind," he says. We're to think about calming places and experiences. And always he brings us back to our breathing.

Although this is the first time I've ever done anything called "meditation," I realize that I like this stillness. It suits me.

When the session ends, I wander around a little and discover (to my delight) six small view boxes by Volker Kühn (Germany, 2001) on the wall just outside the Screening Room.

These enchanting, whimsical works of art are about seven inches high and five inches wide. Maybe even smaller.

One has a winged violin rising from a broken eggshell, with musical notes and bars inside the shell. It's entitled *Music in the Air*.

One shows laborers cutting or clearing away a thick gray rock mountain, revealing a golden mountain underneath. I can't find the title to that one.

The third is called *Off We Go* and has a man in a business suit riding a champagne bottle cork as it shoots through a wall.

On the other side of the hall, just outside the Hudson Room are the other three.

One is named *Way to the Stars* and shows a female tightrope walker with an umbrella, making her way up a long, steep rope to a diamond far above in the blue sky.

Another, *The Dealer*, shows a tuxedoed gallery owner with six monochromatic paintings hanging on the wall behind him. He's holding a sign that says: "Art is work. To sell it is art."

Heavenly Joy shows painters on a scaffolding, painting the sky blue (and leaving white fluffy clouds. The whole box is white (even the scaffolding is white) but the painter's brush is spreading blue all across the sky.

Every time I discover some new artful treat on board, I take my camera and notepad in search of more. And the paintings, sculptures, blown glass, photographs and other artworks seem endless on the *Zuiderdam*. No matter how many I find and make note of, there's always more to stumble upon with pleasure. I love it!

At 11:30 a.m. we attend the Mariner Society champagne luncheon in the lower Vista Dining

Room. Our table is shared by two other couples and a single lady. The couples – one from Canada and the other from Southern California – are both involved in helping to feed the hungry.

Since Al volunteers at the local food pantry back home, he and the others have a lot in common to share. Everyone seems interested in exchanging facts, statistics and methods of meeting the ever-increasing food needs of families and individuals.

On this cruise, however, hunger does not exist. For lunch I have quiche and Al has short ribs. Dessert is a custard tart and petit fours, with coffee.

At 3 p.m. we go to a lecture on Cortez and his conquest of Mexico's native peoples.

The afternoon and evening rush by, and after dinner, the 8 p.m. show is a "Tribute to the Temptations." We love the music and the high-energy performance, but know that we'll have a hard time getting to sleep early tonight.

AL'S TAKE ON SACHER TORTE

This evening the Vista Dining Room's dessert menu offered a seldom-seen choice: Sacher torte (or

Sachertorte for historical purists). Never heard of it? Well, read on.

It all began in 1832, when Austrian Prince Wenzel von Metternich asked for the creation of a special dessert. The task fell to 16-year-old Franz Sacher, then an apprentice baker, who was equal to the challenge.

Fifty years later, Sacher's torte – cake – had become a Viennese institution. Squabbles arose over the rights to the name "Original Sacher Torte," which wasn't settled (out of court) until 1963. Under the terms of the agreement, "original" tortes were to bear a triangle-shaped seal that reads "Eduard-Sacher-Torte." Everything else is an imposter: the Austrian equivalent of a Hostess Ding-Dong. The entire story is fascinating. And you thought this was just a pedestrian dessert, eh?

The Zuiderdam's Sacher torte is superb (for an imposter, of course). Like the Original, the ship's version consists of two delicious round sponge cakes three inches in diameter (or 7.6 cm for the metric minded).

Again, in accord with the original, a single layer of apricot compote separates the two cakes (please: not apricot jam).

Lastly, the entire concoction is dipped in dark chocolate, which, legend has it, is the secret to a truly great

Sacher torte. I would agree, although the Zuiderdam's chef used only one kind of chocolate. The Austrians use three.

And so: if your waiter brings you something that looks vaguely like a Ding-Dong, do not push it aside. You may have been served a delicious dessert with an equally delicious history.

DAY 11
Friday, October 12

PORT OF CALL: PUNTARENAS, COSTA RICA

**A coffee bean drying slab at the Doka Estate
and Coffee Plantation in Costa Rica.**

The phone rings at 6:45 a.m., our requested wakeup call. We have breakfast at the Lido: oatmeal, fruit and coffee.

By 8 a.m. we've boarded the tour bus for our shore excursion.

This is one of the many things that make cruising appealing to me. I don't have to go in search of a tour, don't have to try to figure out directions or flag down a taxi. The bus is sitting on the pier right beside our ship. We walk off the ship and board the bus.

The seats are comfortable, the windows large. And our tour guide speaks excellent English and has a sense of humor, to boot.

Tour guide Ken explains that his parents had no idea he would be a tour guide when they named him. Ken says that if they'd known, they would have chosen a more appropriate name like Carlos, Miguel or Diego.

As we travel along the Pan American Highway, Ken describes the plant life, government, education system and other interesting aspects of this Central American country.

Today, 27 percent of Costa Rica is designated as national park, biological reserve, wildlife refuge or some other category of protected area, both private and public. This is more than a quarter of the country set aside to protect it for future generations. No other country in the world even comes close to such a statistic.

If that weren't enough, Ken tells us that the nation disbanded its military in 1949 and has since then invested heavily in public education, including university systems as well as technical and vocational training.

Education in Costa Rica is both free and obligatory. As a result, the population of 4.4 million can boast a literacy rate of 96 percent.

As Ken teaches us about the nation he clearly loves, our bus travels through stunning countryside, and neighborhoods filled with modest single-story homes.

THE CHURCH AT PALMARES

Our first stop is in the city of Palmares, where we visit what appears to be the most imposing building in town – the large, gray stone church of the central plaza. Built in 1894 with grout made partially from eggshells, it resembles a European cathedral in size and scope.

The stained glass windows, the statues, the entire atmosphere is one of reverence. Al has a wonderful time photographing the place.

THE DOKA ESTATE AND COFFEE PLANTATION

From the church, our bus drives through fields of sugar cane, then climbs into the mountains, heading to the Doka Estate and Coffee Plantation, Costa Rica's largest coffee producer.

On the way, Ken describes how Costa Rica got its name. He says that when Columbus reported the presence of vast quantities of gold jewelry among the natives, everyone thought the area was rich with gold. "But we're actually a poor nation," Ken says, "which works to our advantage because no one wants to invade us."

He says that coffee was Costa Rica's first major export, and that coffee has been the principal form of wealth in the country well into the 20th century.

When our bus arrives at the Doka Estate, we enjoy a buffet lunch of traditional fare: rice, beans, chicken, squash and plantains. The food is delicious. We sit at large round tables, drinking lemonade and/or coffee. A roof overhead protects us from the sun (or rain), but the open walls enable us to look out over the coffee bushes and enjoy the fragrant fresh air.

Between lunch and the coffee tour, Al discovers an amazing butterfly garden, and leads me to it. The garden is totally enclosed in fine mesh, and filled with beautiful and large butterflies flitting about. We learn later that there are 15 vibrant species in the garden, including Blue Morphos and Owl Butterflies.

They are huge and exquisite. Morpho wingspans can range from five to eight inches. The underside of their wings is dusty brown, with eye spots for camouflage. But the top of their wings – a brilliant, iridescent blue – is both magical and mesmerizing.

Al and I try to capture the insects' beauty, but the butterflies just will not hold still for the camera. They fly about more like bats than butterflies – climbing and dipping and coming right up to us and then flying away. It's almost as if they delight in teasing us. I keep hoping one will land on Al so I can get a good shot, but it doesn't happen.

Just before leaving the garden, however, one large butterfly lands briefly on my shoulder, and I feel blessed by its beauty and the intimate moment we share.

WE LEARN WHERE OUR MORNING COFFEE COMES FROM

Ken starts our coffee tour at the seed bed, where small coffee plants are sprouted. From the seed bed area, we walk to the full-grown plants to see the clusters of green cherries growing along plant branches. Coffee beans are really seeds, called cherries, from the coffee fruit.

When the cherries are ripe (when they've changed from green to a deep red), they are picked by hand. Ken tells us that a good picker can fill eight 20-pound baskets with fruit in a day.

From the coffee plants we walk to the historic water mill, processing plant and roasting areas. Al has a blast with all the historic equipment that's still in use. His camera clicks continually.

Once the cherry clusters are picked, they are rinsed and soaked in huge vats of water. From the water vats, they go to the peeling machines. After peeling, the seeds look like beans – coffee beans.

The peeled beans ferment in water for about 34 hours. Then they are spread on a huge cement slab in shallow rows, to dry in the sun. A worker rotates the beans every 15 minutes, using a rake-like tool.

If it's raining, the seeds can be dried in a centrifugal drier, but we are told that the sun-dried beans are the best.

Once dried, the beans are put into a pressurized air chamber where "the first skin" of the bean is removed. The beans are then packaged and shipped to customers all over the world, to be roasted, repackaged and sold again.

Of course, Doka roasts some of its coffee to sell to tourists like us. And by the time we complete the tour, we are eager to buy a couple of pounds to take back home.

Ken says that 65 percent of Doka Plantation production is sold to Starbucks, an interesting info-tidbit.

I doubt I'll ever look at a cup of coffee the same way, now that I know all the work that goes into producing the beans.

LA GARITA BOTANICAL GARDEN

Our last stop on the tour is the La Garita Botanical Garden, a beautifully landscaped series of gardens that took more than 35 years to develop. Formerly a coffee plantation, the lush area now contains walking trails through a variety of ornamental and tropical plants, including gingers, palms and heliconias, in addition to dozens of species of orchids. The paths wind through a bamboo forest, past a serene pond and through bushes laden with orchids – bright pink, deep purple, snow white and warm peach.

The garden contains about 75 native orchid species and another 75 exotics.

Did you know that vanilla comes from a Mexican orchid? We learn this during Ken's lecture as we walk the garden trails.

This striking place also houses rescued birds – parrots and macaws, among others. They call loudly as we approach.

Although most of the paths and trails are easily navigated, there are some steep stone steps that cause difficulty for elderly people with walkers.

La Garita is famous for its plant nurseries. Here you can view orchids in all stages of development, from fresh seedlings through full-grown plants.

There is a small and airy café where we buy ice cream. The café also sells sandwiches and salads.

And (of course) a souvenir store. But this store has, in addition to typical souvenirs, fragrant orchids in lovely pots, just waiting to be taken home and planted.

After exploring the gardens in all their serenity, we climb aboard the bus, ready for the long, relaxing ride back to the ship.

DAY 12
Saturday, October 13

AT SEA

Our dinner at Canaletto began with this flavorful appetizer.

We wake up thinking that tomorrow is the Big Deal reason for this cruise. Tomorrow we get to sail through the Panama Canal!

Throughout our cruise, whenever I've had a chance, I've asked other women why they chose a cruise that goes through the Canal and without exception, they each have pointed to their husband and said, "He's a retired engineer and has always dreamed of going through the Canal."

What's so funny is that Sweetheart Al is a retired engineer (among other things), and he's always dreamed of going through the Canal, too. So we're a boatful of couples, heading toward one of the engineering wonders of the world. And tomorrow's the day we've been waiting for since we climbed aboard.

This morning we'll go to a lecture about the Canal by former *National Geographic* writer and editor Sabin Robbins.

And later, in the afternoon, we'll go to another lecture, which will tell us what to expect tomorrow as the *Zuiderdam* actually makes its way through the Canal.

Breakfast at 7 a.m. in the Lido. Oatmeal and coffee for Al, Mueslix and coffee for me. I've fallen in love with Mueslix (a mixture of rolled oats, raw almonds, sunflower seeds, dried cranberries and apricots). I add bananas and milk ... and just love this perfect and satisfying breakfast meal. I think I might even make my own after we get back home to California.

A vase of fresh purple and white orchids adorns our window table (and all the other tables in the Lido). We learned yesterday that orchids are the national flower of Costa Rica (and the clay robin is the national bird – a robin with no red feathers at all).

This morning's Lido is packed with lively, garrulous people sharing breakfast and happy conversation. The place vibrates with enthusiastic energy. Former strangers chit-chatting over bowls of fruit and platters of eggs and ham.

As quickly as uniformed staff clear away used dishes and wipe tables clean, new people with breakfast bowls and platters take them.

A man wearing a pink baseball cap and green tee-shirt proclaiming "Party Animal" brings a cup of coffee to a woman wearing a hairnet and a zebra print XL blouse.

Most hair here is white or gray or dyed. The women dress more colorfully than the men, in reds, oranges, blues and purples, prints and silks. But the men look comfortably pleased with their beige and chocolate or checkered shirts and Docker slacks or shorts.

The staff, in black slacks and orange jacket uniforms, pushes coffee refill carts through the Lido.

A tall guy with a white goatee carries a white platter bearing two waffles heaped high with strawberries and topped with a generous crest of whipped cream. Now, there's a breakfast dessert if I've ever seen one.

Smiles and laughter fill the Lido from one end to the other. There is so much positive energy here it's almost contagious. What a great way to start the day.

After breakfast, Al goes off to Mass. I go off to exercise.

We meet at the Vista Lounge about 9:45 a.m. The theater is packed, everyone eager to hear the lecture "The Panama Canal, Eighth Wonder of the World."

After reading two books and numerous online articles, I feel that Al and I probably know as much about the building of the Canal as the lecturer.

I know that the French tried to construct the Canal between 1881 and 1889, but failed. Among the many reasons they failed:

- Disease: yellow fever and malaria, among others
- Weather: the suffocating heat and torrential rains, often filling the trenches with chest-deep mud
- The Chagres River, which crossed the Canal's route, flooded during the rainy season, sometimes rising as much as 25 feet in a day, destroying much of the digging work
- Cost: Despite the many investors, the project ran out of money.

The Americans built on the French construction work, spending 10 long years and thousands of laborer-lives creating what President Teddy Roosevelt envisioned as a great opportunity for America. He felt the Canal would give the U.S. command of the seas, and pressed forward with plans to build it.

Taking advantage of the work the French had done, the U.S. completed the Canal by 1914. The first ship – a cement carrier, the *S.S. Ancon* – made the official inaugural passage on August 15, 1914.

That historic passage was not front-page news, however, because World War I had just exploded across the world stage. Stories of the War took up all of page one. The Canal opening was mentioned farther back in most papers.

From the books we read and the maps we consulted, I know that our ship will approach the Canal through the Bay of Panama. We'll go through two locks (the Miraflores Locks) and emerge into Miraflores Lake. Then we'll go through the Pedro Miguel lock.

After that, we'll sail through the Culebra Cut (now called the Gaillard Cut). This nine-mile Cut, dug through the mountains of the Continental Divide, was by far the most difficult part of the Canal to build. I wonder what sailing through it will be like.

We'll emerge from the Cut into Gatun Lake. This is the 24-mile-long lake that was created by damming the Chagres River.

After sailing through the Lake, we'll take our place in line for the Gatun Locks (three of them). They will lower the *Zuiderdam* down to the level of the Atlantic Ocean. And we'll sail out into Limon Bay.

The transit will take most of the day.

Turns out that Sabin Robbins is an excellent lecturer. We're enthralled with his presentation.

He points out that during the construction of the Canal, yearly rainfall in the area averaged 17 feet.

"The place had killer mosquitoes so thick that they blotted out the lights at night," he says. "And everything, absolutely everything, had to be brought in for building the Canal. Once it got there, everything rusted and rotted."

The Calebra Cut was a hellhole of heat and racket. He says, "For seven years the Calebra Cut was never silent."

And tomorrow we'll be going right through it. I can hardly wait.

After the morning lecture, and lattes and open-faced salmon sandwiches in the Explorations Café, we wander out to the windy observation deck.

Finding chairs where we can sit under gray skies, we watch the choppy sea and ponder the pleasures of this cruise.

It is so luxurious to have nothing but time – time to read a whole book. Time to stare at a whole churning ocean. Time to take a class or wander the decks in search of art. Time to sit with a cup of coffee until it cools.

At the afternoon lecture we learn that we're scheduled to enter the Canal around 7 a.m. tomorrow and will leave the Gatun Locks and head for Cartagena, Colombia, around 3:10 p.m.

The ship's crew will open the bow on Deck 4 beginning at 5:30 a.m. so that those who want an up-close and personal experience of passage through the locks can have one. We decide to take advantage of the opportunity, and phone the front desk for a wakeup call at 5.

DINNER AT THE CANALETTO

To celebrate tomorrow's Big Day we go to dinner at the Canaletto. Reservations are required at this Italian-themed restaurant, but when we arrive at 5:30 p.m., there is only one other party in the room.

Actually, this specialty restaurant is a walled-off portion of the Lido. However, its design, the linen tablecloths, the maître d', the waiters dressed in black-and-white striped shirts like Venetian gondoliers ... everything contributes to a quiet, casual, almost playful change-of-pace. It seems worlds apart from the busy, bustling Lido.

Our ocean-view table beside the floor-to-ceiling windows comes with personal attention and, for the most part, delicious food.

There's a nice selection of antipasto, including calamari, mozzarella, mushrooms, eggplant, asparagus and tomatoes, along with garlic bread.

Appetizers include soups and salads. The minestrone soup is much too salty for my taste.

Our main course choices included seafood linguini, veal Milanese, lasagna, chicken Marsala scaloppini and spaghetti with meatballs.

I choose the spaghetti. It's excellent.

Al has seafood linguini and says it is outstanding.

Even as the restaurant fills with couples and families, the atmosphere remains pleasantly quiet, calm and gentle. Electric candles flicker at all the tables, adding a tenderly romantic touch.

For dessert I have three variations on tiramisu. Al has gelato. The waiter brings us a large fluffy ball of cotton candy. How's that for playfulness?

We finish our meal in time to get a good seat in the Vista Lounge for Shirley Dominguez and her electric harp. Electric would be the word for her performance.

The magma-red harp and her matching gown light up the stage. She gives us an evening of lively Latin music that keeps toes tapping and hands clapping. It is truly amazing what she can do with that harp! Totally changes our assumptions about harp music forever.

DAY 13
Sunday, October 14

TRANSITING THE PANAMA CANAL

Heading into the first of the Miraflores Locks.

AL DESCRIBES HIS BUCKET-LIST ADVENTURE

We *are jarred awake by the buzzy ring of our cabin's telephone, which Sunny snags quickly. Five a.m. and time to get going! We are finally at the Canal!!*

A quick brush of the teeth, throwing on of clothes and we dash for Deck 4, where the door to the bow of the ship is scheduled to be opened (bow access is normally reserved for the crew). There we will find an unobstructed view of our passage through the Canal.

What we actually find is a long line of fellow passengers already waiting at the door: many others had the same idea we did. (Obviously, they ordered earlier wakeup calls!)

When the crew opens the door, everyone scurries out into the bow's predawn light, each claiming a bit of the ship's rail. All spots immediately fill: ship's security is kept busy keeping the adventurous from unsafe viewing spots. There are other places to watch the transit, of course, but only on the bow is the view an unobstructed 360 degrees.

Though the sun isn't yet up, the sky behind us is pink-peach and the water gray-blue. Dozens of ships ride at anchor nearby, each awaiting her turn to either go through the Canal or unload at the container port on the Pacific side. The smell of anticipation mingles with a hint of wet jungle. This is what we've come to see!! Bring on the exotic!

In short order, a small boat powers alongside and our pilot boards. Neither vessel slows for the exchange.

Each ship making the transit is assigned a pilot whose job it is to safely guide the vessel from Pacific to Atlantic (or vice-versa). It doesn't matter how many times our captain has gone through the Canal: the pilot is in charge. One can only assume the captain's job is to look nautical and serve coffee. "Cream or sugar, sir?"

"Entering" the Panama Canal actually takes place several miles from shore. A major (and ongoing) dredging operation keeps the shipping channel deep enough. We don't see any sign of dredging or dredging vessels, though we would, later, in the Canal itself. Silt, the result of heavy tropical rains, steadily accumulates and must constantly be removed. I am reminded of my email spam folder.

As we churn toward the coast and the entrance to the Canal, Panama City appears on our right. It's a huge, skyscraper-capped metropolis that seems completely out of place. We'd read several books in preparation for this voyage, and expected something more ... simple, perhaps primitive. Two-story white pine buildings, facing onto mud streets. Pith-helmeted engineers in puttees. A jungle canopy, something like the one I'd seen in 'Nam. Nope. Civilization has happened, on a very large scale. Another myth bites the dust.

Looking ahead of the Zuiderdam, the huge arch of the Bridge of the Americas emerges from the morning haze. This bridge carries the Transamerica Highway over the Canal. Passing under it was and is symbolic, in a way: reminiscent of our passage under the Golden Gate Bridge, leaving San Francisco. This seems to be the true task of bridges: to indelibly mark the boundary between "A" and "B." Such is the Bridge of the Americas. Once passed, we've truly entered the Canal.

We later learned that the Zuiderdam's passage under the Bridge of the Americas had to be timed for low tide. Even then, the clearance between the top of the ship's (smoke)stack and the understructure of the bridge was reportedly only five feet.

If Panama City was an unexpected surprise, the huge cargo terminal that appears on the far side of the Americas Bridge is even more unexpected. Instead of the tropical forest we'd anticipated, a forest of steel cranes bobs up and down, hard at work plucking cargo containers from stacks piled high on freighters from around the world.

Once plucked, those containers are sent by rail across the isthmus to another container port in the Atlantic side (or the other way). It's cheaper to send freight across the *isthmus on the railroad than sending ships through the Canal. Panama has clearly come a long way from the one-track choo-choo that trudged its way through the swamp (not always successfully) at the turn of the 20th century. (See "another myth bites the dust," above.)*

Just beyond the cargo terminal, we notice what appears to be a log, or perhaps a small telephone pole, floating by on the starboard side. No, wait, it's moving!! Look, Ma!! It's ... m'god ... a Panamanian alligator! Exotic at last!! Blissfully ignoring our cruise liner, off it swims toward the Pacific, completely unimpressed by 82,000 tons of steel steaming past. A new definition of "nonchalant" for the dictionary.

As the sun rises, Zuiderdam's staff sets up a table with coffee and Panama Buns. This creates a problem for singles-at-the-rail. Leave (and lose) one's choice viewing spot for a cup of desperately needed coffee? Or stay and tough it out? Couples, of course, don't have the problem. I hold the rail. Sunny dashes for coffee. No sooner has she left than someone asks, "Would you mind if I stepped in your wife's spot to take one picture?" This is called the camel's-nose-in-the-tent ploy. By the time wife and refreshments return, our rail space had been halved. We stay put from then on.

Our ship approaches the first of the locks through which we'll pass, a double set called the Miraflores Locks. There are actually four locks: two sets of two, side by side, allowing two ships to pass through at the same time. Each of the two locks lifts (or lowers) the ship in it about 28 feet, so the total lift of the Miraflores set is about 56 feet.

These are just numbers, but look at it this way: in a matter of a few minutes, our 82,000 ton (ton, not pound) ship, more than 900 feet long, will be gently lifted the height of a three-story building. As Popeye would probably say, that takes a lot of spinach.

But first we have to get into the lock. From our vantage point on the bow, it doesn't appear the Z will fit. She appears a tad too "full-figured." We knew, from the books we'd read, that the lock is 110 feet wide. Our ship is 106 feet wide, so the numbers look good, but from our vantage point of view it still looks like five pounds of tomatoes in a four-pound sack.

The key, of course, as every parallel-parker understands, is keeping the vessel centered in the lock. We know that little electric locomotives, called "mules," positioned on each side of the lock, somehow provide that centering, but we have no idea how they do it.

And then—here we have the height of incongruity—we see a little rowboat, a dinghy, to be proper, with two men aboard. One rows and the other holds the end of a rope, whose other end is tied to the quay. A hawser, in nautical-speak. These gentlemen row from the quay to the ship, pass the end of the rope to someone aboard, and row (quickly) out of the way. The little rope becomes a bigger rope, which quickly becomes a skein of steel cables linking ship to mules on each side, and – voila – there we are, held as snugly in the middle of the lock's bay as a baby in Mama's arms.

What makes all this especially challenging is that it is all happening as the Z steams under power into the first lock (you will understand why the folks in the dinghy got out of the way quickly). We don't stop outside the lock and let the mules pull us in. Nope. As Admiral Farragut is reputed to have said, "Damn the torpedoes, full speed ahead!" Or in our case, "Watch out for the dinghy, but keep going."

Here I had a small memory of my father, who was a captain with American President Lines back before I was born. I once asked him "How do you stop a ship?" He went into an elaborate explanation that I immediately lost, but it had something to do with reversing the engines at the right time. I did get the idea that the "right time" was the key. Too late and you'd ram the dock; too early and you'd drift alongside. Either would qualify you for your next career as a used-car salesman. The job has to be done perfectly.

And so the Zuiderdam. Gently in, gently stop. Perfectly. It is clear that the man on the bridge has done it before.

While we're entering the first Miraflores lock, we watch the Splendid Ace pull into the lock alongside ours, a few minutes ahead of the Zuiderdam. The Ace, a car carrier probably full of Kias or Toyotas, resembles nothing as much as an eight-story office building on its side. How on earth could something that utterly huge fit the lock? She is wider and longer than the Z, but slides into the lock like it has been greased, rises, slides out, steams into the second lock, repeats the process, and steams out into Miraflores Lake. Even Slick Willie would be impressed.

Let's pause a moment to consider the word "steamed." Your only experience with this word might have been in connection with foods like "steamed clams" or broccoli.

However, steam power was the first means of propulsion for ships after the days of sail. Early ship's steam engines were exactly like those used on railroad locomotives. A boiler, wood- or coal-fired, made steam, which drove pistons, which spun the propeller, and away she went: steamed away.

The term has stuck, even though steam-powered ships have been replaced with newer technology. The Zuiderdam, typical of her generation, has gas turbine engines and electric drive. "Prius of the Sea," she might be called.

And so we shall continue with "steamed," though the only steaming done aboard is, yes, back to clams and broccoli. There is, after all, a certain romance to the phrase "steamed away." To say the ship "gas-turbined away" lacks that smell of salt air and adventure the old term carries.

Here we are, steaming (and smoothly stopping) into the first Miraflores lock. The massive lock doors before and behind the ship swing smoothly closed, and the lock bay, now a concrete-and-steel box, fills with water. With repeated clanging of signal bells, the four electric mules, wire-cabled to the four corners of the ship, adjust their support, keeping the ship centered as she gently rises. In minutes—five, perhaps; no one checks their watch—we've risen the requisite 28 feet.

As soon as the water stops filling the lock bay, the doors at the front of the first lock ponderously open. The water level in the second lock bay is already at the same level as the water in the first lock bay, so with many clangs from the mule's bells the Z slowly moves into the second lock bay. The doors between the lock bays, now at the rear of the ship, swing closed.

Approaching the second Miraflores Locks.
The Centennial Bridge lies ahead.

Just as before, water pours into the second bay filling it to the melodious clangs from the mule's bells, as these "muscular" little locomotives keep the ship centered. And then, there we are, up another 28 feet, smooth as silk.

The second bay's front doors open with a grace that belies their bulk, the mules disconnect their cables and off we steam into Miraflores Lake, 56 feet above sea level.

I am struck with the routineness (if I may) of that first double-lock transit. It was an orchestra in hydraulic technology, played in two parts, with the utter certainty and confidence that comes from years of practice – 98 years, in fact. Every player – dinghy rower, mule operator, lock door controller, ship's pilot – knew his part and played it flawlessly. But this was no string quartet: this was an orchestra of such magnitude that my mind – our minds – had difficulty taking it in. Poet Mary Oliver writes of her desire to be a "bridegroom to amazement," and so we were.

Miraflores Lake, where the Zuiderdam now sails, is a channel between the second and third (or first and second if you're coming from the Atlantic and heading into the Pacific) Miraflores Locks. At the Atlantic end of the Canal, all three locks (the Gatun Locks) are grouped together, one right after the other. The geography of the Pacific end, however, requires a small space between locks. Thus the Lake.

Once in Miraflores Lake, many on the bow dash off for food, coffee, a restroom or sunscreen.

We stay put.

The sun is now fully up and its heat is steadily building, along with the humidity. We have the uneasy feeling that a chicken slowly turning on a rotisserie must have. A brief shower spritzes us, but provides no relief from the heat: some flee for the air-conditioned Crow's Nest on Deck 10. Hardier folks, ourselves included, soldier on.

The third lock from the Pacific side of the Canal is called the Pedro Miguel lock. With a lift of 31 feet, it connects Miraflores Lake with the Culebra Cut, perhaps the best-known feature of the Canal.

Our transit through the Pedro Miguel is an exact duplicate of the two preceding lock transits. As Caesar would have said, "I came, I lifted, I departed" (or "Veni, allevavi, relinqui" for Latin buffs). Since we've seen how it is done from deck level, I dash back and down to Deck 2 and watch the electric mules at work, busily keeping the ship centered. The visual perspective is interestingly illusional: as the ship rises, it appears that the mules are sinking.

Exiting the Pedro Miguel lock, the Zuiderdam steams into the Culebra or (as it is now known) the

Gaillard Cut, the most difficult, time-consuming, and costly (in both lives and dollars) part of the Canal's construction.

The Cut goes through the mountain spine running north to south through the Americas: we call our portion of this spine the Rocky Mountains.

But before we enter the Cut, we pass beneath the Centennial Bridge, also known as the Freedom Bridge. This stunningly beautiful cable bridge spans more than 1,000 feet across the Canal. It was built in 2004 to relieve traffic crossing the Bridge of the Americas, traffic, which had more than tripled since the Canal's opening. Many, ourselves included, take the elevator up to Deck 10 and go out on the observation deck to observe the Centennial as we passed under it. Unlike the Bridge of the Americas, the Freedom Bridge has been built to clear today's bigger ships, so there is ample clearance for the Z to pass beneath.

By now we are thoroughly dehydrated, so we head to the Lido Deck, where we find an outside table, there to watch the Culebra Cut as we steam through. I make a lemonade run, bringing as many glasses back to our table as I can carry in one trip. Then, having had nothing to eat but Panama Buns on the bow at daybreak, we *fill our plates from the buffet and watch the mountains go by.*

This was something I'd – we'd – never expected, much less imagined: our 82,000-ton steamship is steaming through mountains. They aren't snow-capped peaks, but they are clearly mountains, rising on both sides of the ship. And we aren't in any sort of Scandinavian fjord: this is plainly a manmade channel, cut through solid rock.

The French, whose first attempt to build the Canal in the late 19th century envisioned a sea-level canal from the Atlantic to Pacific, failed in their effort, magnificently (Vive la France!!), for many reasons, perhaps foremost the impossibility of making a sea-level cut through Panama's spine.

When the U.S. picked up the task, we slowly realized that raising the Canal's route with locks at each end meant less spine-cutting. There was still, however, a staggering amount to cut. Worse, as the Cut got deeper, Panama's torrential rains caused mammoth landslides, which, in turn, meant further widening the Cut, which, in turn, meant more debris ("spoil") to cart off. It's a fascinating story, especially for anyone who goes through the Canal.

About halfway through the Cut, I recognize Gold Mountain. When the French attempted to build the Canal, a story was spun that a certain craggy spire in the middle of the Cut was solid gold. Investors lined up like sheep, eager to be fleeced – and were, in large numbers. There was, of course, no gold, but France was a long way from Panama in those days, and who wants to be the first to acknowledge that he was un idiot? You'll recognize Gold Mountain these days as a sort of Babylonian ziggurat, a neatly-terraced granite spike on the east side of the Cut (remember that the Canal runs north-south).

Leaving the eight-mile Cut, we steam into Gatun Lake, a mammoth manmade lake that spans the width of Panama, which was created by damming the Chagres River. Surrounding this lake is lush tropical jungle: palms, banana trees (with bananas!), exotic birds, and surely more Panamanian alligators (we look but are not able to see another).

Buoys mark the channel, which is clogged with ships going both directions. Our route zigs around hilltops, which we soon realize were once mountaintops before the dam was built and the area flooded. I can't help but think of the Canal's staggering ecological impact. This was all once virgin tropical rainforest.

About halfway across Gatun Lake, a passage that takes all afternoon, we pass the bridge over the Chagres River at the place it empties into the Lake. In its natural state, the Chagres was an uncontrolled river, rising or falling dozens of feet in a few hours, regularly washing out the trans-Canal railroad. Gatun Lake Dam now controls the level of Chagres River and thus Gatun Lake, adjusting the amount of water released to the Atlantic Ocean.

At long last, the low-lying Chagres River Dam appears on our left, an unimpressive gray line. This huge earthen dam was built from Culebra Cut debris. The dam includes two powerhouses that provide electricity for the Canal. Nearing the dam, the Zuiderdam swings to starboard (right, for you landlubbers) and approaches the first of the triple Gatun Locks, these also in side-by-side sets.

By this time all those aboard are experts in the mechanics of transiting a lock, but this is a new experience: we are going down. I would describe the experience as a watery staircase descent: enter lock, close door, drain, open door, go into next lock, close door, drain, open door, go into third lock, drain, open door and exit. We are there!! El océano Atlántico!!

As we steam out into the channel leading to deep water, a fireboat pulls alongside, spraying water from multiple nozzles in celebration of our transit. It is in every way both a grand goodbye to the Canal and a grand sendoff for the final leg of our voyage. We are dutifully impressed. Several thousand photos are taken.

A small boat pulls alongside and our pilot disembarks, without benefit of slowing down. Our captain resumes command and, in the tradition of the sea, rings the engine room bells for more speed. And away we go, a "bone in her teeth" (spray from the bow) as the old mariners would say. Or at least I so envision. In all probability, the watch officer probably turns command of the ship to the computer. I'll stick with the romantic version.

And thus the Panamanian jungle fades into the growing dusk. Ahead lies the gray-blue of the open sea.

Somewhere ahead of us is Colombia, but that is another day. Right now, everyone aboard the Zuiderdam is exhausted from the day's heat and activity. All stagger into either (a) a shower, (b) a bar or (c) the dining room. Or all three. We settle for shower and food.

I'd waited a lifetime to make a transit of the Panama Canal. Now that I've done it, what are my thoughts?

The one thing that comes to mind (and has remained) is how effortless the journey from Pacific to Atlantic was. Sunny and I had read stories of the earliest trans-Panama crossings on foot, horseback and, later, the frequently-washed-away train. If malaria didn't kill you, yellow fever probably would. Thousands upon thousands of workers, laboring in the mud and the hellish heat. The results? An absolute marvel of applied engineering. And there we were, a boatload of AARP tourists, sipping lemonade in the cool of the Lido, taking it all in.

SUNNY'S TAKE ON THE TRANSIT

We jump up as soon as we get our 5 a.m. wakeup call, dress and hurry down to Deck 4. Today is the only time that the ship's crew opens the doors to the bow so that passengers can go outside for a close look as we move through the Canal. Scores of people who got up even earlier than we did crowd the hall ahead of us.

At 6 a.m. sharp the doors open and out we rush to stake our places along the rail.

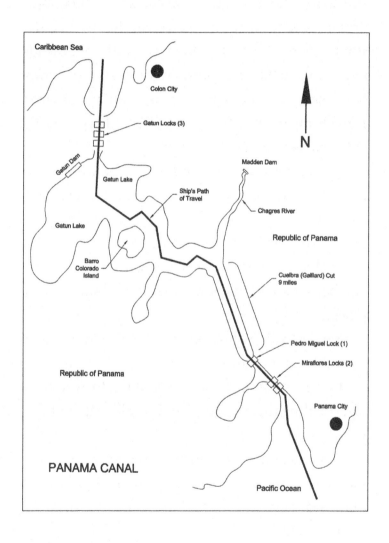

Caribbean Sea

Colon City

Gatun Locks (3)

N

Gatun Dam

Gatun Lake

Madden Dam

Ship's Path of Travel

Chagres River

Gatun Lake

Republic of Panama

Barro Colorado Island

Cuelbra (Gaillard) Cut 9 miles

Pedro Miguel Lock (1)

Miraflores Locks (2)

Republic of Panama

Panama City

PANAMA CANAL

Pacific Ocean

Sweetheart and I claim a very good spot on the starboard side. From here we can see – and photograph – every stage of our transit. Behind us, the sun turns the horizon golden. Great thunderheads rise, pink, white and lemony-yellow in the gray dawn sky. The sea behind us is calm as a mirror. It holds an array of freighters and tankers, waiting their turns to enter the Canal.

I'm surprised at how industrial the whole area is. All the old photos I'd seen made the Canal look like a watery path through the jungle, but here we are surrounded by cranes and cement and iron and cable. Metallic mules, men, rails and lights and bells. I could never have imagined such a busy place.

Yet, crowding close on either side is the jungle, a tumble of greenery.

I love standing at the rail, looking forward and aft, smelling the morning air. I just love it out here. It feels so free.

The big ship going through the lock next to us looks like a building. In fact, when Al pointed it out, I was certain it was a building, not a ship, but I was wrong.

I notice lots of white herons, obviously locals. Tall, graceful and totally unimpressed by these vessels, the slim, snow-white birds sit solemn and sophisticated atop the lock doors.

When we enter the first lock, the water pours in like a rushing waterfall. As our lock fills and we rise, I feel like we're all being carried on a magical, undulating carpet. The little railroad engines (silver mules) running on tracks on either side of the locks keep us centered by way of steel cables.

There is, however, one unpleasant reality of our rail position: the deck is filled with people who want to be right where we are. They push and shove, trying to squeeze in (and in the process, squeeze us out). They press against me, but I try not to budge. They step on my toes. Little by little, they finagle a way to shrink my space.

A stocky man with a big camera crowds in to get a shot, pushing me into Al, without so much as an "excuse me" or "sorry." What's worse, he does not leave the space once he's taken his picture. He now occupies half the space I used to have.

When I decide to get us coffee and a couple of Panama Buns, I give Al explicit instructions on how to save/maintain what little space we have left at the rail. "I'm not going to go get us breakfast if you don't promise to save this space," I say in my sweetest voice.

He sort of spreads out his arms and legs to hold our spot. I hurry over to the table where crew is serving up coffee and to-die-for Panama Buns.

Panama Buns are good-sized pastries – about two-by-four inches of flaky creampuff-type pastry – filled with a cream-and-orange custard that is so delicious I can't begin to describe it. I grab one each and carry them atop the two cups of coffee. Back at the rail, we sip and sigh. Although he assures me he preserved our space, it seems a lot smaller to me than when I left to get us coffee. It's not long before I have to try to save our space while Sweet-tooth Al heads to the table for more Panama Buns.

When it grows too hot for comfort, we relinquish our spot at the rail and go to the Lido for lunch.

As we sit munching our lunch, the ship slowly makes its way through the Cut. We're actually going through the mountains – the Continental Divide – on an ocean vessel. It's the weirdest sensation. Like living a fairytale.

Al and I talk about the fact that we've had nothing but perfect weather. When we prepared for this cruise, we read about the frequent and intense rainstorms that occur in Panama and throughout the equatorial region. But we've had only clear, sunny skies. How lucky is that?

The Canal view from the Crow's Nest,
high above the ship's bow.

From the Lido we go to the Crow's Nest on Deck 10 for a head-on (from the inside) view of our Canal transit. The place is packed – everyone chattering in their native tongues. I hear French, Japanese, Dutch, German and English, and other languages that I can't distinguish. Everyone's as excited as we are about going through the Canal.

People with cell phones, cameras, tablets and video cameras all take pictures as we sail along. And everyone's talking, sharing what they know about the Canal and the transit. It's so much fun! Like one big, happy party!

It seems as if we sail through Gatun Lake for hours, and as the ship approaches the Gatun Locks, rainclouds gather thick and threatening. Al and I go back down to Deck 4 and out onto the bow. There are far fewer people on deck now.

Suddenly there's a downpour.

I run inside, but Al stays.

It rains and rains and rains. We're so glad we packed our raingear. At least Al will get some use of it. Most of us passengers watch from inside, as our ship enters the locks that will lower us to Atlantic Ocean level.

The Canal view from the Seaview Pool at the ship's stern.

At the end of the day, as our ship heads toward Colombia, Al and I return to our cabin. It's been quite a day! We download pictures from our cameras and find that together we've taken 342 photographs of today's Canal transit.

DAY 14
Monday, October 15
PORT OF CALL: CARTAGENA, COLOMBIA

A typical street scene in Cartagena's Old Town. This walled colonial district is filled with Spanish colonial architecture.

We are officially in the Caribbean. Again, calm seas and clear, cloudless skies.

We were so tired after yesterday's excitement that we slept almost 12 hours. Breakfast in the Lido (omelet with peppers and smoked salmon) and the *New York Times*.

Al does his daily church service. He says his congregation numbers about 20.

At 9 a.m. we go to the Culinary Arts Center to learn how HAL chefs make cinnamon rolls. We watch the baker (who has been with Holland America for 15 years) illustrate the creation of these tasty morning staples. Al is amazed that the guy lets the dough rise three times. Giant Culinary Arts Center TV screens give us an intimate, close-up view of what the baker is doing while he's describing the process.

We, of course, do not have to wait through all this. The baker's got rolls in the oven, about to come out. When the cinnamon rolls are drawn hot and fragrant from the oven, our mouths begin to water in earnest. He lets the rolls cool a few minutes, and then frosts them. All of us in the audience line up for our sample of these delicious pastries. We also get the recipe for the rolls, the filling, and the cream-cheese frosting.

CARTAGENA

Today's port of call is the old walled seaport on Colombia's northwest coast.

Even though we had promised ourselves to spend no more money on shore excursions, we bought "A Stroll Through the Old Walled City," a two-and-a-half-hour walking tour. It costs 55 dollars each and starts at 12:45 p.m.

I had been tempted by "Medieval Cartagena by Horse Carriage," which costs about 15 dollars more apiece. I could picture a leisurely horse-drawn carriage, taking us to churches and restaurants and galleries, showing us parks and other picturesque places. But the description sounded like we weren't allowed to leave the carriage, and I like to walk around and explore. I want to go inside the churches or other buildings. We both like to photograph the places we visit and that would require free rein.

The tour coordinator for Holland America warns us against trying to do a self-guided walkabout. She says that the ship, which is docked in an industrial area to refuel and take on other supplies, is a long way from town, and the area between our

169

ship and Old Town is dangerous. So dangerous, in fact, that should we try to hire a taxi, we must remember to lock the doors and roll up the windows the minute we climb inside. The warnings convince us to buy the shore excursion tour. With the tour, we can step off the ship and onto a bus that will whisk us safely to Old Town and our walking-tour guide.

So we sign up and climb on the bus.

After our excellent Costa Rica tour, this tour is a disappointment. Despite the fact that Cartagena has a fascinating history preserved in ancient forts, churches and palaces, our tour guide is not as conversant in English as Ken had been, and seems to know very little about the places he is showing us.

In addition to his lack of knowledge, we are hounded by aggressive vendors from the moment the tour starts.

Skinny, unshaven men with dirty hands and dirty jeans try to sell jewelry, belts, leather purses, hats and other items. They come right up to us and grab our arms or our hands, insisting that we buy something.

Women in native dress with huge bowls of fresh fruit on their heads ask us to photograph them and pay for the pictures. The size of the bowls, and the mountain of fruit they contain, look as if the women are carrying 25 or 30 pounds on their heads. Actually, the women are beautiful and I do photograph one, paying her for the privilege.

But wherever we go with the tour guide, we are harassed. There are men trying to sell drawings, paintings, fans and many different kinds of lacy tablecloths.

So many vendors grab my elbow or arm that I become both paranoid and angry. Instead of my gentle "*Gracias, no,*" I glare angrily at them, shaking my head and saying repeatedly, "No! No!" And then feel like an Ugly American because my rudeness matches theirs.

Despite the annoying, clinging cloud of insistent vendors, both Al and I love the exquisite 16th- and 17th-century Spanish colonial architecture throughout the Old Town.

Bright sunshine-yellow buildings with white balconies, cheery orange buildings with lime

green trim and balconies, bright red-brick buildings with purple flowers tumbling over white
balcony railings – the narrow streets and bright
buildings vibrate with beauty.

One delightful surprise of Old Town is the
abundance of artistic sculptures. There are metal
people playing chess, listening to old fashioned
radios, playing musical instruments in a band. All
of the close-to-life-size sculptures add a sense of
playfulness to the plazas and street corners where
they are displayed.

One huge brass sculpture of a super-Ruben-
esque reclining nude attracts men like a cherry
pie attracts flies. Men want their picture taken
beside the voluptuous brass woman, her smiling
face turned heavenward. They want their picture
taken kissing her chubby cheek, or resting their
hand on her generous bosom or derriere.

The plaque for this oversized sculpture reads:
"Figura Reclinada 92" and describes that the
sculpture was donated by the artist, Fernando
Botero, to the city of Cartagena on April 14, 2000.

As our tour group wanders up one narrow, picturesque street after another, I find it intriguing

that the roadways are so empty. We seem to be the only people around. On this Monday afternoon, we see few, if any, locals shopping or eating in restaurants or sitting in the plazas enjoying coffee. But there are lots of tourists following their guides.

Our guide is most knowledgeable about a weird and spooky museum: Palacio de la Inquisición. This is one of the "must see" places in Old Town, according to tourist brochures and websites, but I could do without it. This beautiful historic building displays, among other things, many gruesome instruments of torture. Our guide describes in detail how each had been used to punish heretics and others who failed to "keep the faith."

In the lovely outside courtyard stands a gallows and a chopping block, reinforcing Cartagena's role in the Spanish Inquisition.

Not far from this museum is Plaza Bolivar. Filled with 100-year-old palms that provide both lush beauty and welcome shade, this park features a huge statue of South America's liberator, Simón Bolivar, astride his horse. It rises to the treetops, towering over the park plaza.

Today, dozens of little kids laugh and giggle as they feed pigeons at the foot of the statue. The birds strut, peck and flutter between the children and Bolivar's brass head. The children's happy laughter, the fluttering wings of the pigeons, the beauty of the day ... all remind me in some way of the magic of San Marco Square in Venice, Italy.

Close to the plaza stands a picturesque cathedral and a gold museum.

As we continue our stroll through the beautiful streets of Old Town, we see the people who signed up for a horse-and-buggy ride. Unlike my preconceived idea of a gentle, romantic ride, there are close to 30 horses-and-buggies in a train-like procession, trotting swiftly "bumper to bumper" through narrow streets. The poor horses, their ears laid back in anger or distress, rush along to the snap of whips. The people in the buggies look unhappy too.

"Aren't you glad we took the stroll instead of the buggy ride?" I ask Al. He nods.

Our tour includes a stop at a colorful shopping arcade. Forty-seven painted archways open into small and varied souvenir shops. Some are well-stocked with emeralds and gold, some with Botero knock-offs, hammocks, hats and other sundries.

We buy coffees and chocolates and other goodies for friends back home.

For shoppers, this arcade can offer fun browsing.

Back on the ship, we shower and dress for dinner. As I comb my hair, I notice my upper arm is covered with small bites that itch.

"Where do you suppose I got these bites?" I ask Al.

He takes a quick look and says, "You're sweet. Insects are always biting you."

It's true. We go outside in the evening and I come in with a bunch of mosquito bites, while Al has none. We go for a walk along the beach, and I end up with bites on my ankles or wrists.

And now my upper arm is covered with little swollen, itchy bites. I wonder if one of the vendors, with his dirty hands, has given me some dread disease.

I slip on a light jacket, and we are off to the dining room. Another wonderful meal with couples from Calgary, Canada and Sacramento, California.

During dinner, one of the men at our table (a retired contractor from Iowa) says this is his first cruise and two things have surprised and delighted him: the interesting people he meets at dinner and the evening shows.

I agree with his assessment. Completely.

After dinner, we enjoy a comic and juggler, Benji Hill, in the Vista Lounge. Benji proves to be a true showman. I can't believe how entertaining his (somewhat silly) act is. His jokes have me laughing until tears run down my cheeks.

When we finally get back to our room, we almost drop into bed we're so tired. Of course, we have to eat our chocolate first, and admire the towel animal our room attendant has created for us.

Then it's lights out.

DAY 15
Tuesday, October 16

HELP! BUGS IN OUR BED!

I see it moving slowly on my sheet – a little red-brown bug that resembles an apple seed. Al had gotten up before me, and had just come out of the bathroom, drying himself from his morning shower. I threw back the white sheets and sat up, intent on heading for the bathroom for my own shower, and there it was – a little, dark apple-seed-shaped bug on a broad white expanse of sheet.

"Al, we've got bedbugs!" I cry. "Look! Look!" I point at the tiny insect. Al comes over to inspect it. Afraid it will scurry off somewhere under the bedding and disappear, I say, "Quick, get a baggie so we can capture it!"

Al searches through his bedside stand and pulls out a baggie filled with small bottles of aspirin and other things. Deftly, he empties the baggie on his side of the bed. "What makes you think it's a bedbug?" he asks.

I have him hold the clear plastic baggie open while I slip a piece of paper under the bug, and then gently tap it so the bug falls into the baggie.

"I saw a documentary a few weeks ago on bedbugs, and the one thing I remember from it is that bedbugs look like apple seeds. And just look at that insect. What does it look like?"

He nods, saying, "Exactly like an apple seed." Then he grins, "But I can't imagine why anyone would want to watch a documentary on bedbugs."

Upset at the thought (and the reality) of having bugs in bed with me, I wave away his comment and phone the front desk. When the happy female voice answers, I ask, "Whom do I contact about bedbugs?"

"What makes you think you have bedbugs?" she asks politely.

"Because I just caught one and it looks like a bedbug. I have it here in a baggie."

"I'll send housekeeping right up," she says.

Quickly, I dress, comb my hair, brush my teeth and try to calm myself.

Soon the housekeeping supervisor and our room steward stand in our room, examining the little bug in the baggie. The supervisor, a middle-aged man of average build, peers into the baggie as he shines a flashlight on the little creature, turning the baggie this way and that. He does not look happy.

"Can you give us a few minutes?" he asks.

Al and I head off to the Lido for breakfast.

There, over oatmeal and coffee, we try to figure out how bedbugs could have gotten into our room. I think I got them from one of those aggressive salesmen yesterday. Al thinks they may have been brought in with a change of laundry. Who knows how they got there? I scratch at my upper arm, now a patch of red and itchy welts. I've also noticed itchy welts on both legs, too. What a mess!

After breakfast, Al goes to Mass and I go to the gym for a few minutes of exercise.

When we both return to the room, we find mammoth plastic bags stuffed with bedding and pillows in the hall outside our room. Obviously, our cabin is being stripped.

An attractive woman, probably in her late thirties, wearing a Holland America uniform, is talking with the housekeeping supervisor. When she sees us, she introduces herself as Joena Gonzales, supervisor of Guest Relations. She says that, unfortunately, we've got bedbugs and everything in our room has to be cleaned. The room itself has to have deep cleaning with heavy chemicals, making it unavailable.

She says the ship will provide us with another room. We need to move. We also learn that all our clothing needs to be cleaned.

Her manner is professional, but also caring.

Still, I'm extremely upset. I explain that we have an evening reservation for the specialty French restaurant, Le Cirque. She assures me that our evening attire will be delivered back to us in time to keep our dinner reservation.

As Al and I look at each other, trying to figure out how to get all our non-clothing stuff out, she asks, "Would you like to see the room you'll be moving to?"

We say "sure," and follow her to the other end of the ship. As we walk from our bedbug infested room, 5005, to our new room, 5175, I wonder if the little critters are hidden away in my hair, and determine to wash it a.s.a.p.

When we arrive at room 5175, she unlocks the door and motions us in. We enter a stateroom twice the size of ours, with a balcony. It is called a Deluxe Verandah. Quite a difference from our inside cabin!

We walk straight through the room and out onto the balcony. The warm Atlantic sun welcomes us.

"Is this acceptable?" she asks.

How could we turn down such a spacious and beautiful room and with a balcony, no less? The size and beauty of our new accommodations softens the bedbug shock and the trouble of moving.

When I show Ms. Gonzales the itchy welts on my arms, she urges me to go to the ship's infirmary for help. She says she'll call ahead and make sure that we are not charged for the care or the medicine.

During the next couple of hours, Al and I transfer our stuff – toiletries, medications, jewelry, books, notebooks, pencils and pens, cameras, laptop and anything else that can't be dry cleaned or laundered – to our new room.

How can a few original belongings, neatly packed into three medium-sized bags, expand to mountain-range size? I can't believe how many armfuls of stuff we haul from one room to another. Our old (bedbug infested) room is at the front of the ship and our new room, on the same deck, is all the way to the back end of the ship ... something like 800 feet away. But, back and forth we go.

There are problems with the new room key, but Ms. Gonzales quickly and courteously resolves them.

Before she leaves, I ask her how common bedbugs are on a cruise. She says that in her 16 years with Holland America, this is only the second time she knows of that guests have found bedbugs in their room.

Once all our stuff is in our new cabin, Al and I move out onto the balcony and watch the sparkling waves as our ship sails through the sunny Atlantic.

The phone rings. When I pick it up, I'm told that the housekeeping supervisor wants me to meet him at our old cabin to itemize all our clothing, shoes, etc. for cleaning. I walk back to our old room and, piece by piece, help him list every item of underwear, outerwear, evening dress, raingear, even our shoes and suitcases – all are to be cleaned.

When that task is finished, Al and I head to lunch.

Today, there's a special curry bar set up next to the Lido Pool. Since both of us really love curry dishes, we load our plates. I have dahl, rice, curried vegetables, tandoori chicken and curried lamb. And naan. For dessert: warm rice pudding.

As we sit savoring this special lunch, I think how nice it is that the ship's chefs continually prepare food that is both interesting and varied. While I have heard some of our friends complain that cruise food gets boring, there has been nothing boring about the food on this cruise. I've loved it all.

I'm also grateful for a delicious curry meal. It comforts me on this very upsetting day.

After finishing our flavorful lunch, we sit and people-watch for a while. Then I decide it's time to go to the infirmary and see if I can get relief for my itchy bites.

"Meet you back at our new room," I say and head down to the bowels of the ship.

The infirmary is not the easiest place to find. But I find it on Deck 0, where huge palettes of supplies sit, and where behind-the-scenes workmen labor. When I walk into the infirmary, no one is at the reception counter. I simply stand there and scan the empty waiting area, with chairs lined up neatly against two facing walls.

On one wall, above the chairs, hang watercolor prints of a Dutch fishing village (a windmill in the background). On the other wall, five colored etchings of Venetian scenes (could be pen-and-ink drawings, extremely fine, tinted with wash or watercolor). The pictures are just beautiful!

I find it amazing that even in this rather pedestrian area of the ship, hidden away from the daily hustle and bustle of the cruise, lovely art is on display. I'm so glad we chose the *Zuiderdam* for our cruise!

I'm suddenly aware of a lot of intense activity going on in a small room nearby. Someone is lying on a table (I can only see his feet), and several medical personnel are working on him.

A woman comes out from the room and says that everyone is very busy with an emergency. I tell her I can come back.

Just then the doctor comes out of the room and asks what I've come for.

"I have some insect bites. Bedbug bites," I say, feeling apologetic for taking their time. "I can come back when you're less busy."

He runs his hand through his hair and says, "We're going to be busy all day and into the night with this one."

I can sense his concern.

"I'll come back tomorrow."

"Thank you," he says.

Back in our new room, I wash my hair, and hope that no bedbugs have hitchhiked to our new location.

"You need to wash your hair too," I tell Al. "Just in case those little buggers are hiding among the shafts."

"I did it before you even got out of bed this morning," he laughs. "I'm way ahead of you."

We sit on the balcony, soaking in the day's warmth. I can't get over how tired I am. Moving all our stuff feels like the most exercise I've had all cruise long, despite my daily visit to the gym. Al closes the book he's been reading. He's now finished two books from the ship's library. Soon, I'll finish the book I've checked out.

When it approaches 4 p.m., I worry that our clothes have not yet returned from the cleaners. Our dinner reservation is for a little after 5 p.m.; I try not to stress. We continue enjoying our balcony, watching the sea rush by, quietly lost in thought.

Al writes an email to all our friends (no doubt telling them the bedbug story, and how it has netted us an outside room with a balcony).

After a while, he looks up and says, "We're really hauling the mail. I think this is the fastest the captain has had us going all cruise long."

Just then an announcement comes over the intercom. We walk inside to hear it better.

"This is your captain, Christopher Turner, and I just want to let you know that we have altered our course and are proceeding full speed to Kingston, Jamaica. We have a patient on board who requires urgent medical assistance. We are too far out for helicopter assistance. This may mean that we miss the Half Moon Cay stop scheduled for tomorrow, but I'm sure you understand. Thank you."

"So!" we both say in unison. Now I understand what was going on in the infirmary. Now Al knows why the ship is really "hauling the mail."

The captain's intercom message reminds me of an airplane emergency that happened many years ago on a flight from California to Chicago. As I approached the gate area, I noticed a heavyset older woman in a wheelchair, wheezing and coughing. She seemed quite ill. I wondered if she was flying somewhere or if she had just arrived and was waiting for someone to help her get to the baggage claim area.

Soon we boarded and I was in my aisle seat with my seatbelt fastened, ready to go. As usual, I had a good book with me and kept my nose in it as we took off and headed for Chicago.

I don't know how long it was after we took off, but suddenly I realized that the plane was in a nosedive. Anyway, that's what I would call it. We seemed to be on a roller coaster, heading down fast.

The pilot came on the intercom: "This is the captain. We have been granted permission to land at Salt Lake City. One of our passengers is having a medical emergency. I know this will be a great inconvenience to you, but I'm sure if you were having the medical emergency, you'd want us to land at the first possible place. We'll be in and out of Salt Lake as quickly as possible."

And down we went.

When we landed, a team of paramedics came on board with a narrow gurney. They moved up the aisle, loaded that same elderly woman I'd noticed at the gate onto the gurney and headed out the door.

It took only a few minutes to get her off the plane and into the waiting ambulance.

It took much longer for the plane to get back into the sky.

As I sit on our balcony in the warm Caribbean sun, remembering, I hope that today's medical emergency has a happy ending for all concerned.

At 4:55 p.m. our clothes arrive.

We hurriedly put them away, and pull out our evening garb. Within minutes we're all gussied up and ready to go to Le Cirque. It's then that we realize Al doesn't have his good shoes. He only has the athletic sneakers he's been wearing all day. Obviously, we forgot them and they're back in our old room (for which we no longer have a key). Or they're being cleaned along with our suitcases. Whatever the explanation, they're not here.

Nothing we can do about it now. We head for our second big night out, sneakers, bug bites and all.

LE CIRQUE

For one night on each cruise, the Pinnacle Grill is transformed into a kind of French "Le Cirque" (in partnership with the critically acclaimed NYC restaurant of the same name).

On this special night, menu offerings, wine selections, table decorations and the restaurant setting is tailored to create an authentic Le Cirque dining experience.

Even the china is different. In place of the Pinnacle Grill's blue-accented Bvlgari Rosenthal china, Le Cirque china is a lively orange and white, bearing impish monkeys, a hint of the restaurant's circus connection.

Like our Pinnacle Grille dinner, this special Le Cirque dinner comes compliments of Holland America.

Before our appetizer, we received a gift from the chef: a layered combination of foie gras and rhubarb chutney in a glass.

My palate is not sophisticated enough to appreciate this offering.

However, my appetizer is wonderful. I choose the Le Cirque Lobster Salad. It's a cold dish: poached lobster tail on a bed of bib lettuce, surrounded by crisp green beans, sections of grapefruit and pieces of avocado, tomato and potato.

Al's appetizer is "le trio" (caviar, smoked salmon and pâté). He says it is equally delicious.

We both order butternut squash soup with huckleberries, and are charmed at its presentation. It arrives in two segments. First, our waiter brings a bowl with huckleberries sitting in a circular dollop of green sage chantilly in the bottom. Then, using a beautifully styled black-iron tea pot, he pours steaming butternut squash soup into the bowl.

The bright yellow-orange soup lifts the circular dollop of sage chantilly and red huckleberries as it fills the white bowl. The red berries and creamy green sage chantilly float in the center, fresh, cool (in contrast to the hot soup) and delicious.

The soup is spectacular! I could end the meal with the soup and be fully satisfied. But there's more to come.

From our window seat, we watch the sun float gently on the horizon, sending streamers of light across the sea. The gilded clouds, billowing profusely, fill me with happiness.

We are among the first guests of the evening, and love the empty serenity of the place.

But by the time our entrées arrive – Al has rack of lamb, I have chicken under a brick – couples occupy many of the nearby tables. The clink of wineglasses and the gentle babble of intimate conversations fill the restaurant.

Al says the rack of lamb is perfect. My chicken under a brick is a delightful dish, heavy on vegetables and very tasty.

While we concentrate on our entrees, the sun sinks behind a jumble of gilded clouds, sending a flat spray of light across the waves in geometric shapes of dull orange and gold.

And night begins to gather above the waves.

For dessert I have Crème Brûlée Le Cirque and Al has chocolate soufflé. Both are the perfect ending to a flawless dinner.

Every dish has been delightful in its presentation and its taste – truly a feast for both eyes and palate.

By the time we finish our dessert and coffee, our ocean-view window holds only darkness. The restaurant is now full and bustling, and it's time for us to head to the Vista Lounge for tonight's performance.

A HARD DAY'S NIGHT (A TRIBUTE TO THE BEATLES)

As always, the Vista Lounge is packed. Even though we're there half an hour before the show, it's difficult to find two empty seats together. Obviously, this cruise is filled with Beatles fans.

Once we find seats, we quickly claim them. All around us passengers are sharing Beatles stories with each other.

As we wait, I look around at the beautiful design of the theater, its artistic lights and generous stage. Even here, stunning art is on display. On either side of the theater, large statues sit in recessed niches above the audience.

On one side a woman, much larger than life-size, sits knitting. Opposite her on the other side of the theater is a larger than life-size workman in hardhat and overalls, reading a newspaper. These sculptures sit serenely in their places. Are they connected? Is she married to him? Is he an admirer of hers? Why such "ordinary" people sitting above the eager audience night after night? I'll never know the answers to my questions, but I love the statues and their locations. While the people in the seats chatter, the knitting woman and newspaper-reading man sit quietly, at peace, in their niches.

[I learn later that both sculptures are by Lebigre & Roger, the internationally recognized artists from Italy who also created the intriguing sculptures near the mid-ship elevators – the woman sitting on the crescent moon; the happy clown, Bip; and others. This husband and wife team (Gilbert Lebigre and Corinne Roger) live in Tuscany, work in a studio near Pisa, and provide much of the contemporary sculptural beauty found on the *Zuiderdam* and other Holland America ships.]

Before the 8 p.m. show each night, Holland America waitstaff walks the aisles, taking orders for wine or after-dinner drinks. But once the lights go down, it's showtime.

Tonight the Beatles tribute band "Hard Day's Night" takes the stage and actually re-create Paul, John, George and Ringo, looking and sounding so much like the originals that we're all transported back in time.

To help with the transport, the performance is punctuated by historic videos of the lads from Liverpool appearing on *The Ed Sullivan Show* and being interviewed later in their career. There's also a charming video of people on the streets of Great Britain in the '60s telling the camera what they think of the Beatles.

The high-energy show is fantastic – lots of people in the audience cheering and singing along with the four on stage. Obviously this is a love fest – for the Beatles, for the '60s, for our youth.

AL'S TAKE ON THE FAMOUS CHOCOLATE EXTRAVAGANZA

At 10:15 p.m. (that's 2215 in nautical time), Tuesday BD (that's Bedbug Day), we head up to the swimming pool on Deck 9, the Lido, for the famed Chocolate Extravaganza.

The Extravaganza is featured on all Holland America cruises, and while I'm not sure what it's all about, I'm ready. The very name is rich with promise: "Chocolate" and "Extravaganza" combined in one savory event.

To understand the CE (as it shall be henceforth abbreviated), one might start by looking up the word "extravaganza." The dictionary says: "extremely or excessively flamboyant," "outrageous," or, rather less enthusiastically, "exceeding the normal bounds" or even "immoderate." These definitions approximate, though rather inadequately, what is to be found at the CE.

The ship provides 15 minutes to photograph the ensemble before the forks are turned loose. It isn't nearly enough time. This is a photographic opportunity to challenge the food editor from the New York Times. To shoot it all I would have needed a Sears Die Hard battery for my flash camera.

The ship's main swimming pool – Olympic class size – is encircled with tables sagging under the weight of desserts of every size, kind, and shape, most encrusted with, or built entirely of, chocolate. Words cannot adequately describe the bounty which spreads before us in all its brown-and-golden loveliness. Backlit ice sculptures further add to the beauty. It is an art gallery for eye and belly.

Where to start? Petite Fours. Life-size chocolate crowns. A cake in the form of a book. Statues. Puddings. Pies. Eclairs. Bundts. Sheet cakes. Fruit cakes. Things that looked like giant Ding-Dongs. There are chocolate custards, chocolate drinks, chocolate-covered fruits. Imagine: hundreds of people, pointing at this and that, all going "Oooooooh."

Scores of people in tuxes and gowns photograph the beautiful and fragrant display. Chefs take cakes out of their pans and make space for them amid the crowd of other cakes, two and three layers high, drizzled or slathered with chocolate frosting. We ended up taking nearly 200 photos. The pungent chocolate fragrance saturates us. Believe me, it's divine dining on chocolate.

For those who aren't quite up to the CE's caloric excess, a huge case of cheeses sit in one corner: enough cheddar to satisfy the craving of every mouse in the past three ports. There are also little sandwiches and other munchies for those who prefer a more rounded diet (at this stage we are all getting a bit rounded, truth be told).

It's almost inconceivable that the ship's 1,900 passengers could even begin to make a dent in the overflowing horn of plenty standing before us. We are, however, eager and willing to give it a shot. After all, most of us haven't eaten in at least two hours. The only decision is: Where to start?

Sunny and I sample, roam and eventually give up, taking the elevator back to our spacious new cabin. If we'd stayed on, we'd have needed a forklift to get home. It is nearly midnight, the latest we've stayed up, and a beautiful night at sea. And only seven hours to breakfast, come to think of it. In the morning, will we find leftover chocolate dessert instead of oatmeal? And with that, to sleep, perchance to dream, of ... chocolate. Extravagantly.

DAY 16
Wednesday, October 17

AT SEA

We were so exhausted when we got back to our room last night that we knew we wouldn't wake up in time for breakfast. So we filled out a room service request for breakfast and hung it outside our door just before we fell into bed.

And this morning, right on schedule, breakfast is delivered: my veggie omelet, Al's French toast, along with our grapefruit, orange juice, English muffins, toast and coffee. The breakfast tray comes with a lovely fresh orchid in a vase.

As we eat, wearing our comfy bathrobes, we watch CNN news, listening to the various pundits discuss last night's presidential debate between President Obama and Mitt Romney. Every once in a while, it's nice to switch on the set and see what's happening back home and what folks are saying about it.

After breakfast, Al heads to Mass. I head to the infirmary. There I find a woman named Janet behind the reception desk. She takes my temperature and blood pressure, then gives me some pills (Benadryl, 25 mg) to help end the itching.

I ask how often bedbugs show up on board and she says it's rare, but they do occasionally appear.

"They're usually picked up in a motel and transferred to the ship," she says. As I head out the door with my pills, she says I should come back at 10 a.m. to see the doctor.

Climbing the stairs to the fifth deck and walking toward our new room I realize that I've totally lost track of the days of the week.

What's today? Tuesday or Wednesday? What's the date? I don't know. I'll have to check the calendar in our room to find out. And you know what? I don't even care. It's wonderfully freeing to not know.

When I return to the infirmary at 9:55 a.m. there are two people ahead of me: a large man in white tennis shoes, beige shorts, a dark blue polo shirt and glasses, and a woman in beige pedal pushers and a light brown sweater.

We're all sitting in the waiting area, under the beautiful pictures, thinking our own thoughts (which in my case means thinking very little). Another man enters, sits down next to the man in beige shorts, and the two begin talking about yesterday's change of course to help an ailing crewmember.

"I heard the problem was appendicitis," the new man says. The one in beige shorts says he had assumed it was something like a heart attack.

Then I hear my name. I look at the reservation desk and see the doctor from yesterday. He motions for me to follow him. We walk to a small supply room with a metal desk and two chairs. We both sit next to the desk and he asks my age and general state of health.

I explain the bedbug problem and that this morning I'd been given some pills for general itchiness. He examines the bites on my upper arm.

I ask if he might have a more topical medication that I can put on my bites. He goes to a metal cabinet and searches the shelves. "I have some cortisone cream I can give you," he says. I take the tube of cream, gratefully. Then he says Al and I need to wash the clothes we were wearing yesterday.

I ask if the patient he'd been dealing with yesterday is all right.

"This cruise has been the E-ticket ride for me," he says, "because we got him to the hospital and he's going to survive."

He smiles when he says that.

I ask, "Was it appendicitis?"

He replies, "It was a little more serious than that."

Then he asks if Al and I are planning to go to Half Moon Cay tomorrow. When I say "I think we will," he says to be sure and put on lots of sunscreen.

"We always get a lot of sick people after Half Moon Cay because they ignore the need for sunscreen and come back to the ship burned to a crisp," he says.

"So they end the cruise in pain?"

He nods, and I assure him we'll use plenty of sunscreen.

Back in our room, I load a laundry bag with the clothes we wore yesterday and hang it on the outside of our cabin door. I sure hope the bugs, their eggs and everything else connected with them are gone, gone, gone.

Al and I sit on our balcony enjoying the day. We can see two rainstorms on the horizon. I watch their black, fist-like shapes pour gray waterfalls into the ocean. But here, close to the ship, the sea is calm as we resume our leisurely trip heading for Holland America's private island – Half Moon Cay – in the Bahamas.

Even though yesterday was unpleasant, and even though I have itchy bites all over my arm and in a couple of places on my leg, it's wonderful to have this big cabin and this balcony for the last couple of days. It makes the bedbug shock and disruption less traumatic. The *Zuiderdam* staff has done its best to turn a most unpleasant situation into something ultimately pleasant.

In the Vista Dining Room for lunch, we eat at a small table for two. The dining room relaxes us. Our meal is marvelous.

We spend the afternoon in our new cabin or out on our balcony. It's very humid, but not too hot. I don't think I'd enjoy living near the equator. The constant humidity can be oppressive. As the afternoon grows overcast, I decide it's time to take a nap. Al joins me.

At 3:45 p.m. the captain wakes us from our nap when he announces over the ship's intercom that we are passing Cuba's eastern edge. We walk out on our balcony to watch the island as we pass. The sea is a deep, royal blue. I just love the way it constantly changes – from blue to gray to silver to green to royal blue to black. I can understand why people want to spend their life near or on the ocean.

The evening show is a big, Las Vegas–type music and dance production. Al and I are too tired to attend. We take a light supper in the Lido and then come back to our cabin to sit on our balcony in the dark.

After a long time of doing nothing but watching the star-sprinkled sky, Al says, "The humid air feels soft and comforting."

And it does. It is a lovely feeling.

When we go back inside, our bed has been turned down, chocolates lay on our pillows and the steward has left a little gold box from Le Cirque for us. The accompanying card thanks us for dining at Le Cirque. When I open the door on the little gold box, I find two small gold drawers. In each drawer lays a rich chocolate truffle.

"Now that's class," Al says.

DAY 17
Thursday, October 18

PORT OF CALL: HALF MOON CAY, BAHAMAS

Enjoying the warm turquoise water at Half Moon Cay.

The last full day of our cruise has arrived.

We awaken to find the ship anchored just off Holland America's private island – Half Moon Cay.

This long, low, sandy island, once called Little San Salvador Island, has been renamed after

Holland America's logo, which depicts explorer Henry Hudson's ship, *Halve Maen* (Half Moon). The name also reflects the island's spectacular crescent-shaped, 2½-mile white-sand beach.

Gazing out from our balcony, the island looks like something out of a Walt Disney movie.

Strange as it may sound, I've never been attracted to the Caribbean. I grew up on a lake in Michigan, learned to swim about the time I learned to walk, spent the first 10 years of my life either swimming in or ice skating on the lake, and all the pictures I've ever seen of the Bahamas and Caribbean resorts look artificial (almost plastic) to me. So I've never been tempted by that "Let's float all day in the warm ocean" advertisement.

However, we are definitely going to take advantage of this last stop on our itinerary.

It's the Lido for breakfast. We both, for the first time in the entire cruise, order waffles with fresh blueberries and strawberries. They are scrumptious. After breakfast, we read our last *NYT* condensed paper, then return to the cabin, pack our bathing suits, sunscreen and sheltering hats in a little HAL tote and head for a tender.

The morning is absolutely perfect, warm but not yet hot. Gentle breezes. From our orange-and-white tender, we can see the long white-sand beach, lined with lounge chairs. And behind it, acres of greenery.

This 2,400-acre flat and sandy island is one of about 700 islands that make up the archipelago of the Bahamas.

Holland America Line bought it in 1996 for six million dollars. The island lies 100 miles south of Nassau.

Our tender putt-putt-putts toward Half Moon Cay, then into a narrow inlet passageway. We slowly make our way through palms and other lush trees to the marina, where we disembark.

About 50 acres of the island have been developed with trails and misting stations, cabanas and four bars. As we enter the island's welcome area, we notice a small straw market and an ice cream shop, but we, along with everyone else on our tender, head directly for the beach. We pay five dollars for a little locker to put our shoes, clothes and watches in, find the changing rooms, get into our bathing suits and head for the water.

I've never seen such water – clear turquoise and welcoming-warm.

We drop our towels on two lounges at the water's edge, and just walk right out into that clear, warm (about 81 degrees) liquid. The ocean's gentle swells lift us and set us down and lift us and set us down, and then we swim. Fun! Free! Fabulous!

I haven't had this much swimming fun since I was a kid.

The beach is full of people. The water is full of people. People swimming. People standing chest-deep and talking. People snorkeling. And yet, despite all the people, the place feels spacious and open.

We swim. Dog-paddle. Sidestroke. Backstroke. Breaststroke. Swim under water. Stand around in the warm, beautiful, magical water, and then swim some more. And eventually, wander out and drop onto the beach lounges to let the warm air dry us off.

Not only do I find the water of fairytale quality, but the sand is magically soft. Gentle as talcum powder, it coats my feet and toes like a soft, white slipper.

When Al decides to head back into the water, I take off to explore. Wearing nothing but my bathing suit and a hat, I meander along paved trails, reading the names of the various plants.

Much of the island is a nature preserve. Among the exotic vegetation found here are coconut palms, hog palms, mangroves, sea oats, buttonwood trees, sugar apple trees, avocado trees, sour orange trees, Persian lime trees, banana trees and more.

Half Moon Cay is also a migratory bird reserve and waterfowl nesting area. I hear lots of birds singing or cawing, but can't identify a single one. However, experienced birders can see sooty terns, noddy terns, roseate terns, shearwaters, Bahamian pintails and many others.

I love wandering along the various paved paths, almost as much as I loved the swimming. I haven't walked barefoot like this since I was a kid. My trail winds past a couple of bars, some picnic areas, a little chapel and a playground.

If I had wandered farther, I could have found the horse riding area, the three water sports centers, the stingray cove, the 5K running course, the basketball and volleyball courts and more. But I'm satisfied to simply meander, reading the posted names of various local plants and enjoying being barefoot.

When the sun grows too intense for me, I head back to the beach and find Al, and both of us decide it's time to leave the beautiful, brilliant water behind.

Changing back into beach clothes and shoes, we're off to lunch. First, however, I have to show Al some of the plants I've discovered. Then we stop by one of the little grass-roofed bars, to sit and share an icy Coke.

As we head for the outdoor covered food pavilion, we're surprised and pleased to see some folks in wheelchairs with large balloon tires, made especially for beach-sand use. When we ask, we're told the wheelchairs are available at the information center. Isn't that fabulous? Even mobility-limited passengers can enjoy a day at the beach on Half Moon Cay.

The lunch pavilion is packed with hungry, smiling people, but we are able to find what we want quickly. A BBQ section serves beef and chicken, a grill area serves hamburgers, hotdogs, sausages and fish. There's a large salad area that includes unbelievably delicious fresh fruit (mango, pineapple, etc.). And for Al, of course, a dessert bar serving cookies and brownies.

I heap my plate with melon and coconut salad, coleslaw and barbecued chicken. Al's plate is equally mountainous.

We share a shaded picnic table with a couple from Ottawa, Canada. They are celebrating their 55th wedding anniversary with this cruise, and say they've had the time of their life. The wife's sister and her friend have also come along.

After finishing our lunch, we all sit at the table talking about what a perfect ending to our cruise this morning at the beach has been.

"We feel like kids again, at a picnic," the husband says.

And that's exactly how I feel. Barefoot at the beach. Lots of good food nearby. Warm, wonderful water to swim in. And nothing to do but play and have fun.

Back onboard, Al downloads the pictures from our cameras and announces that during the course of our cruise, "we've taken 1,405 pictures."

"We're going to have a lot of fun sorting them out, and deciding which ones to put in our book," I say.

Then we sit side by side and click through them all on our laptop, oooohing and ahhing and laughing. What a great time!

Then we stretch out on the bed for a nap.

When I was 10, a Bun candy bar was the epitome of wealth. If I had a Bun (chocolate-covered maple or chocolate-covered mint), I felt rich and happy and satisfied. Now, more than 50 years later, there's no luxury to equal an afternoon nap.

DISEMBARKING INFORMATION

At 4 p.m. we, and hundreds of others, make our way to the Vista Lounge for the disembarking informational. If I thought the place was packed for the 8 p.m. show each night, I hadn't seen anything. Every seat is full. People sit on the stairs and stand along the walls.

While we wait for our disembarkation instructions, the cruise director entertains us with jokes and interesting statistics about our cruise. He says that cooks have used 120,000 eggs during this cruise. He says that the staff served 13,000 meals each day of the cruise. I quickly work out the numbers and figure out that, if it's true, the 1,936 people on board ate more than the equivalent of six meals a day.

Eventually he tells us what to expect tomorrow, how we should pack and set our bags outside our doors and when we can expect to depart.

It just doesn't seem that long ago that we were lining up to get briefed on emergency procedures, and now we're getting briefed on leaving the ship.

LETTER FROM THE GUEST RELATIONS MANAGER

After a Lido salad supper, we find our end-of-cruise bill and a separate letter from Guest Relations. Opening the letter, we read:

Dear Mr. and Mrs. Lockwood,

On behalf of Guest Relations in Seattle and on-board, we would like to apologize once more for the inconvenience you have experienced in your previous accommodation.

As a gesture of goodwill, please be informed that a shipboard credit of $300.00 total will be applied toward your onboard account and which is redeemable if not fully used.

We are truly grateful for your patience and consideration of the situation you were put through; we hope that this regretful incident has not clouded your otherwise favorable view of Holland America Line and of the MS Zuiderdam's staff and crew.

We wish you safe travels whatever your plan is tomorrow in Fort Lauderdale, Florida.

Sincerely,

> *Cindy Castro*
> *Guest Relations Manager*

"Well, how about that," Al says. "They are really trying to make it up to us."

I'm also impressed. The 300 dollar credit pretty well wipes out what we spent on shore excursions and other extras. This is, indeed, a pleasant last-night-onboard surprise.

We spend the evening packing and filling out customer satisfaction surveys.

We also turn on the TV to watch the Detroit Tigers wipe out the New York Yankees and head for the World Series. I'm thrilled. Having been born and raised in Michigan, I love the Tigers. And having lived in California for the past 40 years, I love the SF Giants. So, no matter who wins the World Series, I'll be elated. This is too cool!

DAY 18
Friday, October 19

THE CRUISE ENDS: FORT LAUDERDALE, FLORIDA

Up at 6 a.m. The ship is maneuvering into port. Al watches the activity from our balcony.

After our last breakfast aboard, we wait in our cabin for our disembarking group (gray 1) to be called.

By 9:15 a.m. our group is heading off the ship and into a warehouse where our bags are waiting.

Then we stand in line to go through customs. We have little to declare and move through quickly. Then it's out the door and into a waiting cab.

The cruise has reached its end.

But OH! The memories!

AL'S AFTERTHOUGHTS
(penned in January 2013)

*I*t's been three months since we docked in Fort Lauderdale; ample time to reflect on voyage and ship. El bueno, el malo y el feo *as the Spanish language has it, or for the language-challenged, the good, the bad, etc.*

One of the things that comes to mind immediately is the experience of 17 days at sea. I've done shorter cruises (up to two weeks), but a cruise of this length settles the soul in ways that nothing else does.

Some might ask "Isn't a ship confining?" but the Zuiderdam is a wholly contained village in 11 decks. There was always some place to go, something to do, or (my favorite) something to eat, preferably dessert. Every few days we'd stop, get off, play turista, and toddle back to the very same room we left that morning. And if we didn't want to go ashore, well, there was the (air-conditioned) library. This might have been a drag for the young and restless, but for the old and tired (which most of us were) it was a marvel.

A decided negative was our discovery that everything cost extra, and sometimes a great deal extra. Perhaps elsewhere you get an eggroll with #2, but on Holland America that eggroll would be an additional five dollars please, plus 15-percent gratuity. It is possible to go the entire voyage without running additional charges (beyond the standard room tip), of course, but if you wanted a latte or a drink (soda or otherwise) or a minute's Internet time, you'd hand over your card/door key and it would be added to your tab. Shore excursions were (to our thinking) expensive, though many offered good value for the money.

Offsetting the extra expenses, the Z made it a practice to promptly care for our every wish and need (success in the casino and weight management excepted, of course). Soft bathrobes in every cabin, meals in the cabin if desired at no extra cost, attentive staff wherever one went, fluffy towels at poolside.

Though it wasn't an issue with us (we don't drink alcoholic beverages), those who like an afternoon bebida or a glass of wine with supper or a wee bedtime nip should be prepared for both some difficulty and significant expense. It is not permitted to bring alcoholic beverages aboard or to consume them out of your own stock, in your cabin or elsewhere.

Liquor is sold on board, but it, and anything alcoholic purchased ashore, is kept under lock and key until the voyage ends. If you like to drink, there are bars and wine stewards aplenty, but be prepared to pay.

A very solid plus for this trip and, I gather, for HAL, was the quality of the food – the careful choice of ingredients, the variety, the presentation, the care with which the ship's chefs saw the thundering herd fed. Holland America's guests tend to be older, which means somewhat more discerning in their eating habits, and perhaps a bit pickier, too. Sunny and I heard many an exclamation of delight when a dish was laid on the table, and words of praise were common fair. It takes a lot to keep 1,900 palates satisfied – no, happy – and the Zuiderdam was fully equal to the task.

Finally, a few more words about shore excursions. I would call my impression a mixed bag. As earlier noted, many are expensive, but then, they may represent a once-in-a-lifetime opportunity to see something unique. Wandering ashore by yourself is fine if you're able to handle the heat and feel safe, especially so if you have some of the local language. Often when we got off the ship, we were besieged by local vendors, a problem somewhat less acute when we were on excursion. We needed to remind ourselves that in the eyes of the locals we were all rich beyond their wildest dreams, for which reason we would gladly hand over sums of money for this, that, and the other. It could be, and was, draining at times.

On the whole, my post-voyage summary is this: "When can we go again?" I would repeat this voyage in a heartbeat, on Holland America, and would unhesitatingly recommend it to friends of my age. "Of my age" is important. To more youthful cruisers, our ship may have been Senility of the Seas, but to us it was just perfect.

SUNNY'S AFTERTHOUGHTS

Bedbugs and aggressive Colombian vendors aside, I had an absolutely wonderful time on this cruise.

In addition to the fun we had on board and the discoveries we made at our various ports of call, I learned a few things that will stay with me the rest of my life. I learned how satisfying it is to actually do something you've long dreamed of doing. It's life-enhancing to transform wishes into actuality. At least it is for me. On this cruise, I found myself more energetic, more curious (and curiosity is one of my stronger traits), and more enthusiastic. We both felt like kids making all kinds of fascinating discoveries.

And the pace of the cruise (and our discoveries) was comfortable. We had plenty of time to explore, learn, and experience without feeling rushed. Whenever things started feeling too frenetic for me, I simply found a chair on deck or in the library and spent an hour or two with a good book.

I learned that 17 days without a computer is liberating. Although Al did some emailing, I stayed totally computer-free. That freedom gave me more time for such blissful experiences as watching the ocean change colors, sharing playful conversation with my Sweetheart and visiting with other passengers. To say nothing of luxurious afternoon naps.

I learned that when one is freed from the ordinary domestic duties of life – shopping, cooking, cleaning, -- the imagination blossoms. If you want to feel like a kid again, free to pursue your own interests with no obligation to clean up after yourself and no restrictions about being home before dark, take a cruise.

Even though there is so much we didn't mention in this book – the casino (and its beautiful Neptune sculpture), the spa, the many musical acts that performed in various bars and lounges throughout the ship – I hope you've been able to experience the essence of a lovely (if complicated) cruise.

And, in case you're wondering, I did gain weight – one pound.

Sweetheart, however, remains his rail-thin self. I just smile and shake my head.

☆ ☆

What follows are a few factual details about the *Zuiderdam* and the Panama Canal. Enjoy.

DETAILS ABOUT THE *MS ZUIDERDAM*

Captain: Christopher Turner

Hotel Manager: Kees van Saten

Power: *MS Zuiderdam* has five diesel generators (3×16,000 hp and 2×12,000 hp) and one gas turbine (18,000 hp) for a total of 90,000 hp.

Propulsion: 2×ABB Azipods (2×17.5 mw) for total power of 46,000 hp.

Fuel Consumption: the diesel generators use 90 tons (57,000 gallons) a day

Water Production: potable water production totals 1,700 tons (or 450,000 gallons) a day

Water Consumption: 750 tons (or 200,000 gallons) a day

Gross Tonnage: 82,000

Length: 935 feet

Width: 106 feet

Maximum speed: 23 knots

Number of guests: 1,936
Number of crew: 823

MS ZUIDERDAM FEATURES

The Culinary Arts Center, presented by *Food & Wine Magazine*: Deck 2, a state-of-the-art demonstration kitchen offering interactive gourmet cooking lessons taught by master chefs or culinary guests.

Explorations Café, powered by the *New York Times*: Next to the Crow's Nest on Deck 10, a comfortable, coffeehouse environment where you can browse through an extensive library, surf the Internet and check email or simply read the morning paper.

Greenhouse Spa & Salon: Deck 9, features beauty treatments and wellness rituals. Enjoy a facial, hot-stone massage, steam in a thermal suite and have your hair and nails done for a special evening.

Vista Show Lounge: Decks 1, 2, and 3, features talented vocalists, dancers, illusionists, comedians and variety acts.

Queen's Lounge: Deck 2, features cabaret-type entertainment in the evenings. (During the day, it doubles as the Culinary Arts Center.)

Crow's Nest: Deck 10, above the bow, offers sweeping views during the day, and becomes a hip, fashionable nightclub each evening

Club HAL: Deck 10, *Zuiderdam*'s dedicated youth facilities, filled with supervised activities for kids ages 3 to 12.

The Loft: Deck 10, designed exclusively for teens (13 to 17) to have fun, socialize and hang out with people their own age.

MS ZUIDERDAM BARS

For those who enjoy a cocktail, glass of wine or beer or an after-dinner drink, there are plenty of places on board to quench your thirst. And in the evening, many of these venues include live music along with the libations.

However, alcoholic beverages (like soft drinks and designer coffees) are not included in the price of the cruise.

Here's a list of the onboard bars:

- Lido Bar
- Crow's Nest
- Ocean Bar
- Sports Bar
- Pinnacle Bar
- Atrium Bar
- Explorer's Lounge
- Piano Bar
- Northern Lights

PANAMA CANAL DATA
(according to Elizabeth Mann's book *The Panama Canal*)

- Length: 50 miles
- Length of Culebra Cut: 9 miles
- Length of Gatun Lake: 24 miles
- Area of Gatun Lake: 64 square miles
- Elevation of Gatun Lake: 85 feet above sea level
- Amount of water used by one ship going through the Canal: 52 million gallons
- Total number of locks: 12
- Length of each lock: 1,000 feet
- Width of each lock: 110 feet
- Depth of locks: 70–80 feet
- Minimum depth of water in Canal: 45 feet
- Rise in elevation of ship going through Canal: 85 feet
- French construction: 1881–1889
- American construction: 1904–1914

ACKNOWLEDGMENTS

This book has been a labor of love and sharing; the operative word being "labor." Although our cruise was perfectly unforgettable, turning happy memories and personal observations into a book others might enjoy reading is not an easy task.

Of course, we encouraged each other through the long year of writing, re-writing, editing, tossing out and starting over.

But we are most grateful for the helpful support and wise advice we received from others.

Poet Barbara Alfaro read an early draft and said our manuscript was both engaging and entertaining. Her reassuring words, especially as we were just beginning our project, meant so much and kept us going even when we were weary of the work.

Novelist Robbi Bryant read two later versions of the manuscript, contributing ideas on content and style and helping us polish the text. Her thoughtful suggestions improved our manuscript.

Illustrator Janie Berry created a book cover design that captures the beauty, drama and gastronomical delight we experienced on our cruise.

Lou Gonzalez, eBook formatter extraordinaire, worked his magic with our manuscript, turning it into an appealing eBook. Lou, himself a writer of depth and sensitivity, is all about encouraging indie authors.

Copyeditor Mark Burstein made sure our facts, grammar and punctuation were as close to perfect as possible. In addition to his editorial expertise, his love of books and languages and cartoon art made our collaboration both educational and lots of fun.

We and our book have benefitted greatly from these talented friends who took the time to help us with this project.

And in addition, we gratefully acknowledge the contribution of Holland America Line. Their many hours of assistance—interviews, information, helpfulness—were essential to this project.

Keeping 1,900 septuagenarians entertained and fed is a big enough task without the extra burden of two curious writers doing research, but they met our requests with friendly aplomb.

Made in the
USA
Monee, IL